The Complete
Belgian Tervuren

American Belgian Tervuren Club
Education Committee
Karen P. Johnson
Barbara A. Krohn
Edeltraud Laurin

ABTC Editor
Kay K. Maves

HOWELL
BOOK HOUSE
New York

Howell Book House
Macmillan Publishing Company
866 Third Avenue, New York, NY 10022
Collier Macmillan Canada, Inc.

Library of Congress Cataloging-in-Publication Data
The complete Belgian tervuren/American Belgian Tervuren Club, Education
  Committee; editor, Kay K. Maves.
      p. cm.
    ISBN 0-87605-051-8
    1. Belgian tervuren.   I. Maves, Kay K.   II. American Belgian
Tervuren Club. Education Committee.
SF429.B42C66   1990
636.7'37—dc20   89-35293   CIP

Macmillan books are available at special discounts for bulk purchases for
sales promotions, premiums, fund-raising, or educational use. For details
contact:

                   Special Sales Director
                   Macmillan Publishing Company
                   866 Third Avenue
                   New York, NY 10022

10 9 8 7 6 5 4 3 2 1

Printed in the United States of America

Contents

Foreword

THIS BOOK PRESENTS the history of the Belgian Tervuren in the United States. We have highlighted pedigrees of dogs that have made a great contribution to our breed over the years. We discuss dogs whose influence on the breed is significant, and in doing so we cover a wide range of breeders and dogs.

It is hoped that the book fulfills its intent by providing every reader with additional knowledge on this wonderful breed we know as the Belgian Tervuren.

A Belgian Tervuren herding sheep. Drawing by Alison Freund, 1980. *Courtesy Janina Laurin*

Drawing of a Belgian Tervuren with a Sealyham Terrier, by Marguerite Kirmse, illustrator of books by Rudyard Kipling. *Courtesy Janina Laurin*

Preface

WHEN I THINK of the history of the Belgian Tervuren in America, the same words always come to mind. Among them are "adversity," "determination" and "courage."

Certainly our breed has known adversity. In Europe, where it always has been considered a coat and color variety of the Belgian Sheepdog breed, it nearly foundered from neglect for many years when the Groenendael and Malinois were far more favored. Revived after World War II, it was imported to the United States and came close to being banned as an illegitimate member of the Belgian race. Only by being designated as a separate breed by the American Kennel Club did it manage to survive intact.

It survived because of the determination and courage of early breeders and enthusiasts. Theirs is the glory, and they will be forever honored for their staunch defense of the animals they knew to be as worthy of acceptance as any other. Now, at last, thirty years after Tervuren were given recognized status by the American Kennel Club, we have a book about them. It has been crafted by our national breed club's Education Committee—an anonymous name, to be sure, but composed of three long-time members whose credentials virtually chronicle the Belgian Tervuren in America. They are Karen Johnson, Barbara Krohn and committee chair Edeltraud Laurin.

Although she has bred a number of litters whose members boast enviable records in breed and obedience, Karen Johnson's interest has focused on serving the national club and excelling in obedience competition. A dedicated and active contributor to the breed since 1960, she has held nearly every office in the ABTC except president (which she has refused) and performed innumerable tasks, all of which have contributed immeasurably to our progress. In the obedience arena, she has proved her expertise by winning twelve *Dog World* awards with her Tervuren. Karen exemplifies the "silent force" present in any breed. Working quietly behind the scenes, such individuals provide the glue that holds us all together. Without them we truly would be lost.

Barbara Krohn and her husband, Bob, generally are regarded as the senior mentors of the breed. As two of the pioneer breeders of Tervuren in this country and cofounders of our national breed club, they have made an enormous impact with their breeding and activities in behalf of Tervuren. Their commitment to the breed began in the mid-1950s and continues today. They are prominent in this book.

Edeltraud Laurin also is a name to be reckoned with. Since 1963 her Chateau Blanc kennel, whose foundation stock came from the Krohns, has been a major force in the breed. It is widely regarded as a producer of many of the most influential dogs in the history of American Tervuren. In addition to her highly successful breeding program, Edeltraud has served the breed in many capacities—from president of the American Belgian Tervuren Club to membership on the present committee. Like the Krohns, her name will be found here many times.

These individuals and the breed they so proudly represent are truly special. Without such people, no breed can survive. It has been an honor for me to work with them.

Kay K. Maves
Editor

Acknowledgments

THE COMPLETE BELGIAN TERVUREN is the result of the joint efforts of the American Belgian Tervuren Club (ABTC) Education Committee and many breeders and fanciers. Special thanks are expressed to the board of directors of the ABTC for supporting this endeavor, to ABTC president Janina Laurin for her help and patient prodding, to the ABTC archives committee, Cheryl Cawley, Merrelyn Clark, Terrie Janssen, Mara Lee Jiles, Bob Krohn, Nancie Mages, Sue Morlan, Jeanne Ohmann, Judith Lee Smith, Barb Van Eseltine, Marcelle King (Great Britain), L. E. Stanbridge (Canada), Judith Lee Specht for her consultations with Jean-Louis Vandembenden (Belgium) and to the many sources of ABTC historical information.

Reference material was used extensively, particularly the *Belgian Tervuren Registry* manuals, the ABTC *Belgian Tervuren Genealogy Books,* as well as *The Berger Belge Anthology* by Sally Mitchell Perry and Adrienne A. Pagel. We greatly appreciated the efforts and research put forth by the authors and contributors of these materials.

Our editor, Kay Maves, deserves special mention. An owner, fancier and student of the breed since the mid-1960s, Kay took personal interest and great care in her work. Her questioning and curious mind forced us to look deeper to produce needed detail. Her ability to put our many writing styles into a sequence and flow of words that would make sense to the reader was invaluable.

To all these Tervuren fanciers, and others too numerous to mention, we extend our deepest gratitude.

THE ABTC EDUCATION COMMITTEE
Karen P. Johnson, Barbara A. Krohn,
and Edeltraud Laurin, Chairperson

The varieties of Belgian Sheepdog in their homeland: the Groenendael and Laekenois in front, Malinois and Tervuren standing. Drawing by Alice Rasmussen, Denmark, 1985. *Courtesy of Specialklubben for Belgisks Hyrdehunde (Danish Belgian Shepherd Club)*

1

European History

FOR DECADES REFERRED TO in Belgium as *Chien de Berger Belge a poil long fauve charbonne,* the Belgian Tervuren originally was a sheepherder. Today it plays many other roles. It is a family companion and protector, competitor in breed shows and obedience trials and an aide to the handicapped. It also excels in such diverse pursuits as search and rescue work, skijouring and dogsledding. Its herding instincts are still very strong, however, and are maintained by the use of the dog in herding trials.

EARLY TERVUREN

To trace the origin of this remarkable dog, we must return to the nineteenth century. All sheepdogs on the European continent probably evolved from the same common ancestors. Gradually, however, different groups developed that possessed traits common to all herding dogs. These characteristics can be found in the Belgian, German and Scottish sheepdogs of Western Europe and the Hungarian and Russian sheepdogs of Eastern Europe. In the late 1800s the shepherd dogs of Belgium were listed in the stud books and at dog shows as *Le Chien de Berger des Races Continental* (Continental Shepherds), a classification that also included German Shepherd Dogs, Hollander Herders, Beauçeron, Bouvier des Flandres and Briards.

During this period, nationalistic movements arose in the countries of Western Europe and created fierce national pride. Citizens of each country vied for dominance and recognition in many arenas, including a concentration

1

of time and energy to perfect native dog breeds. Sheepdogs were no longer being used heavily for their traditional work because sheep and cattle drives were no longer necessary, ranges were fenced and predators were not a menace. Luckily, the owners of these dogs developed a profound interest in training them for police work and in dog shows. The dogs' superior intellectual and physical abilities permitted them to adapt quickly to their new roles, and their survival was thus ensured.

The native Belgian Sheepdogs are reputed to be the first to be employed in police work. In the mid 1890s M. Ernest van Wesemael, chief police commissioner of Ghent (whose squad of police dogs was said to be the finest in existence), used them extensively. Van Wesemael, a lover of dogs, trained by kindness. It was said that if any of his officers was known to strike a dog, that officer was dismissed. Some sources mention that Rittmeister von Stephanitz, the developer of the modern German Shepherd Dog, requested demonstrations and instructions from the Ghent police to aid in training his dogs.

THE BELGIANS EMERGE

Nineteenth-century Belgian Sheepdogs were a diverse collection of coat colors, lengths and types. Because they were bred specifically for herding ability, their owners paid little attention to appearance. Tails often were docked, as well. The breed as we know it today may never have evolved except for the developing interest in dog shows. Belgian owners formed a club, the Club du Chien de Berger Belge (CCBB) on September 29, 1891, to preserve Belgium's shepherd dogs, organize working trials and exhibitions and stress uniformity of the dogs' characteristics.

Professor Adolphe Reul, a professor of zoology and a veterinarian, provided expert leadership. He asked other veterinary surgeons to give him details on the sheepdogs they saw in their practices, and asked owners to show their dogs. He judged these dogs many times over a ten-year period. The first gathering of the country's sheepdogs was held on November 15, 1891, at Cureghem, Belgium, where 117 of the best dogs of old Belgian stock were brought together. As a result, type was established and breeders were advised to select stock according to three coat lengths, as classified by Reul: long, short and rough. He had not specified desired colors, which ranged at the time from fawn to black, including brindles and grays. Reul later gathered his information and published the results in a book, *Les Races des Chiens (The Dog Breeds),* in 1894.

In April 1892, the General Assembly of the CCBB established a standard for the breed and advised breeders to attempt to produce uniform type and eliminate the practice of docking tails. It made the decision to admit only the three following coat lengths and colors: long-coated black, short-coated fawn and rough-coated ash gray. At the time, Mendel's hereditary theories were still new and not widely known; otherwise it would have been clear that it was not

Piccard d'Uccle, the Groenendael, and his son, Duc de Groenendael. Painting by A. Clarys, 1896.

Tomy, a Malinois (1898), perpetuated the dark mask and warm color for short-coated Belgians that was passed down to the Tervuren.

3

possible to connect color with coat length. Thus, naiveté led to the exclusion of both long-coated and rough-coated fawn dogs. Their owners were forced to start a club of their own; in July 1898 the Club de Berger Belge (BBC) was formed to preserve Belgians of all varieties.

Several years afterward, the CCBB dissolved because of internal dissent, and the newer BBC took over guidance of the breed. The club had the wisdom to establish the principle that the fawn color was one of those basic to the Belgian Sheepdog, and reinstated them to their proper place with the other colors and coats. At the club's first location, Le Maison Rouge, a show was, at last, also organized for the rough-coated dogs. Later the club moved to Schaerbeek, where shows were held annually. The newly recognized rough- and long-coated fawn dogs were well represented among the entries.

EARLY BREEDING PRACTICES

Differing breeding practices regarding correct Belgian coat and color produced strong prejudices that deserve considerable mention. These are the historical facts.

Early in their history, Belgians of various coat lengths and colors were bred together regularly, based upon each breeder's ideals. Dogs often lacked kennel names, the last names of their breeders/owners serving to distinguish one dog from another, as many "call names" were repetitious. Registration practices were what would be considered lax today, and some unregistered subjects were bred.

ORIGIN OF DISTINCT VARIETIES

By the 1890s M. Nicolas Rose, owner of the restaurant Chateau de Groenendael, had been raising long-coated black sheepdogs for several years. In 1893, a litter was whelped from two of his dogs, Piccard D'Uccle and Petite. It produced Duc de Groenendael, a dog destined to play an important role in the future of the long-coated varieties.

Even as Rose was raising his blacks, M. F. Corbeel, who owned a brewery in the town of Tervueren (now spelled Tervuren), was raising litters from his pair of long-coated fawns, Tom and Poes. In 1895 they produced the pup named Miss. She would lead to the establishment of Tervuren, for her son Milsart (whose sire was Duc de Groenendael) was the first Tervuren to be awarded a championship and became forefather of all Tervuren.

In 1898 a short-coated charcoaled fawn sheepdog with black mask, called Tomy, caught the eye of Professor Reul, who proclaimed him to be an

4

excellent specimen of the breed. Tomy, the son of a short-coated brindled fawn (Samlo) and a short-coated brindled gray-brown (Diane), was the first dog of this color to be so recognized. His markings were to become regarded as typical of the dogs of the Malines region, known as Malinois. These colors were transmitted through several generations to Minox, a Tervuren (born in 1921), and became the typical Tervuren coloring as well.

In the Parc du Laeken section of Brussels, sheepdogs with rough fawn coats were being raised. Vos I, a rough-coated fawn, was used at stud with Lieske (Lise) de Laeken, a short-coated brindle. They produced both short- and rough-coated offspring. One of the offspring was the rough-coated Spits; another was Diane, a short-coated brindle gray brown. Diane was the same bitch who became the dam of Tomy, the Malinois mentioned in the preceding paragraph. Vos I and Lieske can be considered as a foundation couple of both the Malinois and Laekenois varieties.

The Société Royale Saint Hubert (SRSH), governing body of pure-bred dogs in Belgium, recognized only the following three varieties of sheepdog in 1901: long-coated black, short-coated blackened fawn and rough-coated ash gray. This exclusion of other coat colors was probably due to both a lack of understanding of hereditary theories, as well as the Société's preoccupation with contemporary hunting dogs and other more established breeds from elsewhere. Pressure was brought upon them by a federation of many individual specialty clubs, including the BBC, which formed for the protection of the many varieties. In 1907 the SRSH accepted short-coated blackened fawn, long-coated black, long-coated fawn, rough-coated fawn and rough-coated deep ash gray. A year later, the federation of specialty clubs for the long-coated fawn and rough-coated gray joined the Saint Hubert Society when their dogs were recognized. (The many specialty clubs that had formed to preserve varieties have since dissolved and the Royal Groenendael Club now represents them.)

VARIETY NAMES

As breeding continued into the 1900s, lengthy discussions were held to select names for dogs of different colors and coat lengths. Eventually the various types became known by the cities or area names associated with their beginnings. By 1910–1911, long-coated black dogs were designated as Groenendael, short-coated fawn and black were Malinois, and rough-coated fawn were Laekenois. The rough-coated ash gray and short-coated black dogs were not given special names. At this point, the long-coated fawn dogs were called just that—long-coated fawn. As time went on, the name Tervuren gained usage and has alternately been used to refer to the fawn color as well as other nonblack colors, with the fawn color being the one most accepted and associated with the name.

Jeck, whelped in 1907, by Bibi (a Milsart grandson) x Betsy. Breeder: Van Tricht.

Inspector of Police Walter and his Tervuren, Albert, pictured about 1923

TERVUREN COLOR EVOLVES

Early on, the fawn color had been rather undistinguished, tending toward shades of pale grayish yellow, yellowish brown and grayish brown. This dull coloring could not compare with the glistening Groenendael or the brilliant charcoaled fawn Malinois with black masks. Thus it attracted little public interest and, consequently, few breeders.

To add to the Tervuren's problems, Groenendael and Malinois breeders occasionally produced excellent long-coated fawn dogs but used them to improve their breeding lines without bothering to register them. They simply provided their names and "origin unknown" for their ancestors. Tervuren were thus widely and anonymously dispersed among kennels devoted to the main varieties and prevented from producing a viable line of their own.

After recognition by the Saint Hubert Society, long-coated fawn breeding centered primarily on Milsart, who had been bred repeatedly to his sisters, dam and granddaughters to fix his type and color. His grandson, Jeck, was a major winner in shows between 1911 and 1914. Jeck combined excellent structure with a noble appearance and a magnificent coat of well-blackened reddish fawn, which has come to be accepted as the preferred color for the Tervuren. Although until recently this color was frequently called "long-coated fawn," we will refer to it as "Tervuren" from here on to avoid confusion over terminology.

The magazine *Le Chien* mentioned only forty-nine Tervuren winners at Belgian shows between 1919 and 1939. Nine were of unknown origin or from parents not registered with the Saint Hubert Society. Four were from pure Groenendael parentage and twenty-two were from Malinois. Only fourteen dogs were direct descendants of the pure Tervuren stock that had existed before 1914. Most of the latter group were descendants of Vici du Val Clos des Sarts, whose dam, Mitsy du Val Clos des Sarts (through her granddam Furia), traces directly to the early lines resulting from Milsart inbreeding.

Vici was an important stud. He represented the merger of the bloodlines of the Jolimont Malinois kennel and the Tervuren line of Mitsy. Long-coated offspring from Malinois litters generally had the same black masks and charcoaled fawn color that their breeders had originally fixed in their dogs, and this contributed to the same homogeneity of type and color in Tervuren (note Vici's pedigree in Chapter 2).

AFTER WORLD WAR I

Despite early relative disinterest in Tervuren, two dogs did distinguish themselves during the period between the two world wars. A Dutch Tervuren, Albert, was a police dog in Amsterdam. Trained as a tracking and defense dog for the judicial police, he died in the line of duty. After his death, a memorial was erected in Amsterdam to honor his achievements. His master, Inspector of Police Walter, wrote that he had owned Dutch and German Shepherd Dogs in addition to Albert, but wanted no breed other than a Tervuren.

The other Tervuren to achieve distinction was Gamin des Etangs Noir, who did so by becoming the first dog with an LOB number to win the international champion title for the new Union Canine International for dogs. LOB refers to the stud book of the Belgian Kennel Club, a professional club started in 1908 whose stud books are not recognized by the Saint Hubert Society, the FCI or the American Kennel Club.

After World War I, M. Felix E. Verbanck, who had been an active dog breeder before the war, began to breed Malinois. In 1931, he produced his first Malinois litter with the kennel name Ecaillon. In later life, Verbanck became a judge and valued adviser on the breeding of Belgians. He researched the history and foundations of the varieties and encouraged European breeders, as well as the fledgling breeders in the United States. His numerous articles on breeding are just as applicable today as they were when he wrote them years ago.

AFTER WORLD WAR II

Before World War II, and for a time afterward, very few Tervuren were bred in Belgium. M. E. Desees of the town of Tervuren did breed two to four litters every year at his Ferme Termunt kennels, and a few other breeders, whose dogs were used to revive the Tervuren after World War II, deserve mention. They were M. Rombaux of Cité de Gilles kennels, M. Duchesne of Val Clos des Sarts and M. Ficheroulle (who produced Urvinioul and Urvinor, offspring of Vici, who was mentioned earlier).

In 1947 M. Philemon van den Eynde's Malinois kennel, Brigade (in Belgium), produced its first Tervuren litter based on a Malinois named Crigga. Crigga, who became a working champion in 1931, was from Belgian parents of unknown origin. She was exhibited at a small show, however, and was awarded a third-excellent rating, thus qualifying her for a LOSH number and for breeding. She was bred to several excellent Malinois studs. With Ivan de L'Ecaillon (a dog with a half-long coat) she produced Mabel de la Brigade, who also had a half-long coat. (Short coats are dominant to long coats, but imperfectly so. Occasionally breedings of long- and short-coated dogs produce offspring with half-long coats.) Mabel remained at the kennel and was bred to a short-coated fawn named Matelot. The breeding produced Tjop de la Brigade, a well-built, long-coated dog of pale color, the kennel's first Tervuren.

As a stud fee from Matelot's breeding to the Malinois, Leorita, the kennel took Tosca du Bon Flair as pick of the litter. She was a typical Tervuren of medium size with small ears and a good coat of ideal color. Tjop was bred to Tosca and, thereafter, the kennel devoted itself to breeding Tervuren. The pair's best known and most important offspring was Xylander de la Brigade,

Tjop de la Brigade, grandson of Crigga and grandsire of Neth. Ch. Brigadier de la Brigade (U.S.)

Lola, born of blacks, was the great-granddam of Willy de la Garde Noire, also born of blacks.

9

used as a stud by Brigade and many other kennels. One of Xylander's sons, Netherland Ch. Brigadier de la Brigade, was brought to America, where he became a foundation sire for American Tervuren.

EARLY FRENCH KENNELS

Sang Bleu

The French must be credited with the firm establishment of the Tervuren variety. In France, as in Belgium, only a few early kennels were devoted to these dogs, although a good specimen would appear now and then. Shortly after World War II, M. Wasels began his Sang Bleu kennels with long-coated blacks. In 1945 he produced the long-coated fawns, Teck and Tanya de Sang Bleu. Born of black parents, they were grand offspring of a Tervuren named Lola. Lola was the origin of many fawns that were generations removed from her. Her fawn genes were transmitted through Groenendaels, but her great-granddam, Ch. Manon de la Sente, was a daughter of the fawn Lakme, who in turn was a daughter of the fawn Minox.

Wasels imported Voltigeur and Vedette de la Brigade, and Ugine de Montplairsir, another granddaughter of Lola. Bred to Voltigeur, Ugine produced the fawn Walhalla de Sang Bleu, who was sent to the Saint Jacques kennels. Two years later Vedette was bred to Willy (Stalick du Mordant x U'Sapho de la Maison Blanche) and produced Yvraie de Sang Bleu, who became the foundation bitch of the Cledeville kennels.

Saint Clair

In 1948 M. Gilbert Fontaine's new Saint Clair kennels furthered the renaissance of Tervuren by importing Willy de la Garde Noire from Belgium. Willy was born of black parents (Samy du Mordant x Ura du Chemin des Dames); however, Lola was his grandmother on both sides of his pedigree. By using Willy with Unique and Unica (both Vici daughters), the Saint Clair kennels produced dogs that captured numerous CAC and CACIB awards.

Fontaine also imported Altesse de la Brigade, a Xylander daughter, and bred her to Willy de la Garde Noire. One of their sons was Caprice du Clos Saint Clair, the only offspring to win over his famous sire. Another breeding of Willy to his daughter Youpette produced D'Jinn du Clos Saint Clair, used by several kennels as a stud.

One of the last big winners for Saint Clair was Kactus, who was awarded best young male at a breed specialty in 1962. Kactus was from a breeding of Jimmy de L'Assa (a Tervuren from Malinois parents) to the Tervuren Fauvette du Clos Saint Clair. Many of the dogs from the Saint Clair kennels became foundation dogs for newly created Tervuren kennels in France. This continued the Saint Clair line even after poor health forced Fontaine to close

Willy de la Garde Noire, whelped 3-14-48, sire of import Hety du Clos Saint Clair, early American producer

Caprice du Clos Saint Clair, whelped 10-3-53. This was the only son of Willy de le Garde Noire ever to win over his famous sire.

his kennels in 1964. The Saint Clair kennels also exported several dogs to the United States. Littermates D'Jimmy (later owned by Dorothy Hollister) and Daloue, and Hety and Hiarka (also littermates), went to Rudy Robinson. Miky went to June Betsworth.

Saint Jacques

Saint Jacques, a kennel established after World War II, began with long-coated blacks but became a prime breeder of Tervuren. Its owner, Charlotte Muller, regularly bred blacks and fawns together and whelped her first all-Tervuren litter in May 1950. She purchased two Tervuren: Witan de la Garde Noire (a brother to Willy), as a stud for her bitches, and Walhalla de Sang Bleu.

The kennel imported Ami du Clos Saint Clair (Willy de la Garde Noire x Unica) in 1951 and bred him to Walhalla in 1953. The resulting "C" litter produced Crigga and Chrysis du Clos Saint Jacques, imported to America by Rudy Robinson. Cheri du Clos Saint Jacques (from another breeding) had been sent to America three months earlier. In 1952, a litter by Swiss Ch. Urvinioul (Vici du Val Clos des Sarts x Rouline) out of Yalou du Clos Saint Jacques (Witan x Walhalla) contained the sisters Braise and Bale du Clos Saint Jacques. Their offspring gave the kennel great prominence in France and Switzerland, as well as in the United States. Dandy du Clos Saint Jacques, a Braise son, was sent to America, where he became the major foundation stud for American Tervuren.

A son of Ami and Braise, Faune du Clos Saint Jacques, was retained by the kennel. CACIB winner at many specialty shows in the provinces, he also was an excellent stud for both fawn and black bitches. Faune's son, Ch. Gin du Clos Saint Jacques (out of Fanny du Clos Saint Jacques—a black), was a very elegant and typey winner in shows between 1959 and 1963, and CACIB in Paris in 1960.

Cledeville

In 1950 Mme. A. Le Moro began her Cledeville kennel with Yvraie de Sang Bleu, a Tervuren with excellent body proportions. Yvraie was bred to her nephew, Xylander de la Brigade. The two produced some very good dogs, including the perfectly built Berengere de Cledeville, who was kept by the kennel.

Berengere was bred three times to D'Jinn du Clos Saint Clair. The pair produced CAC and CACIB offspring. They also produced Eros and Hans de Cledeville, who remained at the kennel as studs; Ivan, who went to a French breeder; Habra, who became a champion in Luxembourg; and several prominent bitches. Bred to his dam Berengere for her last litter, Eros produced Jasmine de Cledeville, who was sent to Bob and Barbara Krohn in America. With Ismene du Clos Saint Jacques (a Faune daughter), Eros produced Kenny

Ch. Crigga du Clos Saint Jacques,
whelped 1928, owned by policeman
Philemon van den Eynde

Int. Ch. Beaute Gin du Clos Saint Jacques, whelped 10-1-57. Breeder: C. Muller; owner:
Mme. Blot.

Quow Boy du Long Spinoy, whelped 8-8-67, by Ogam de d'Artamas (black) x Kinnie de la Ferme Termunt. Breeder: Mme. Bottemanne.

Int. Ch. Tarass de la Pouroffe, whelped 1970, appears in pedigrees of many American dogs. Sire: Quow Boy du Long Spinoy; dam: Riquitta du Val des Aubepines. Breeder-owner: Mme. Bottemanne.

de Cledeville, imported to America by Lou Hawkinson. This was the last litter produced by Cledeville kennel.

OTHER POSTWAR KENNELS

Among other kennels producing Tervuren after World War II was the Parceval kennel of Gerard Couturier, who had bred some fawns from his blacks. Of note was Ungoh de Parceval, the first male fawn to win a CAC after the war. Ungoh's dam was a granddaughter of Lola. Ungoh was bred to Unique at the Saint Clair kennels to produce Witty du Clos Saint Clair, who became a stud for the kennels.

Val d'Orge, owned by M. Maurice Jolivet, produced blacks, grays and some fawns from intervariety breedings. One of the fawns, Ouka du Val d'Orge (Milord des Masques de Sable x Magda du Val d'Orge), was sent to Edeltraud Laurin in the United States.

The Trois Fleuves kennel of Mme. Deyas owned Tervuren for twenty years. It produced few litters, but they were of good quality. The kennel's principal stud, Heros du Clos Saint Clair, sired Loris de Marquisere, who proved to be an excellent producer. One of her daughters, Quadhia des Trois Fleuves, was imported by Lou Hawkinson to the United States.

Interest in Tervuren continued to increase during the 1960s and became even more evident in the 1970s and 1980s. Many more kennels in Belgium and France, originally breeding long-coated blacks, added Tervuren as well. Some of the more prominent kennels in Belgium producing Tervuren were Bonmoss, Val des Aubepines, Landas, Talion, Long Spinoy, Pouroffe, of the Two and Ferme Termunt.

Prominent French kennels include Bois du Tot, Gorges de Lure, Horizons Boises, la Colla Dona, Masques de Sable, Parc de l'Hay, Parc de Sceaux (grays), Puits d'Ombelle, d'Artamas, Cher and Hauts de Bievre.

Furia, whelped 5-9-24.
Breeder: de Pauw.

Swiss Ch. Urvinioul, a son of
Vici, whelped 9/5/46.
Breeder: Ficheroulle; owner:
Deprez.

2

Understanding European Practices

ALTHOUGH THE DEVELOPMENT OF Belgian Tervuren in the United States began in 1953 with the importation of European stock, most American breeders soon lost contact with the breed's homeland. For over two decades the American fancy was content to develop the breed from the early imports, and not till recently have European dogs been imported in significant numbers. To this day the activities of the breed in Europe remain a mystery to many of our fanciers. What follows will, we hope, give readers a greater understanding of and appreciation for the breed closer to its homeland.

TRACING PEDIGREES

Tracing the history and pedigrees of the ancestors of our Tervuren beyond U.S. borders can be confusing to many Americans. The primary reason for this is that Tervuren, Groenendael and Malinois are separate breeds in the United States and cannot be interbred. Most of us are accustomed to reading pedigrees of American-bred Tervuren, whose all-Tervuren ancestry in this country dates back as far as the mid-1950s. This is not so when we look at pedigrees of European Tervuren. There (and elsewhere) they are considered to be one variety of a single breed, as is the case of smooth- and rough-coated Collies in the United States. One must then trace pedigrees back through Belgians of many coat colors and lengths and readjust one's thinking to the concept of the generic "Belgian Sheepdog" rather than the Belgian Tervuren.

Those attempting to locate each of the "Tervuren" in a particular European pedigree will face even more difficulty because owners were not always required to keep exact records of the color varieties. The designation "Tervuren," which most Americans interpret to be a dog of fawn to mahogany base color, was applied to grays and other coloring, a detail not always spelled out in individual records (this is also true in American pedigrees).

The reader must also know that registration practices vary from country to country. In Europe and in Canada variety is specified on a dog's registration according to its actual coat type and color, regardless of the variety of its parents. In the United States, dogs are registered under the parents' breed name. Thus, when the occasional black, gray or other color is born to Tervuren parents, it is registered as a Tervuren. In the same way, long-coated puppies of Malinois parents or "other than black" offspring of Groenendael (Belgian Sheepdog) parents are registered under the breed name of their parents. Such offspring are ineligible for showing and considered undesirable for breeding.

THE NAME GAME

History shows that the name "Tervuren" frequently referred to all acceptable colors other than black. "Tervuren" was not used in the stud books of Belgium until 1952 to describe a specific color hue. "Long Haired Fawn" was used for what we accept as proper Tervuren color, while other shadings, such as sable, beige, cream and gray, were described as "Other than Fawn or Black." In 1952 the fawns were referred to as "Tervuren."

The French, conversely, called all shades other than black "Tervuren" until 1950. At that time, the "Other than Fawn or Black" designation was given to the other colors. In 1966 the FCI moved both "Tervuren" and "Other than Fawn or Black" into a single classification—"Other than Black"—since the shadings of fawn to gray are often difficult to distinguish. The Belgian and French kennel clubs followed the lead of the FCI and finally, in 1975, the designation "Other than Black" was renamed "Tervuren—Long Coat Other than Black." Thus they are today.

A PURE TERVUREN LINE

The genes for the Tervuren coloration accepted by Americans come from a breeding of two fawns, Tom and Poes, whose fawn daughter Miss was bred to the black Duc de Groenendael and produced Milsart, the forefather of all

Pure Tervuren Pedigree of Vici du Val Clos des Sarts (T)

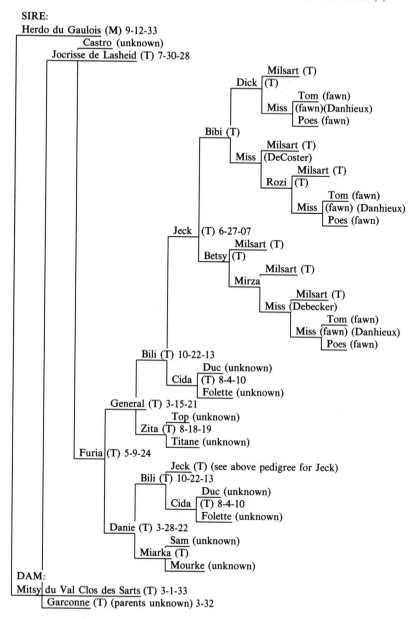

SIRE:
Herdo du Gaulois (M) 9-12-33
    Castro (unknown)
    Jocrisse de Lasheid (T) 7-30-28

                                  Milsart (T)
                       Dick (T)
                                    Tom (fawn)
                              Miss (fawn)(Danhieux)
                                    Poes (fawn)
                  Bibi (T)
                                    Milsart (T)
                       Miss (DeCoster)
                                    Milsart (T)
                       Rozi (T)
                                    Tom (fawn)
                              Miss (fawn) (Danhieux)
                                    Poes (fawn)
              Jeck (T) 6-27-07
                          Milsart (T)
                       Betsy (T)
                                  Milsart (T)
                       Mirza
                                  Milsart (T)
                            Miss (Debecker)
                                  Tom (fawn)
                              Miss (fawn) (Danhieux)
                                  Poes (fawn)
           Bili (T) 10-22-13
                        Duc (unknown)
                     Cida (T) 8-4-10
                        Folette (unknown)
        General (T) 3-15-21
                      Top (unknown)
                    Zita (T) 8-18-19
                      Titane (unknown)
      Furia (T) 5-9-24
                  Jeck (T) (see above pedigree for Jeck)
                Bili (T) 10-22-13
                      Duc (unknown)
                    Cida (T) 8-4-10
                      Folette (unknown)
        Danie (T) 3-28-22
                  Sam (unknown)
              Miarka (T)
                  Mourke (unknown)

DAM:
Mitsy du Val Clos des Sarts (T) 3-1-33
    Garconne (T) (parents unknown) 3-32

Elderly Tervuren and owner on street in Tervuren, Belgium, 1988. *Bob Krohn*

Show ring, Paris show, September 1988. Note spectators and assistants in ring.

Temperament tests, Paris show, September 1988. *Bob Krohn*

Belgian Tervuren. Their genes were transmitted through successive generations of Malinois and Groenendael (the predominant varieties until after World War II), occasionally surfacing as a long-coat born to Malinois parents or a fawn born to Groenendael parents. World War I and II nearly wiped out any pure lines of Tervuren tracing directly to Tom and Poes, and as this chapter demonstrates, most breeders were indifferent about perpetuating the variety for a long time. Thus, most modern Tervuren will trace their lineage through predominantly Groenendael and/or Malinois lines.

Vici du Val Clos des Sarts appears in the pedigrees of some of the early imports to the United States. He is the only dog through which we can find a pure Tervuren line to Tom and Poes. This line was brought to America through four of Vici's offspring—two daughters (the sisters Unique and Unica out of the Tervuren bitch Sandai de la Cite des Gilles), and two sons (the brothers Urvinioul and Urvinor out of the Tervuren bitch Rouline).

Vici's pedigree is partially presented here to illustrate his all-Tervuren link to Tom and Poes. Each dog's variety and birthdate (if known) follows the dog's name: (T) for Tervuren, (M) for Malinois, (G) for Groenendael and (unknown) if the variety is not known. In the case of the name Miss, the owner's name follows for clarity. For the sake of simplicity, we do not continue the pedigree of any dog not known to follow this pure Tervuren line. We stop whenever we reach Milsart, the forefather of the Belgian Tervuren.

The reader should note that even Vici was sired by a Malinois and had other varieties in his pedigree. It actually is fortunate that the Tervuren was not bred "pure" for color and coat type all the way back to Tom and Poes because Vici's pedigree demonstrates the inbreeding that was necessary to fix and perpetuate this color. Had this continued, our breed as we know it would have evolved out of a pure interest in color, a circumstance that would not have created a healthy genetic base for a working breed whose beauty must be balanced with soundness, intelligence and working ability.

THE FCI BREED STANDARD

Today, all countries belonging to the FCI use the standard of Belgium, the breed's country of origin. It accepts fawn, black, brindle and the whole gamut of shadings from fawn to gray to black. It states, however, that "for the Tervuren the fawn with the black overlay being the most natural, remains the preferred one."

The standard requires all nonblack dogs to have a good mask. It specifies that "the mask must tend to comprise the upper and under lips, the corner of the lips and eyelids in one black area," that is, a solid black muzzle. The strict minimum for the Tervuren variety is "pigmentation of the head area of both ears, two top eyelids, the two top lips and the two bottom lips must be black," a definition that is unacceptable under the U.S. standard.

INTERVARIETY BREEDING IN EUROPE

The practice of interbreeding Belgian varieties in Europe and other countries has been debated and changed over the years. It has also fascinated and confused Americans. History has shown that judicious intervariety breeding produced dogs of exceptional type and quality. Certainly the Tervuren as we know it would not have evolved without the contributions of its Malinois and Groenendael ancestors.

Genetic factors control the outcome of intervariety breedings and, for the uninitiated, may yield unexpected results. For example, a solid black dog may lack the genes needed to produce a black mask, dark overlay or richness of base color. Although this would present no problem in the production of black offspring, it could result in surprises in some of its fawn-colored offspring. Likewise, mating dogs of differing coat types can yield other surprises.

Intervariety breeding of the Belgian varieties has been prohibited in Europe since 1964, as a general rule. In most European countries (including Belgium, France and Holland), such a breeding must be approved by the Breeding Commission of that country's specialty club. The Breeding Commission consists of one member of the national kennel club (for example, the Saint Hubert KC in Belgium), two breeders of Belgians and one expert on temperament. Both the male and the female must have been designated "selected for breeding" (which appears on pedigrees as "s.r."). To receive this recommendation, dogs must not only be considered outstanding physical specimens but must also have passed a temperament test. The potential breeder must be highly regarded, with an outstanding record, and prove that he or she has specific needs that can be achieved only by the intervariety breeding.

Few such breedings have been approved—perhaps one or two per year in Belgium and six to eight in France. A breeding between a long-coat and a short-coat is rarely permitted, and intervariety breeding is even more rare between long and rough coats (Laekenois). In recent years, however, Belgium has permitted some Malinois-Laekenois breedings to broaden the Laekenois gene pool.

The majority of permits for intervariety breedings have been given for dogs of the same coat type—that is, long-coated blacks to long-coated "other than blacks." These breedings have resulted in an increase in long-coated sables, creams and silver grays, particularly in France. Among the prominent winners and top-producing studs with these colors have been Quarry van Nekkerberg Ter Lie, Milko du Parc de l'Hay and Swiss Ch. Vici des Hauts Bievre.

These stamps were issued in Belgium in October 1986 to honor the dog breeds developed in that country. In addition to the Belgian Sheepdog stamps, there is a stamp of the Bouvier des Flandres.

AMERICAN IMPORTATION PRACTICES

Tervuren have been imported to the United States on a regular basis since the early 1950s, shortly after French kennels became interested in them. Americans, then, also played a significant part in the development of a long-ignored Tervuren. Because no interbreeding of the AKC Belgian breeds is allowed, and more than thirty years of pure Tervuren breeding can be recorded, it is safe to say that the Belgian Tervuren has been developed as a singular breed more in the United States than in any other country. Since 1980, all imported Tervuren must have three generations of Tervuren ancestors to be permitted AKC registration.

American breeders continue to import puppies and adults from proven European winners. Bernadine Paull's Ch. Tanzy De Landas, UDT, played a principal role as foundation bitch for her homebred Hi Times litters in the 1970s. Another dog, brought back from Belgium by Thomas and Katherine Walker around 1976, was Am. Ch. Yamin van 'T Hof Melyn. Koning, as he is called, has made a tremendous contribution to improvement of type and is an all-time top-producing stud. Likewise, later acquisitions of Dauphin and Duchesse de la Belle Edita, and Dali and Darass de la Pouroffe, imported by Mary Linda Adams for Janet Barringer and Steve Sorenson (Dali), have contributed many favorable qualities.

From time to time, other Tervuren have been imported from France, Belgium, Sweden, Switzerland and Italy. All have contributed to the future of American Tervuren.

3

The Breed Comes to the United States: The Early Years

THE ROOTS of the Belgian Tervuren breed in America can be found in the 1950s. During that decade the number of enthusiasts and dogs were small, but their activities laid the foundation for all the dogs and kennels that followed. This chapter is a chronicle of the events, people and dogs of the era that gave the breed its start and propelled it forward.

FIRST AMERICAN REGISTRATIONS

The first confirmed record of a Tervuren to be registered by the American Kennel Club (AKC) is from the early 1920s, when Oliver Ormsby Page brought a dog named Cesar into the country. Page used Cesar at stud with a long-coated black bitch, La Terrible Lionne, and produced a litter of both long-coated blacks and blackened fawns. Not until mid-century, however, did fanciers begin to seriously import show and breeding stock from the Continent.

Rudolf Robinson (1903–1973) with friends, 1950

Cheri du Clos Saint Jacques, whelped 4-8-53

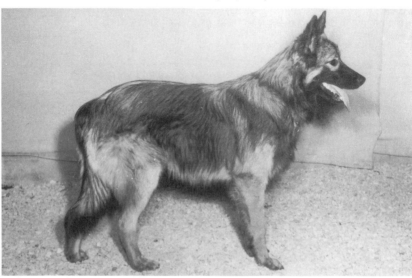

Candide Kennels

Principal among these early breeders was Rudolf (Rudy) Robinson and his Candide kennels. Rudy had owned a Belgian Sheepdog in 1924 but concentrated on breeding German Shepherd Dogs until the mid-1940s, when he began to import a number of black Belgians.

Rudy corresponded with several kennel owners in France, including Felix Verbanck, secretary of the Royal Groenendael Club in Belgium, for information and history on the breed. M. Verbanck furnished him with extensive historical material and pedigrees on the breed's early foundation dogs. The pedigrees extended over many generations and identified the variety of each dog listed.

Rudy started a newsletter, *Today's Belgian,* and sent it to Belgian Sheepdog owners. He also wrote articles for *Popular Dogs* and had them printed into pamphlets. One was titled "The Complete Story of the Belgian Sheepdog."

Rudy's primary importance to our breed, however, rests on his decision to import Tervuren to the United States and establish them as legitimate members of the Belgian Sheepdog family. He had continued to correspond with various European breeders (especially Verbanck) and became convinced that Tervuren, with their fine temperaments and contrasting bright colors, would appeal to many breeders in this country. Before he actually imported any Tervuren, however, Rudy arranged with Robert and Barbara Krohn of Los Alamos, New Mexico, to take a female Tervuren puppy. The Krohns already owned one of Rudy's imports, a beautiful Groenendael named Ch. Zamorane, CDX (Juli). His secretary, Marge Coyle, was to take another female.

After several months of consultation with Verbanck, Rudy decided to import Tervuren from Charlotte Muller's Saint Jacques kennel in France. Early in 1953, Cheri du Clos Saint Jacques arrived at the Candide kennels. He was sired by Asko du Bois de l'Arsot, out of Avocette du Clos Saint Jacques. Cheri was followed a few months later by the litter sisters Crigga and Chrysis du Clos Saint Jacques. Crigga went to Mrs. Coyle, Chrysis to the Krohns. A rather charming aside to these events is that Chrysis arrived in New Mexico via Railway Express. She had made the long journey from France, via Chicago, in a wicker picnic basket, an experience that failed to dampen her spirits.

The pedigrees of these first imports reveal that they were produced from the same foundation stock that helped revive Belgian and French Tervuren kennels after World War II. The background of these foundation dogs was almost entirely Malinois and Groenendael lines. The demise of dogs descending from the original Tervuren bloodlines was caused, in part, by the loss of valuable stock in the two world wars and, as has been noted, by a lack of breeder interest in the Tervuren variety.

Chrysis du Clos Saint Jacques, CD

```
                          Samy du Mordant (G)
                Willy | de la Garde Noire (T)
              |         Ura du Chemin des Dames (G)
      Ami du Clos Saint Clair (T)
      |                 Vici du Val Clos des Sarts (T)
      |         Unica (T)
      |                 Sandai de la Cite des Gilles (T)
CHRYSIS DU CLOS SAINT JACQUES CD (France) whelped 5/20/53, breeder C. Muller
      |                 Tjop de la Brigade (T)
      |         Voltigeur de la Brigade (T)
      |                 Tosca du Bon Flair (T)
      Walhalla de Sang Bleu (T)
                        Mick (G)
                Ugine de Monplaisir (T)
                        Qualine de l'Etoile Blanche (G)
```

28

Ch. Dandy du Clos Saint Jacques, BAR

```
                              Willy de la Garde Noire (T)
                  Ami du Clos Saint Clair (T)
                        Unica (T)
        Chip du Clos Saint Jacques (T)
                              Voltigeur de la Brigade (T)
                  Walhalla de Sang Bleu (T)
                        Ugine de Montplaisir (T)
CH. DANDY DU CLOS SAINT JACQUES BAR (France) (T) whelped 12/25/54, breeder
                              Vici du Val Clos des Sarts (T)                    C. Muller
                  Swiss Ch. Urvinioul (T)
                        Rouline (T)
        Braise du Clos Saint Jacques (T)
                              Witan de la Garde Noire (T)
                  Yalou du Clos Saint Jacques (T)
                        Walhalla de Sang Bleu (T)
```

Neth. Ch. Brigadier de la Brigade, C-BAR

```
                              Matelot (M)
                     Tjop de la Brigade (T)
                              Mabel de la Brigade (M)
             Xylander de la Brigade (T)
                              Matelot (M)
                     Tosca du Bon Flair (T)
                              Leorita (M)
NETHERLAND CH. BRIGADIER DE LA BRIGADE C-BAR (Belgium) whelped 3-6-52
                              Samy du Mordant (G)     breeder, P. van den Eynde
                     Willy de la Garde Noir (T)
                              Ura du Chemin des Dames (G)
             Arka du Clos St. Clair (T)
                              Vici du Val Clos des Sarts (T)
                     Unica (T)
                              Sandai de la Cite des Gilles (T)
```

Hety du Clos Saint Clair

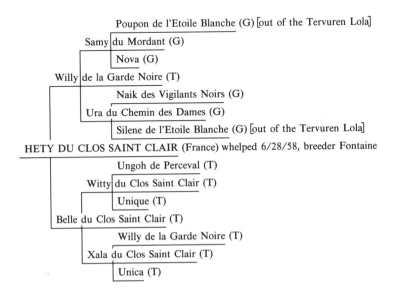

Poupon de l'Etoile Blanche (G) [out of the Tervuren Lola]

Samy du Mordant (G)

Nova (G)

Willy de la Garde Noire (T)

Naik des Vigilants Noirs (G)

Ura du Chemin des Dames (G)

Silene de l'Etoile Blanche (G) [out of the Tervuren Lola]

HETY DU CLOS SAINT CLAIR (France) whelped 6/28/58, breeder Fontaine

Ungoh de Perceval (T)

Witty du Clos Saint Clair (T)

Unique (T)

Belle du Clos Saint Clair (T)

Willy de la Garde Noire (T)

Xala du Clos Saint Clair (T)

Unica (T)

THE INTERNATIONAL FRIENDSHIP TROPHY

The first exhibition of Tervuren in the United States occurred in March 1954, when Chrysis was shown at the Wisconsin Kennel Club show. A month later, Cheri and Crigga joined Chrysis in exhibition at the Belgian Sheepdog Club of America's specialty at the International Kennel Club of Chicago show. At that time, all Belgian Sheepdog varieties—Groenendael, Tervuren and Malinois—were shown together in the same classes, a circumstance that would prevail for another five years.

At this show, a unique award was presented. The Club de Francais du Chien de Berger Belge (Belgian Sheepdog Club of France) had a bronze sculpture made by M. Fath, brother of the famous dress designer Jacques Fath. Inscribed "International Friendship Trophy," it depicted a Belgian Sheepdog standing watch over a flock of sheep. It was offered by the CFCBB to the Tervuren judged to be the best at this show. Of the three Tervuren entries, Crigga was judged the best, and her owner, Marge Coyle, was given the plaque. She later gave it to Rudy Robinson, who passed it on to the Krohns two years before his death.

EXHIBITION AND BREEDING IN THE 1950s

Cheri, Crigga and Chrysis each earned the CD degree at less than or near one year of age. Chrysis was the first to do so, at ten months of age, in three straight shows. Chrysis also was the first Tervuren to receive championship points (1955) and was the dam of the first American-bred champion bitch.

In September 1954 Crigga whelped the first American-born litter of Tervuren. Cheri was the sire. In the same year Rudy began to import more Tervuren to establish a broader breeding base. Littermates D'Jimmy and Daloue du Clos Saint Clair arrived from Gilbert Fontaine's kennel in France. They were followed in early 1955 by another brother and sister, Dandy and Dolly du Clos Saint Jacques. The last Tervuren imported by Rudy were littermates Hety and Hiarka du Clos Saint Clair, brought from France in 1959.

Rudy showed D'Jimmy frequently in conformation against the better-known Groenendael. Under the ownership of Betty Hinckley, D'Jimmy won his championship in June 1958, thus becoming the first Tervuren in the United States to achieve this title.

Rudy bred his imports into the early 1960s, when ill health forced him to stop. In addition to his own stock, he made use of Netherland Ch. Brigadier de la Brigade, brought from Holland to the Chicago area by his owners, Mr. and Mrs. M. W. Ch. Peters. Brigadier's bloodlines were somewhat different from those of Rudy's dogs, and he proved to be a useful stud for Rudy and other kennels as well.

The following are some of the noteworthy dogs produced by Rudy's kennel:

International Friendship Trophy, awarded in 1954. *K. P. Johnson*

Ch. Jory Candide, whelped 5-21-56

Ch. Jory Candide and Ch. Thistle Candide (owned by William and Opal McGee)

Tammi Candide (owned by Cliff and Lou Hawkinson)

Ch. Topper Candide, CD (owned by Howard Pinc)

Ch. Zorro's Mark of Candide (owned by Rudy)

Ch. Hollie Candide (owned by Nancie Mages)

Ch. Lancer Candide (owned by Bill and Joan Kennedy of Canada)

A Tribute to Rudy Robinson

In 1973 the American Belgian Tervuren Club published the first of what would be several volumes of the *Belgian Tervuren Genealogy Book*. Volume I was dedicated to Rudy Robinson with the following inscription:

> This book and its love for the Belgian Tervuren are dedicated to Rudy Robinson, who gave us the Belgian Tervuren in the United States.
>
> It was Rudy's intellectual curiosity about all types of Belgian Sheepdogs that moved him to import the Tervuren. He loved the Tervuren immediately and promoted them with skill and knowledge.
>
> Rudy had more influence on the Groenendael and Tervuren than any person ever had in this country. He brought the foremost European breeders into contact with the American breeders, gleaned volumes of knowledge from European breeders and was *Ambassador Extraordinaire* for the sheepherding dogs of Belgium.
>
> His importance to the Tervuren will never decrease with time.

THE BELGIAN TERVUREN BECOMES A SEPARATE BREED

In the 1950s Tervuren were being bred and shown in increasing numbers in several parts of the country. The Malinois was being bred mainly in the eastern states and a few other areas. The black Groenendael was already quite well established in the United States, with breeders concentrated primarily in the Midwest and the East. At the time, a number of influential Groenendael breeders lacked an understanding of the history of the Belgian varieties, varietal roles in the breed and intervariety breeding in Europe. They objected to the intervariety breedings being made in the United States and to the presence of Tervuren and Malinois in the show ring.

A group of these breeders complained to the AKC's Board of Directors about the intervariety breedings and the fact that dogs of different coat lengths and colors were being shown together. In response, the AKC sent out a questionnaire to members of the Belgian Sheepdog Club of America (BSCA) in 1958, asking their opinions on intervariety breeding and conformation competition.

First Tervuren champions: Ch. D'Jimmy du Clos Saint Clair, CD (*standing*), and Ch. Fidelite de Fauve Charbonne, CD.

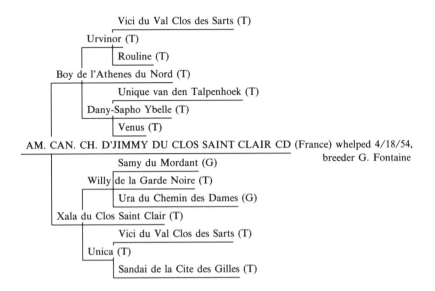

Vici du Val Clos des Sarts (T)

Urvinor (T)

Rouline (T)

Boy de l'Athenes du Nord (T)

Unique van den Talpenhoek (T)

Dany-Sapho Ybelle (T)

Venus (T)

AM. CAN. CH. D'JIMMY DU CLOS SAINT CLAIR CD (France) whelped 4/18/54, breeder G. Fontaine

Samy du Mordant (G)

Willy de la Garde Noire (T)

Ura du Chemin des Dames (G)

Xala du Clos Saint Clair (T)

Vici du Val Clos des Sarts (T)

Unica (T)

Sandai de la Cite des Gilles (T)

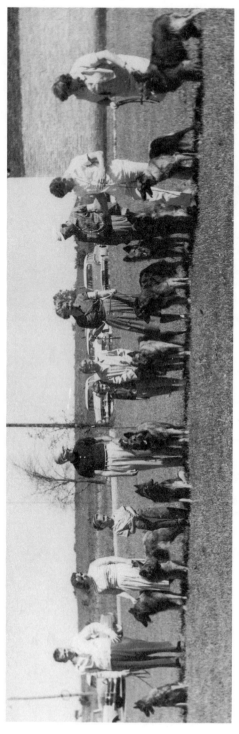

Living up to their promise to AKC, owners united to bolster Tervuren entries. This early photo was taken at the Chain O'Lakes KC, June 19, 1960. *Left to right:* Tammi Candide with Cliff Hawkinson, Ch. Storisende Timothy and Bronze de Laubenfels with Dorothy Hollister, Zorro Candide ("Pete," owned by the McGees) with Patsi Harris, Ch. Gironde de Lafayette with Lee Harris, Ch. Imp Rouge de Fauve Charbonne, CD, with Di and Jacquie Krohn, Ch. Dandy du Clos Saint Jacques with Barbara Krohn, littermates Hiarka and Hety du Clos Saint Clair with Rudy Robinson, Dolly du Clos Saint Jacques with Rudy's helper and Ch. Jory Candide with Opal McGee.

Although less than half of the BSCA membership responded to the questionnaire, the Board of Directors decided that the varieties must be separated into breeds to end the complaints. The Groenendael would retain the name Belgian Sheepdog. Tervuren and Malinois were not to be permitted to use the breed name and were to be relegated to the Miscellaneous Class in conformation showing.

Tervuren owners banded together to protest this decision. They wrote letters, presented documents on history and breeding to the AKC and promised that their dogs would continue to be shown extensively if they were allowed to compete in regular breed classes.

Finally, the AKC agreed. Beginning on July 1, 1959, the breed was to be called Belgian Tervuren and its representatives shown in regular classes as part of the Working Group. The word *Tervuren* was chosen by the AKC to be used as both singular and plural for the breed. The Malinois were named Belgian Malinois and remained in the Miscellaneous Class because of their small numbers at the time. The few Laekenois in this country were entirely denied recognition and registration.

THE AMERICAN BELGIAN TERVUREN CLUB IS FOUNDED

With the Krohns as spearheads, the American Belgian Tervuren Club (ABTC) was established in 1959 with twelve charter members. The club moved quickly to draft a breed standard for AKC approval and begin activities to help establish the fledgling breed. It started a newsletter, named then as now *Tervuren News Tales (TNT)*, promoted supported entries wherever dogs could be gathered and held sanctioned matches in breed and obedience.

The first national supported show was held in 1961 and each year thereafter until 1972, when it was allowed to hold its first national specialty show. In 1978 it held its first independent national specialty. Since then, independent nationals have been held each year across the country. Without the persistence and faith of those early breeders and breed enthusiasts, the story might have ended in quite a different fashion.

EARLY KENNELS

Bar-K Kennels (Fauve Charbonne)

While Rudy Robinson's importation of Tervuren gave the United States its foundation stock, it was Robert and Barbara Krohn's breeding program that provided a foundation for nearly every early American kennel.

In March 1956, the Krohns' Chrysis produced the country's second litter of Tervuren, sired by D'Jimmy. Several members of this first "Fauve Charbonne" litter were sent to various parts of the country. Fidelite went to Dorothy Blew Hollister in Illinois, Fillette to Marion Glover in Oregon and Flair to the East Coast. Fidelite and Flair would go on to become champions. Fidelite would become foundation bitch for the Val de Tonnerre kennels, and Flair would become foundation stud for the Chateau Blanc kennels. A later breeding of Chrysis to Netherland Ch. Brigadier de la Brigade, in 1959, would produce Ch. Imp Rouge de Fauve Charbonne, CD.

In an effort to obtain more refinement of type and elegance of head structure, the Krohns imported Jasmine de Cledeville from Mme. Le Moro of France in 1961. Jasmine's offspring gave them what they wanted. From her first litter, sired by Dandy, came five champions. The bitches were Ch. Kandice, CDX; Ch. Kriquette; and Ch. Katie; the males were Ch. Kappy and Ch. Kim de Fauve de Charbonne, CD. This litter is recognized by the Tervuren fancy as among the most influential ever produced, for the three bitches were to become foundations of other major kennels. Katie went to California to start the Betsworths' Georjune kennels, Kandice to the Laurins' Chateau Blanc kennels and Kriquette to the Dickens' Bonheur kennels. The impact of Jasmine on the breed was so profound that she is highlighted, along with her pedigree, in Chapter 20, "Breeder's Achievement Awards."

Jasmine produced champions in every litter she produced, for a total of thirteen, including Chs. Mars, UDT; Mystique, CD; and Matelot. The Krohns retained Mystique (sired by D'Artagnone du Falaise) for their breeding program. She produced Chs. Quien Es, CD; Scorpio, CD, TD; Satin, CDX; Suzette, CD; Soubrette, CDX; and Sassafras. Later imports of Loyal du Clos Saint Jacques and his first cousin, Lucie du Clos Saint Jacques, added other needed features to the Fauve Charbonne lines.

Barbara believes that her most important stud dog was Ch. Padric O'Bar K Can Do, CD (Paddy), whose pedigree went back to both Jasmine and Chrysis within a few generations. Paddy lived for more than fourteen years and left a legacy of excellent sons and daughters and grand offspring still being shown. He passed on type, color and, most importantly, his strong, outgoing temperament.

The Krohns were actively involved in breeding and exhibiting for twenty-six years, from 1956 to 1982. Although they no longer breed, their influence on the breed remains, and both have become respected judges. At the 1986 ABTC National Specialty, Bob judged the majority of male classes, veteran and nonregular classes. Barbara was honored as the breeder-judge at the 1985 AKC Centennial show and has judged ABTC Sweepstakes classes and the 1988 ABTC National Specialty.

Val de Tonnerre

The 1950s laid the foundation for other Tervuren breeders, as well. Dorothy Hollister's (later English) Val de Tonnerre kennel relied primarily on

Ch. Jasmine De Cledeville, BAR

h. Padric O'Bar K Can Do,
D, whelped 3-17-73, by Ch.
onheur Knight to Re-
ember, CD x Ch. Wayfarer's
weet Alice Can Do, CD

foundation stock from Rudy Robinson's imports. She also was the final owner of Ch. D'Jimmy du Clos Saint Clair, CD, whose last known ring appearance was in 1965 at the Kankakee, Illinois, ABTC Supported show, where he was defeated for the breed by his eight-year-old son, Ch. Flair de Fauve Charbonne.

Dorothy showed her Ch. Fidelite de Fauve Charbonne, CD (Leah), to her championship in September 1958, making her the second Tervuren to obtain the title in the United States, and the first American-bred champion. Leah was shown extensively as a Special. In June 1960, she took a second place in the Working Group, thus becoming the first Tervuren to achieve a Group placing. She also won BOB at the ABTC's 1962 National Supported show and BOS at one other national. Leah was bred once to her sire and produced Ch. Storisende Timothy, who became the first American-bred male champion Tervuren.

Dorothy purchased Nightwatch Tawny Theresa from Marion Glover of Oregon. A puppy from the breeding of Theresa to Timothy, followed later by one out of Theresa bred to Ch. Kis Tam's Candide Pataud, were the first Tervuren to go to Karen Johnson of Sunfire kennels, who remains active in the breed today.

For more than twenty-five years Dorothy bred many champions in the United States and, later, in Canada under the Blackamber prefix. Several of the dogs from Val de Tonnerre became foundation stock for other kennels, including Bonheur and Sanroyale.

Nightwatch Kennels

On the West Coast, Marion Glover began her Nightwatch kennels with a Groenendael bitch, Cuti Candide, purchased from Rudy Robinson. In 1956, she added Fillette de Fauve Charbonne from the Krohns' first litter and, shortly thereafter, Dandy du Clos Saint Jacques.

Fillette was bred to Dandy for her first litter. One of the offspring was Can. Ch. Nightwatch Russet Chevalier, Can. UDTX, a dog who would become famous for his trailblazing accomplishments, which are detailed in the chapters on Canada, obedience and tracking. Val's litter sister, Nightwatch Russet Rondo, also had been exported to Canada. She was bred back to her sire, Dandy, and produced D'Artagnone du Falaise, who was sent to the United States and used at stud to produce a number of champions.

The Nightwatch kennels also used Dandy as a stud with the black Cuti Candide, producing an all-black litter in 1956. A daughter from this litter was bred back to her sire to produce a litter of Tervuren and Groenendael in 1957. One of the Tervuren was Ch. Nightwatch Tawny Theresa.

Ch. Kenny de Cledeville, CD, BAR

Willy de la Garde Noire (T)
D'Jinn du Clos Saint Clair (T)
Youpette du Clos Saint Clair (T)
Eros de Cledeville (T)
Xylander de la Brigade (T)
Berengere de Cledeville (T)
Yvraie de Sang Bleu (T)
CH. KENNY DE CLEDEVILLE CD BAR (France), whelped 8/11/61, breeder
Mme. LeMoro
Ami du Clos Saint Clair (T)
Faune du Clos Saint Jacques (T)
Braise du Clos Saint Jacques (T)
Ismene du Clos Saint Jacques (T)
Cadix des Forges Monceux (G)
Gracieuse du Clos Saint Jacques (G)
Bale du Clos Saint Jacques (T)

41

Tervuren Haven Kennels

Another kennel active during the 1950s was Bill and Opal McGee's Tervuren Haven kennel in Michigan. In the 1940s, the McGees had bought a puppy whose parents, they were told, had been imported from Europe. Some years later, the McGees were attracted to Rudy Robinson's Tervuren, who they thought resembled their original dog.

The McGees purchased Jory Candide (Dandy du Clos Saint Jacques x Daloue du Clos Saint Clair) from Rudy in 1957. King, as he was called, finished his championship quickly. He was BOB at the ABTC's first national supported show in 1961 and placed in the Working Group twice.

King was bred only twice but produced five champions from the two litters. One of these was Ch. Thistle Candide (out of Hiarka du Clos Saint Clair), taken as a stud puppy by the McGees. Thistle was bred twice. From her breeding to Ch. Ami Roux du Val de Tonnerre, the McGees kept her son, Ch. Tervuren Haven's Kactus. Kactus' litter sister Tervuren Haven's Krickit also was shown and used for breeding by the McGees.

The handler for the McGees' Tervuren was Collie breeder Vivienne (Rickie) Richards, whose daughter Terry Harville's fond memories of the breed prompted her to purchase and finish her first Tervuren champion in the mid-1980s. Ill health forced Bill and Opal to abandon their showing and breeding program in the early 1970s, but their steadfast love and interest in Tervuren remained throughout their lives.

THE BREED ADVANCES

With the advent of the 1960s, new Tervuren kennels were established throughout the country, joining those of the 1950s. Although many of these early kennels are no longer active, their efforts were crucial to the establishment of Tervuren in America and are worthy of recognition.

Garde Roux Kennels

In about 1959, Lou and Cliff Hawkinson of Illinois purchased Tammi Candide (Brigadier de la Brigade x Dolly du Clos Saint Jacques) from Rudy Robinson. Bred to Hety du Clos Saint Clair, Tammi gave the kennel its first litter, which bore the Kis-Tam prefix, in January 1961.

Two excellent puppies from this litter—a dog and a bitch—soon proved their value to the breed. Ch. Kis-Tam's Renee, CD, TD, was kept by the Hawkinsons. Her brother, Ch. Kis-Tam's Candide Pataud, CD, was owned and shown by several different persons, including Karen Johnson (Sunfire kennels) in the United States and Bill and Joan Kennedy (Willoan) of Canada. Winner of a number of Group placements, Pataud was BOB at the 1966 and 1968 ABTC National Supported shows, and, at the age of ten years, BOB at

Hiarka du Clos Saint Clair, sister to Hety du Clos Saint Clair

the Belgian Sheepdog Club of Canada's National Specialty show. When bred to Brenda Leedy's Eau De Vie du Val de Tonnerre in 1966, he produced Ch. Rob-Lyn's Ange Acajou, CD ("Misha"), a bitch whose achievements are discussed in Chapter 20, "Breeder's Achievement Awards."

As a mate for Renee, Kenny de Cledeville was imported from France by the Hawkinsons. The first of three litters from the pair was whelped in October 1962, and the Garde Roux suffix was born. The matings of Kenny and Renee produced nine champions. Bred to Misha, Kenny produced BIS winner Ch. Rajah d'Antre du Louve, CD, a major stud for the Sanroyale kennels.

The Hawkinsons' breeding of Ch. Our Valient du Garde Roux to Oralee du Garde Roux in 1967 produced the breed's second BIS winner, Ch. Quincy du Garde Roux. A number of dogs from this kennel became foundation dogs for other kennels, including Bon Chateau and Flambeau Rouge. The kennel was active until the mid-1970s when the Hawkinsons retired to California.

Bon Chateau Kennels

Rev. Thomas Badger established his kennel with Garde Roux and Fauve Charbonne dogs. Kiki de Fauve Charbonne arrived at the end of 1961. A year later Lance and Lu-Tawny du Garde Roux joined Badger's breeding stock. At about the same time, Ch. Dandy du Clos Saint Jacques became available, and Tom quickly bought him. Dandy was entered at most southern California shows. With his beauty and excellent temperament, he became the first outstanding Tervuren show dog and sire in the country. He was bred to Kiki for the "A" and "B" Bon Chateau litters.

Kappy de Fauve Charbonne (Dandy x Jasmine de Cledeville) arrived at the kennel in early 1962, and Tom was to obtain several more dogs from the Garde Roux and Fauve Charbonne kennels over the next few years. The kennel remained active throughout the 1960s and into the early 1970s, when Tom retired from breeding dogs. In that relatively short time, however, the kennel produced some excellent animals, some of which were used as foundation and breeding stock by newer kennels, among them Braise Rouge (Allen), Cavalier (Eklund) and de Grandeza (Kolyer).

Georjune Kennels

June Betsworth established her kennel with German Shepherd Dogs but switched to Tervuren with the purchase of Katie de Fauve Charbonne. Katie was the first bitch to be bred out of the Krohns' famous "K" litter. With the birth of Katie's first litter on December 7, 1962, a new bloodline began. The sire of the litter was Netherlands Ch. Brigadier de la Brigade.

The most influential dog in the litter was Ch. Joker of Georjune, who was the top producing sire in 1971. He won a Canadian Group I to become the first Group-winning Tervuren in North America. Joker was kept by June along with his littermate Ch. Justa Flare of Georjune, the dam of

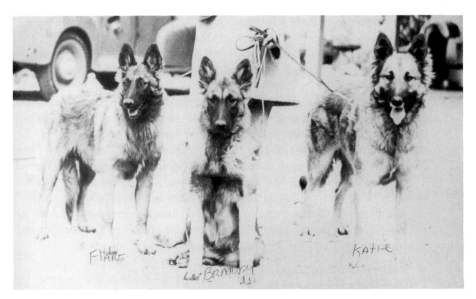

Ch. Katie de Fauve Charbonne, BAR (*right*), with two of her pups, Justa Flare and Jigger O'Brandy of Georjune, sired by Brigadier de la Brigade

Ch. Miky du Clos Saint Clair

Ch. Columbine Nikit, BAR, first Tervuren to win the old Working Group (prior to the establishment of the Herding Group)

twelve champions. Justa Flare and Joker were later bred to produce Ch. Oondine of Georjune, UD, and Ch. Olinda of Georjune, UD, a multiple High in Trial winner. Sometime thereafter, June imported Ch. Miky du Clos Saint Clair from France. He was bred to Justa Flare and produced the Georjune "Q" litter.

June continued to breed and show during the 1970s, but declining health forced her to curtail her activities. She managed to attend any event at which she felt she could help give recognition to the breed. The last dog she handled to its championship was Ch. Xanthos of Georjune, whose daughter, Ch. Pine Acres Daxene of Georjune, was the last champion produced by her kennel.

June Betsworth will be remembered not only for her successful breeding program, with its many champions and obedience titlists, but for producing the foundation stock for a generation of Tervuren owners. Among them are the kennels of Wallendale, de la Corps, Patana, de la Barge, Hilton, Carousel, Liberte and the Canadian kennels of Kingsgate and Chordeiles.

Columbine/du Rochemont Kennels

In the Denver, Colorado, area, Tom Graham and his partner Betty Engels imported Linda du Clos Saint Jacques from France in 1962. They embarked on a limited breeding program with Linda and a young male from the Krohns, M. Beau de Fauve Charbonne, CD. This breeding produced one of the decade's major winners and Group placers, Ch. Columbine Nikit, first Tervuren to win the old Working Group. For her second litter Linda was bred to D'Artagnone du Falaise, an inbred Dandy son from Canada. Later, offspring from the two litters were bred together with good results.

After Tom's death, Betty Engels continued the breeding program and produced several fine studs, including O'Boy du Rochemont, Nijinsky du Rochemont and Ch. Big John du Rochemont. Not long afterward, the kennel ceased breeding altogether.

The first era of Tervuren had drawn to an end. But as it did, its pioneers left a solid legacy on which an advancing generation was to draw. The base they built would permit the next wave of breeders and dogs to establish the breed as one worthy of general acceptance and recognition.

4

The Belgian Tervuren in Canada and Great Britain

IN CANADA, as in most countries of the world, the Tervuren is accepted as the long-coated blackened fawn or gray variety of the Belgian Sheepdog breed, with the Groenendael being the long-coated black variety, the Laekenois the rough-coated fawn or gray variety and the Malinois the short-coated fawn variety. The Canadian Kennel Club registers all representatives of the breed as Belgian Sheepdogs, with the variety designated on the pedigree as (T), (G), (L) or (M). Intervariety breeding is permitted, and the variety designation on registration papers and pedigrees is determined by the actual variety of the offspring, rather than the variety(ies) of the parents. Belgians imported into the country are not required to carry a three-generation pedigree true for any one variety. The parent club for the Belgian Sheepdog breed (which includes all varieties) is the Belgian Sheepdog Club of Canada (BSCC), founded in 1965.

As a variety, Tervuren arrived relatively late in the history of the Belgian Sheepdog breed in Canada. The first recorded Belgian import was a Malinois, Dicko des Banes, who arrived in 1912 but was not registered with the Canadian Kennel Club until 1922. In 1913, a Groenendael, Marc of Montreal, was imported from Belgium. He was followed a year later by a Groenendael bitch, Princess Louisa. In 1918, they produced the first recorded Belgian Sheepdog litter born in Canada. Both were owned by Charles Bourgeois of Montreal,

Can. Ch. Nightwatch Russet Chevalier, UD, TDX

Canadian-bred D'Artagnone du Falaise, BAR

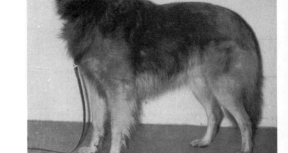

Can. Ch. Lancer Candide

Quebec, who joined with George Domus to establish the Belgium kennel. They subsequently imported other Groenendael and Malinois, and their kennel thrived from 1921 through 1932, producing sixteen litters and exporting a number of dogs of both varieties into the United States. Born in Belgium, these two men were excellent dog trainers and their dogs won many police and working dog trials. However, despite their early efforts to establish the Belgian Sheepdog breed in Canada, none of their Belgians have had an impact on current Belgians.

The first recorded Tervuren to be imported was Snap, produced from two blacks, Kiss-Kitch and Diantina, who arrived in Windsor, Ontario, in 1924. While holding the distinction of being the first Tervuren import, this dog had no impact on the subsequent development of the Tervuren variety or the Belgian breed. In fact, during the period from 1931 to 1952, there were few importations of dogs of any variety and no significant breedings of interest. It was not until the post–World War II period that interest in the breed developed in any serious manner, and then it was limited to the Groenendael variety. In 1954, a black bitch, Cathie de Columbia, was imported from France in whelp by Will du Chemin des Dames. She bore her first litter in July 1954. Although this importation and the subsequent litter had little impact on the development of the breed in Canada, it is interesting to note that this bitch was a littermate to two blacks, Ciana de Columbia and French Ch. Cheik de Columbia, both of whom can be found in the pedigrees of many modern Tervuren.

About this same time, Hugh Monroe of Thorold, Ontario, imported a black bitch, Luci Candide, CD, from Rudy Robinson of Illinois, and a black male, OTCh. Maximillian Bodeux Birbingen, from Mary Dillaway of Massachusetts. With these two dogs he launched a limited but interesting breeding program that attracted a number of enthusiastic puppy purchasers. These purchasers were mainly obedience enthusiasts and achieved excellent results in obedience trials, thereby attracting others to the breed. They also signaled the first important foray of Belgians into the conformation ring and, along with others, formed the nucleus of the BSCC.

In 1956 another American-born Groenendael, Nightwatch Chianti, CD, was imported by Joan McLelland of British Columbia. Born of Tervuren and Groenendael parents (Am. Ch. Dandy du Clos Saint Jacques x Cuti Candide), this bitch was bred back to her sire in 1958 and produced a litter of four fawns and two blacks, thus establishing the first recorded Canadian-bred Tervuren, registered under the prefix of Shelley's.

Obedience enthusiasts Don and Mollie Hudson of Victoria, British Columbia, were acquaintances of Joan McLelland and imported a Tervuren in 1957 who subsequently became Can. Ch. OTCh. Nightwatch Russet Chevalier, UD, TDX, by Dandy bred to Fillette de Fauve Charbonne. Val, as he was known, made history not only for the Tervuren variety but also the Belgian breed. He became the youngest dog of any breed in North America in his time to earn his UD; he became the first UDT of his breed and was the first dog of any breed to earn the coveted Canadian title of TDX. He also excelled in the conformation ring, where he became the first Tervuren to place in the Group and where, for several years, he was the top-winning Belgian Sheepdog in the country.

Val's litter sister, Nightwatch Russet Rondo, was imported in 1957 by William Stewart, also of British Columbia. The Falaise kennel was founded upon this importation, and although the production of this kennel was very meager, it left an important mark on Tervuren history primarily through the descendants of D'Artagnone du Falaise, who was born in October 1959 from Rondo bred to her sire Dandy.

In May 1963 a Tervuren litter was born under the Gui Gredin kennel prefix when the Carleys of Ontario bred their American import, Baden Reine Shad O'Lan (Am. Ch. Jory Candide x Coco Sucre) to Am. Ch. Gironde de Lafayette. From this breeding, Can. Ch. Gui Gredin la Fauve de Willoan, CD, found her home with Bill and Joan Kennedy of Dundas, Ontario. The Kennedys subsequently bred this bitch, affectionately known as Tawny, to their American import, Can. Ch. Lancer Candide, and thus, in 1965, commenced the breeding of Tervuren under the Willoan kennel prefix. Ch. Lancer Candide was a major winner in the Canadian conformation ring and won multiple Group placements. Unfortunately, Lancer was later X-rayed and was found to be dysplastic. The Kennedys were very open about this revelation concerning their dog and this encouraged significant discussion of possible hip problems in the Belgian Sheepdog breed and the subsequent establishment, in 1972, of the Hip Dysplasia Control Registry of the BSCC, as well as a similar registry in America. The Kennedys were among the first members of the BSCC and the first members to own the Tervuren variety.

In June 1967 the Kennedys imported Primavere du Clos Saint Jacques from Mme. Muller of France. This bitch was bred to a male of the Lancer-Tawny breeding, Willoan's Eric, producing litters in 1967 and 1968. The Kennedys also imported other Tervuren from Europe and the United States. Included in these importations were Themis des Hauts de Bievre, Ch. Thesee des Hauts de Bievre, who won BOS at the 1974 Specialty judged by Mme. J. Aubry, and Am., Can. Ch. Ugo des Hauts de Bievre, all from France. Their American import, Ch. Kis Tam's Candide Pataud, CD, was a major winner in the show ring, as was Quella de Fauve Charbonne (Am. Ch. Columbine Nikit x Am. Ch. Mystique de Fauve Charbonne, CD). The Kennedys imported several Groenendael from France as well, with strong Tervuren representation in their pedigrees. Although the Kennedys stopped breeding Belgians in the early 1980s and turned their entire efforts to their other breed, Pembroke Welsh Corgis, many of their imports and their offspring can still be found in the pedigrees of current-day Tervuren.

It was through the efforts of the Kennedys and their promotion of Tervuren that other Canadians became interested in the variety. One such couple was Syd and Marguerite Hope of Hamilton, Ontario. Although they only purchased male Groenendael and Tervuren, and never produced a litter, they were, in the 1970s, tireless workers for the Belgian Sheepdog breed and

Ch. Crocs Blancs Diablo O'Hi Time, C-BAR, winner of two Can. Bests in Show in 1975. Sire: Ch. Chateaubriand, CD, BAR; dam: Ch. Rob-Lyn's Ange Acajou, CD, BAR. Breeders: Danielle Daugherty; Bernadine Paull and Connie Wentling; owner: John McClintock.

Ch. Hi Times Toga De Mont-Blanc, CD, TD, Sch III, wins Can. Best in Show in 1979. Sire: Ch. Hi Times Kanook of Crocs Blanc, CD, BAR; dam: Ch. Hi Times Get It Got It Good, CD. Breeders: K. Lakies and B. Paull; owner: Raymond Wisner III

51

the BSCC. Tervuren owned by them were Ch. Willoan's Eros, UD, Ch. Willoan's Homer, UD and Ch. Leistraum's Anchorman, CDX.

During the 1970s, interest in the Belgian Sheepdog breed continued to grow across Canada, and particularly in Ontario. This was reflected in dramatically increased entries of Belgians in both conformation shows and obedience trials in the province. As a result of this interest and the ongoing efforts of the BSCC to establish relationships across the U.S. border, more and more American Belgians began to take part in Canadian shows and trials, and they achieved good results. In fact, two of the major-winning Tervuren in the Canadian rings during the 1970s were Am., Can. Ch. Hi Times Kanook of Crocs Blanc, Am. CD, and Am., Can. Ch. Crocs Blancs Diablo O'Hi Time. Both dogs paved a new road for the Tervuren variety in the Canadian dog show ring as a result of their multiple all-breed and specialty Best in Show wins. In Canada, all varieties of the Belgian Sheepdog compete together in the same ring. While that system has some critics, Tervuren such as Kanook and Diablo, and before them Val, Lancer and Pataud, have proven that Belgians of any variety, including more recently the Malinois and Laekenois, can win in the breed and the Group providing they are good, sound representatives of the breed.

During the late 1960s and the 1970s, several Tervuren breeding kennels were established. In British Columbia, Pat and Dave King founded their Kingsgate kennel with the purchase and importation of several Tervuren. Most notable of these acquisitions were Ch. Cinderelva of Georjune, Ch. Chordeiles Heide of Kingsgate and Ch. Sanroyale's Falko. Also in British Columbia, Agnes Williams started her Acajou kennel with the importation of Ch. Kajon's Acajou, CD, and Rick and Jan McVean founded their Ambrgai kennel with the purchase of Ch. Acajou's Amphibion.

In Alberta, Roger and Margaret Drury established their Dorak kennel with the acquisition of Ch. Willoan's Dore, and Al and Val Johnson began their Lockview kennel with the purchase of Ch. McLeod Valley's Alterelle.

In Manitoba, Elizabeth Swanson commenced a strong linebreeding program under the Chordeiles prefix, based on Am., Can. Ch. Joker of Georjune with the importation of Ch. Chordeiles Ultra of Georjune and Ch. Chordeiles Valor of Georjune. Joker, an American dog, became the first Tervuren in North America to win the Working Group, which he did in Canada in 1967. In Saskatchewan, Wally English established his Blackamber kennel with the importation of several American dogs, including Ch. Willowview's Allure and Ch. Dante du Bon Chateau.

In Ontario, the Berkshire kennel of Jim and Carol Howarth commenced breeding Tervuren with several imports, including Ch. Impetus de Petite Chalet and Hi Time Crystal Knight N Dale. Barbara Barnes acquired Ch. McLeod Valley's Alterelle, whom she used as a foundation for her Curriewood kennels. In Quebec, Jean Normandin added a French flavor to the expanding interest in the Belgian breed when he added Tervuren to his Groenendael du Pays Brule kennel.

Ch. Whirlwind's Amber O'Frostfire, CD, TD, BAR, wins Can. BIS in 1980. Sire: Ch. Frost Fire's Jasper of Bobkat; dam: Frost Fire's Cher O'Vedette Noir, C-BAR. Breeders: S. Kiley and J. Smith; owner: Steve Sorenson.

Ch. OTCH Hi Times Country Summer, UD, Can. BIS in 1982. Sire: Ch. Hi Times C-Sam O'Crocs Blanc, BAR; dam: Winjammers Ima Hi Timer, CDX, O-BAR. Breeders: Lemmer, L. Morgan and B. Paull; owners: B. Noble and B. Paull.

Ch. Yessit C'Est Tout, TDX, wins back-to-back BIS in Canada and the Canadian Specialty in 1988. Sire: Ch. Bonheur Ruarri MacTire, BAR; dam: Ch. StarBright Black Brocade, BAR. Breeder: L. Barlow; owner: D. Barlow.

Ch. Corsair's Gaiter, CD, first Canadian-owned Tervuren to win multiple Bests in Show (1988) and top Belgian Sheepdog in Canada in 1987 and 1988. Sire: Ch. Dali de la Pouroffe, C-BAR; dam: Ch. Whirlwind's Amber O'Frostfire, BAR. Breeder: S. Sorenson; owner: G. Stark.

Ch. Hi Times Sweet Polly Purebred, C-BAR, won the 1974 Canadian National Specialty under French judge Mme. Aubry. Breeder: B. Reckenbeil; owner: M. Schubert.

Ch. Willoview's Bearbait, CD, a Canadian winner during the 1970s. Breeders: D. and J. Arns; owners: K. and F. Walker, of Ottawa.

Unfortunately, although several of these kennels continued into the 1980s, none of them managed to establish a distinctive Canadian line of Tervuren.

Many other fanciers of Tervuren assisted in the growing popularity of the variety without establishing a continuing line. Worth mention because of their outstanding contributions to the BSCC and their accomplishments in the ring are Frances Walker of Ottawa, Ontario, with her Ch. Willowview's Bearbait, CDX; Ellen Shields of Kitchener, Ontario, with Am., Can. Ch. Frostfire's Worthy Damon, and Brian and Anne Wilcox with Ch. Hi Times Saturn's Dusk, CDX.

In the 1980s interest in all varieties, including the Tervuren, continued to grow. Membership in the BSCC increased, particularly in the province of Quebec and, as a result, all official club correspondence from the BSCC newsletter appears in both French and English. Belgian Sheepdog entries in CKC conformation shows and obedience trials have shown marked increases across the country, and Belgians provide formidable competition to other breeds in Group and obedience class competition.

While American-owned dogs continue to achieve excellent results in the Belgian ring, a growing number of Canadian-owned Belgians are proving their worth. Several new Tervuren kennels have emerged in the 1980s, and each shows promise of establishing a lasting line. The Gemfire kennel of Glen and Lynne Stark of Peterborough, Ontario, is creating a breeding program around its top-winning and multiple Best in Show American import Ch. Corsair's Gaiter, CD. In Quebec, Micheline Riopel is establishing an interesting breeding program under the kennel name Quattpatt, based on her American import Corsair's Hobo Rox, CD.

As a final note to contemporary development of the Tervuren variety in Canada, the recent importations from Europe of a young Tervuren bitch, Cachette des Hauts de Bievre, by the long-established Mi-sha-ook Groenendael kennel of Skip and Elsie Stanbridge of Troy, Ontario, and a young Tervuren male, Marquis Van de Hoge Laer, by Brian and Anne Wilcock of Guelph, Ontario, hold special promise. Both of these Tervuren offer interesting and different alternatives for the future of the Tervuren variety in Canada.

TERVUREN IN GREAT BRITAIN

Despite the added cost of six months' quarantine for imports, Tervuren are firmly established in Great Britain. The first two were imported in 1971 from France by Ann O'Shea and Eric Irvine. These were Ungo and Ula du Clos Saint Jacques. Their first litter, in 1972, produced Zellik Alexis and Zellik Alexandra. Alexis became a successful obedience and show dog, while Alexandra was taken to Belgium where she won a CACIB—the first British-bred Belgian Shepherd to win this rating in its country of origin.

Also in 1971, Mrs. Harris imported Uranus de Braise Rouge from Jack

British Ch. Snowbourn Enchantress of Vallivue, owned by S. and M. Young and bred by M. Brownfill, was Best of Breed at the 1985 British National Specialty under famed French breed authority Dr. Yves Surget. "Farrah" is the dam (bred to Bacchus) of the first Tervuren of English breeding to be exported to the United States as a show and breeding prospect.

British Ch. Norrevang Bacchus of Belamba, owned by Marcelle King, is a son of French Ch. Sam de la Douce Plaine, winner of the 1984 French National Specialty.

British Ch. Bandol de la Pouroff at Snowbourn, Britain's top-producing sire, at ten years of age and Donna Allen of the United States. Shortly thereafter, another American dog, Am. Ch. Qandi de Petite Chalet, in whelp to Am. Ch. Chateaubriand, was sent to Great Britain by owners Pauline McClintock and Carol Schnur.

The next Tervuren to come from Europe was Vanda of Jinga, who was bred to Zellik Alexis. Colombe O'Albions Franglad came from Frances and Gladys Calderwood of the United States and was bred to bitches of the American lines.

These six imports, plus the litter by Chateaubriand out of Qandi, provided the foundation dogs for many of the Tervuren in Great Britain.

In 1977 Bandol de la Pouroff came to Snowbourn kennels and Boris of the Two came to Delator, both imported from Belgium. Bandol became the first male champion in Britain and has proved to be an outstanding sire. During the 1980s, breeders have imported numerous dogs from Belgium, France, Norway, Denmark, Switzerland and Germany.

During this time one noteworthy dog went to England from America. In 1982, Marcelle King of Belamba kennels imported StarBright Dollars Invested (Ch. Bonheur Ruarri MacTire x Ch. StarBright Bouquetiere, CD, TD) from Sharon Redmer's kennel. Dollar set records in the breed ring, where he became the first Belgian of any variety to win Best Puppy in Show. The entry was some four thousand puppies. He also has been a popular stud and has champion offspring in England and several other countries. Dollar's influence on English Tervuren will continue to be felt for many generations.

Challenge Certificates (CCs) were introduced for Tervuren in 1984. To earn a championship, a dog must receive three CCs under three different judges, with at least one CC being obtained after the dog is one year of age. There is no separate class for champions, so unfinished dogs must compete for CCs with finished champions (which may be entered in the Open classes). Because conformation entries routinely number in the hundreds, a championship is difficult to obtain. As of late in 1988, however, thirteen males and seven females have earned the title.

The Belgian Shepherd Dog, as it is called in Great Britain, is considered one breed with four varieties that are the same as those of France. The Kennel Club has allowed intervariety matings to fix needed characteristics until 1990, when the situation will be reviewed. The practice either will be permitted to continue, or subsequent breedings will be limited to dogs of the same variety.

Foundation dogs at Chateau Blanc Kennels, Ch. Flair de Fauve Charbonne, CD, C-BAR (*center*), and Ch. Kandice de Fauve Charbonne, CDX, BAR (*right*), with offspring Amber de Chateau Blanc

Ch. Lancer de Chateau Blanc, BAR, bred and owned by Edeltraud Laurin

5

Famous Tervuren Kennels

THE 1960S WITNESSED the firm establishment of Belgian Tervuren as an active breed in the United States. Many fledgling kennels were founded, and a number of the breed's pioneers of the 1950s remained active, as well. We will look at a number of these kennels in this chapter. Because of its influence during the past twenty-five years, we begin this chapter with the activities of the Chateau Blanc kennel. Please note that the dates that follow the kennel headings identify the year in which a kennel bred its first litter.

CHATEAU BLANC KENNELS (1963)

In 1960 Edeltraud Laurin acquired a five-year-old Belgian Tervuren male, Flair de Fauve Charbonne, and in 1961 Kandice de Fauve Charbonne also found a home with the Laurins. Thus Chateau Blanc kennel was established.

Flair and Kandice are among the most important of U.S. Tervuren. Both finished their championships and went on to be ABTC national supported show winners—Flair in 1964 and Kandice in 1967. (The supported shows were the forerunners of our current National Specialty shows.) In addition, Kandice became the first Belgian Tervuren bitch to hold both the champion and CDX titles.

Flair and Kandice were bred together three times and produced eight champions. These three litters follow the kennel's tradition of naming its litters alphabetically. In the "A" litter the males were dominant, Ami and Akeeta becoming champions. André, acquired late in his life by Bernadine Paull (Hi Time), would be known primarily as a stud.

The "B" litter had three champions with Brigadier, Belle and Bijou (Winners Bitch at the ABTC's 1967 National Supported show). The "C" litter produced Chs. Caprice, Candice and Cyrano. Cyrano was one of the most elegant males of his time, with good neck and color, and is the sire of the breed's first Best in Show dog, Ch. Bonheur's D'Artagnon, UDT. He also sired Ch. Chateaubriand, CD, a top producer for many years who sired in turn two Best in Show offspring, Ch. Hi Times Kanook of Crocs Blanc, CD, and Canadian BIS Ch. Crocs Blancs Diablo O'Hi Time.

Chateau Blanc imported a French bitch, Ch. Ouka du Val d'Orge. Bred to the kennel's Ch. Ami de Chateau Blanc, she produced the "D" litter of Ch. Daktary, Ch. D'Art and Desiree. Daktary went to the Krohns and was the sire of their "S" litter, which included Ch. Scorpio de Fauve Charbonne, CD, TD, winner of two National Specialty shows. Daktary was purchased later by the Masque Noir kennel.

Ouka also was bred to Ch. Cyrano and produced a litter that became known for its bitches, Ch. Faola, Ch. Fauvette and Ch. Fleurette. Both Faola and Fauvette went to Florida to start Pinky Johnson's Pinkcliff kennels. Fleurette remained in the home of her breeder.

The breeding of Ch. Kandice de Fauve Charbonne to Ch. Columbine Nikit produced the "E" litter for the Laurins. It contained Ch. Eros, Ch. Escaut, Eglantine (who stayed with her breeders) and Ch. Ebony de Chateau Blanc, UDT, who was Best of Opposite Sex (BOS) at the 1974 ABTC National Specialty show.

Eglantine was later bred to Ch. D'Art de Chateau Blanc, producing the "G" litter of two males and one bitch. All three became champions. The better known were Ch. Geronimo and Ch. Galaxy, the latter Winners Bitch (WB) at the 1978 National Specialty show. Both Galaxy and Geronimo remained with their breeder. Galaxy was bred first to Ch. Hi Times Kanook of Crocs Blanc. This breeding produced Ch. Lancer de Chateau Blanc, a dog who would make a major impact on the breed and was Mrs. Laurin's favorite Tervuren. She believed him to be the ideal in temperament, movement and color. A top producer and one of the soundest to come from this kennel, he died of cancer at a very young age.

The kennel's "H" litter was the result of a breeding of Fleurette to Ch. Apache Sun of Butkrest (a son of Bijou). It produced the top obedience competitor, Ch. Herzog de Chateau Blanc, UD (owned by obedience judge Jeanne Ohmann and Manetta Tomlison), and Ch. Heureux de Chateau Blanc, owned by Al and Esther Leong of Oregon and important in Masque Noir kennel production.

Lancer's son, Ch. Ovation de Chateau Blanc, CD, equally as sound and possessing more elegance, was a Best in Show dog and twice winner at National Specialties (BOS 1978 and Best of Breed 1980). He was the first Ter-vuren to place in the Group at the prestigious Westminster Kennel Club show at Madison Square Garden.

A breeding of Ch. Galaxy and Ovation produced two dogs, Ch. Quando and Ch. Quintessence de Chateau Blanc. Quintessence was WB at the first independent National Specialty in 1978, at six months and one day of age. She went on to become a Canadian champion as well as a Schutzhund national trial champion.

Chateau Blanc has played a great part in the development of the breed from the early 1960s to the present. Its dogs have been in the winners circle at Specialties many times and have won more than fifteen C-BAR and O-BAR awards (see Chapter 20 for a discussion of BAR awards).

Mrs. Laurin's sister, Gerlinda Hockla, has handled the majority of the kennel's dogs to their championships. A highly regarded professional handler, she always has presented them in the peak of coat and condition.

Edeltraud Laurin has retired from active breeding and now devotes her energies to judging; her daughter Janina carries forward the kennel's breeding activities.

BONHEUR KENNELS (1963)

Bud and Faye Dickens founded their kennel when they acquired Kri-quette de Fauve Charbonne from the Krohns in January 1962. Kriquette played a vital part in the early days of the breed by establishing a successful show career in an area where competition was scarce. All Bonheur Tervuren trace back either to Kriquette or Dentelle du Val de Tonnerre (Lace). Their pedigrees, which combined bloodlines of the early dogs, produced a successful breeding strategy for Bonheur.

Kriquette's first litter was registered under the Weeping Pines prefix, except for one male who was named by its first owner, Sandy Haze Prince of Hearts. Champ, as he was called, became a champion/UD/BAR dog and was one of the early Group placers. The litter also produced Tishaminga de Weep-ing Pines, CDX, Weeping Pines Rory Dawn and Ch. Weeping Pines Friend-ship (Amiz).

A breeding of Amiz to his dam produced the Bonheur "A" litter. It included Ch. Aries Jet de Bonheur, CDX, foundation stud for the Windsong kennel owned by Martha Schubert, and Astral Ember de Bonheur, CD, who began breeder-judge Kay Maves' interest in the breed.

Shortly thereafter, the kennel acquired Dentelle du Val de Tonnerre from Dorothy Hollister. Bred to Champ, she produced three champions. One of these was Bonheur's Bobbins & Pins. She was bred to Ch. Cyrano de Chateau Blanc, CD, and again three champions resulted. They were Maves' Ch. Bonheur's DuBarri, CD, Dickens' Ch. Bonheur's Desiree and the breed's first Best in Show winner—Ch. Bonheur's D'Artagnon, UDT.

Kalyn's Zazarac de Bonheur, CD, BAR, dam of two multiple BIS sons

```
                              Ch. Cyrano de Chateau Blanc CD BAR
                    Ch. Chateaubriand CD BAR
                          Hi'Line Querido BAR
              Ch. Hi Times Kanook of Crocs Blanc CD BAR
                              Ch. Kis Tam's Candide Pataud CD C-BAR
                    Ch. Rob-Lyn's Ange Acajou CD BAR
                          Eau-de-Vie du Val de Tonnerre CD C-BAR
  KALYN'S ZAZARAC DE BONHEUR CD BAR whelped 1/17/73
                              Ch. Gironde de Lafayette
                    Ch. Sandy Haze Prince of Hearts UD BAR
                          Ch. Kriquette de Fauve Charbonne BAR
              Ch. Bonheur's Bea Myne
                              Kurt de Fauve Charbonne
                    Dentelle du Val de Tonnerre CD BAR
                          Bonheur du Val de Tonnerre C-BAR
```

Champ's son Ch. Teddy Edouard Ours Val de Echo was owned by Faye's young daughter, Alleyne. He sired the Best of Breed winner at the ABTC first independent National Specialty show, Ch. Regina's Echo de Bonheur, CD. Gina came to the Dickenses as a stud puppy and went on to become the foundation bitch for the Wilsons' Mont-Cenis kennel.

Champ's daughter Ch. Bonheur's Bea Myne (Bea) was bred to Ch. Hi Times Kanook of Crocs Blanc, CD, to produce Kalyn's Zazarac de Bonheur (Moxie). Moxie was the foundation bitch for Bonheur's second wave. She had twelve points, including two five-point majors before accidents curtailed her career.

Moxie was bred four times, producing only fifteen puppies. From her first two litters by Ch. Kalyn's Whiskey Sour, UDT (a Champ son), came the "well-balanced" Group-placing Ch. Bonheur's Perin de Kalyn, UDT.

By far the best Bonheur litters, however, were the two from Moxie and Ch. Elysee de Mont-Cenis (Gina's grandson). They produced a total of only five puppies; however, among them were Ch. Bonheur Ruarri MacTire, an American and Canadian Best in Show winner and 1984 ABTC National Specialty Best of Breed; Ch. Bonheur Star Treader, CDX, TD, multiple Best in Show winner and the first dog of any breed to go Best in Show from the Herding Group; and Ch. Bonheur Spellbinder, CD (Magic).

Magic, the only bitch from these two breedings, is the cornerstone of Bonheur's future. Her progeny include Ch. Bonheur's Tarot Archana, CD, a Group-placing bitch who was BOS under the first European breeder-judge to preside at an American show.

After twenty-five years of breeding Belgian Tervuren and producing nine conformation and eight obedience BAR award winners, Faye has turned breeding activities over to her daughter Alleyne and is now a breeder-judge.

PATANA KENNELS (1964)

Patana kennels began in 1963 with the purchase of Jigger O'Brandy of Georjune, CD (a littermate to Joker, Javelin and Justa Flare). Its owner, Pat Weymouth, has bred sparingly over the years, producing fifteen litters since 1964. Among them are twenty champions, two Group placers and a number of obedience titleholders.

Among the litters of special interest are the kennel's "F," "J," "O" and "Q" litters. From the "F" litter (Ch. Joker of Georjune x Patana's Yucca of Georjune), Ch. Patana's Fair Heidi O'Carousel and Patana's Fantastic Lady, CD (Tessa), both went to the Carousel kennels (although Tessa later returned to live with her breeder), and Patana's Fame of Georjune went to Cheryl Hepker's Liberte kennels. Fame has achieved both her C-BAR and O-BAR awards. A breeding of Ch. Kajon's Slaughter and Tessa produced the "J" litter and four champions.

Beginning with her "O" litter in 1980, Pat has cobred with her close friends and partners, William and Delores Purvis. The "O" litter was sired by the influential import, Ch. Yamin van 'T Hof Melyn, out of Carousel's Juliana of Patana. It produced three champions and signaled a change in direction for the kennel, which since has strived to produce dogs whose type closely approximates that of the best European Tervuren. Pat retained Ch. Patana's Only You and bred her to Ch. Frostfire's Perpetual Motion for her "Q" litter. Five of the litter have earned their championships.

Not content simply to be involved as a breeder, Pat is active in conformation, obedience, herding, Schutzhund and breed rescue efforts.

SHENANDOAH HILLS KENNELS (BRAISE ROUGE) (1965)

In 1962, Jack and Donna Allen purchased their first Tervuren, Ch. Kim de Fauve Charbonne. Although Kim was not used for breeding, his influence caused Donna to reserve a male puppy from the Krohns' breeding of Jasmine to D'Artagnone du Falaise. That dog, Ch. Mars de Fauve Charbonne, UDT, would become the first U.S. champion/UD/TD Tervuren. In addition to achieving his titles, Mars set standards for the breed by becoming a multiple Working Group placer in three countries (the United States, Canada and Mexico) and also placing in obedience competition in those countries. The first CACIB titles granted to an American Tervuren (FCI shows) went to Mars in Mexico City. He was truly one of the first "well-balanced Tervuren," winning friends for the breed at ringside and in obedience demonstrations. Describing him as a "happy-go-lucky Tervuren whenever he was on display or when his owners indicated a situation was under control," Donna has many charming and touching remembrances of this most special dog.

Mars was the major early stud for the kennel and one of the breed's first great producers. He was used both by his owners and other kennels and left a legacy of twenty-five champion offspring.

Foundation bitch for the kennel was Ch. Aimee du Bon Chateau, CD, a Dandy daughter. Although she produced only one litter, the kennel's first (with Ch. Kenny de Cledeville, CD), she won her BAR award easily, as did two of her bitch offspring and other grand-offspring. From the litter, Ch. Oradea remained at the kennel. Ch. Orellana went to the Petite Chalet kennels (then owned by Jim Davis). The litter is the only one of Donna's production to bear the Braise Ardente suffix. All subsequent litters carry Braise Rouge.

Another bitch important in the kennel was Ch. Wayfarer's Prize Package, CD. Used with Mars, she achieved her BAR as the dam of seven champion offspring and twenty-two champion grand-offspring, some of whom are also BAR recipients.

Through the years Shenandoah Hills has bred more than thirty champions and supplied show and breeding stock to other kennels. Among them are Ch. Chant de Braise Rouge (Commander kennels) and Ch. Rouyn de Braise Rouge (Echo Hill kennels). It also was the first American kennel to

Ch. Chant de Braise Rouge, CDX, C-BAR, top winning Tervuren bitch during 1970, bred by Donna Allen and Lenny Lambert, shown here with Sallyann Comstock

export to European breeders. Raton de Braise Rouge (Mars x Oradea) was sent to Sweden, where he became a champion and a foundation for Swedish Tervuren. His name now appears behind many dogs rated "excellent" in several European countries. A bitch, Peri de Braise Rouge, was the first American Tervuren to be exported to England.

The kennel also has imported Swedish and Danish dogs whose pedigrees go back to Raton and his descendants, blended with excellent European bloodlines.

WAYFARERS' KENNEL (1966)

Owned by Sondra (Hughes) Miller, the Wayfarers' kennel was founded with the purchase of Wayfarers' Nadia and Nabob du Rochemont (from the D'Artagnone x Linda litter) from Betty Engels. The kennel later acquired Otowi de Fauve Charbonne for use with its bitches.

Nadia was bred to Ch. Columbine Nikit and produced the kennel's first litter in February 1966. (Nikit was a major force in the breed at the time and the first Group 1 winner. His Colorado location precluded his being widely at stud; however, some major kennels such as Chateau Blanc were able to use him successfully.) Based largely on Saint Jacques lines, the breeding of Nikit and Nadia produced four champions. Chs. Wayfarers' Pacemaker and Placide were kept by the kennel. Pacemaker achieved a large number of breed wins, including the ABTC's 1971 National Supported show, and sired several champions.

Wayfarers' produced a number of dogs that were used by other kennels with good success. Among these were Ch. Wayfarers' Prize Package, CD (Braise Rouge kennels); Ch. Wayfarers' Sweet Alice Can Do, CD (Can Do kennels), and Ch. Wayfarers' Velvette Angel, CD (Rogues Rouges kennels). The kennel's last litter was whelped in early 1980.

DE LA CORPS KENNEL (1967)

Owned by Linda Franklin, the De La Corps kennel began in 1963 with the purchase of Ch. Javelin of Georjune, UD, who was to become the breed's first American UD and High in Trial dog.

From the beginning, the kennel's activity has focused on the dual tasks of producing dogs of superior working and conformation potential. Linda, by use of judicious culling of her litters, has ensured that only puppies sound in body and mind will carry her kennel's name. With more than twenty champions to its credit, the kennel also boasts an impressive list of working titles. Its dogs have excelled in every arena in which the utility of an animal is tested. One can find them competing in Schutzhund trials and carting demonstrations, as well as more traditional obedience and tracking competitions.

Multiple Best in Show Ch. Bonheur's D'Artagnan, UDT, BAR (*right*), and Belgian import Ch. Tanzy de Landas, UDT, BAR, foundation stock for Hi Time Kennels

```
                            Int. Ch. of Beaute Demon Du Chemin Des Dames
              Jarnac de Iamara
                            Dalila Des Ardennes Du Coitron
     Okey de la Thudinie
                            Joujou De Chemin Des Dames
              Mick de Iamara
                            Jessie De Iamara
CH. TANZY DE LANDAS UDT BAR (Belgium) whelped 10/2/70, breeder Declercq
                            Heros de la Gilde Saint Sebastien
              Belgian Ch. Kurt Des Bonmoss
                            Helyne Du Bos O'Villez
     Suzi de Landas
                            Filou Des Bonmoss
              Kinette Du Talion
                            Doria Du Val Suzon
```

Especially noteworthy among the De La Corps dogs are Ch. Chilure's Fiama, UDT, Ch. Hi Times Let It Be De La Corps, UDT, and Ch. Javondi's Allure De La Corps, UDT. Also bearing her kennel name are OTCH Gabiama's Krista De La Corps, UDT, OTCH Ochiama Legend De La Corps and OTCH Gabiama's Kaiser De La Corps, three of only a handful of Tervuren to achieve an obedience trial championship.

HI TIME KENNELS (1967)

Bernadine Paull acquired a puppy from Karen Johnson's (Sunfire) breeding of Ch. Kis Tam's Candide Pataud, CD, to Tishaminga de Weeping Pines, CDX (Tish was the first dog in the breed to achieve a perfect 200 score in Obedience). Ch. Sunfire Tyee, CDX, would become Bernadine's first champion and sire of the kennel's first litter. That litter, registered under the La Sin prefix, resulted from a breeding of Tyee to Dentelle du Val de Tonnerre, leased from Faye Dickens. It produced Bernadine's Ch. La Sin Bonheur's Dana, TD, who died in an accident at close to one year of age.

In 1968 Bernadine purchased Bonheur's D'Artagnan from the Bonheur kennels. Dart was to become the breed's first Best in Show dog, in June 1971, at the Fox River Valley Kennel Club show with an entry of 1,500 dogs. He would repeat that win again and was a two-time National Specialty winner. His owner is also proud of his multiple High in Trial wins. According to Bernadine, "His overall balance, short back, and impeccable rear movement along with his ability to be showy under all conditions made him a showman for many years." He was the number-one Tervuren in 1971, 1972 and 1973. He sired a total of forty-five champion offspring—a breed record that still stands. One son, Ch. Paulmars Cosmic Vanguard, also became a Best in Show winner.

Hi Time imported Ch. Tanzy de Landas, UDT, from Belgium. She, along with Ch. Rob-Lyn's Ange Acajou, CD (Misha), and Ch. Belle de Chateau Blanc, were among the bitches that would produce many well-known dogs for the kennel, some of whom became the foundations of other kennels, as well. More than 130 champions bear the Hi Time name, and at least half that number have worked in obedience or herding as well.

MASQUE NOIR KENNELS (1971)

In 1970, Lynn-Marie Kara and Luther Sturtevant made a speedy, cold trip from Oregon to New Mexico and returned with Daktary de Chateau Blanc and Satin de Fauve Charbonne from the Krohns. Both would become champions and BAR dogs, with Daktary also earning his CD and Satin her CDX.

Masque Noir litters are named alphabetically. Beginning with their "A" litter, out of Satin by Ch. Big John du Rochemont, in 1971, the owners continued breeding until 1982, with the production of their "M" litter.

Lynn-Marie and Luther regard their foundation dogs to be Satin and Ch. Heureux de Chateau Blanc (Vanya). They are proud of the many fine dogs produced, especially for their qualities of sound movement, dependable temperaments, deep base colors and good blackening and masks.

Probably one of the best-known Tervuren produced by Masque Noir was Ch. Chagall du Masque Noir, CD, foundation stud for the Esprite de Joie kennels in Alaska. His showing was limited by his residence in Alaska and lack of campaigning. In extremely limited showing he did well, however, and won the Working Group at a time when few Tervuren were being placed. Chagall was sire to many excellent offspring, among whom was Ch. Achates Esprite de Joie, a dog widely used and admired.

Masque Noir provided other kennels with breeding stock, including Ch. Hosanna du Masque Noir (Crestar kennels), dam of many fine offspring. Most important to Lynn-Marie and Luther, however, are their dogs and the people they have come to know. Their words express feelings held by many in our fancy:

> Our greatest satisfaction in breeding Tervuren . . . has not been found in dog showing but in the dogs themselves. Satin and Daktary brought immense pleasure to our lives, as does our present twelve-year-old "puppy" Hanukkah.
>
> We will always remember Satin herding pigs out of the blackberry brambles and gleefully carrying ice cubes around the house in her mouth. Daktary's penchant for green crème de menthe will never be forgotten. And Hanakkah's super "tracking" nose, able to discern the presence of a potato bag, or carrots, or onions . . . wherever they might be hidden.
>
> The other reason for our love of Tervuren is the people. We prize the lasting friendships gained through our common love of Tervuren.

SANROYALE KENNEL (1971)

In 1968 Sallyann Comstock approached Dorothy Hollister of du Val de Tonnerre with a request for a bitch to establish a kennel that would produce dogs of intelligence, versatility and soundness of mind and body. The future foundation bitch she purchased was Ch. La Mariee du Val de Tonnerre, CD (Destin du Val de Tonnerre x La Candide du Val de Tonnerre). La Mariee and other dogs such as Best in Show winner Ch. Rajah D-Antre du Louve, CD; Ch. Bonheur's Nova du Sanroyale, CD, and top Herding Group producer in 1981 Ch. Kajon's Kashmier of Sanroyale helped turn Sallyann's initial dream into a reality.

Ch. Rajah D-Antre du Louve, CD, was the breed's fourth Best in Show dog and top producer in 1976 and 1977. Some of his best known progeny were out of La Mariee, including the Sanroyale "H" litter. Among them were Am.,

Bda Ch. Sanroyale's The Hustler, CD, foundation dog for the Von Duncan kennel. A multiple Group and Best in Show winner, Hustler was the top-winning Tervuren in 1981, number-two producer in 1981 of all herding breeds and number-one producer, all herding breeds, in 1982. He is the sire of Ch. Sanroyale's Ulan Bator, also a Group-winning dog and producer of the Group-placing bitch Ch. Wysteria's Annie's Song, CDX.

Also from the "H" litter came Ch. Sanroyale's Humoresque, UD, foundation bitch for the Wysteria kennel. Humoresque was a Group-placing bitch and the top-winning Belgian in Canada in 1976. She took Reserve at the 1976 ABTC National Specialty and proudly earned her Herding Instinct Certificate (HIC) at thirteen years of age. She was bred only once, to Ch. Lancer de Chateau Blanc, but produced five champions and earned her C-BAR.

Humoresque's son, Ch. Wysteria's Le Baron, CD, was bred to Kajon's Kashmier of Sanroyale to produce the Sanroyale "V" and "diamond" litters. From the diamond breeding came the multiple Group-winning and Best in Show winner Ch. Sanroyale's Ruff Diamond. Baron's brother, Ch. Wysteria's Gabriel, went to Chateau Blanc kennels to become a Group placer and stud; Ch. Wysteria's Mystique became the foundation bitch at Jean Dieden's Pine Mist kennel. When Rajah was bred to Ch. Bonheur's Nova du Sanroyale, the "G" litter resulted. It produced the foundation stud and multiple Group-winning male Ch. Sanroyale's Gamblin' Man, CDX, for the Daybreak kennels. Littermates Ch. Sanroyale's Gabrielle, CD, and Ch. Sanroyale's Giselle became foundation bitches for the Joykist and Siberka kennels respectively. It was, however, Rajah's breeding to Ch. Kajon's Kashmier of Sanroyale that was to give Sanroyale the multiple Group-winning Ch. Our Valiant du San-royale, a dog with at least eight championship titles earned internationally, as well as Temperament Test (TT) and HIC certification.

Sanroyale's record to date is thirty-five champions and many High in Trial obedience winners. To Sallyann, the epitome of the well balanced Ter-vuren is Ch. Sanroyale's Yves de Sabre, UDT, who is, as well, a registered therapy dog, Group winner and scent hurdle racer. In his spare time, he also enjoys flyball.

SNOWFLOWER KENNEL (1971)

Carmen Helgesen began as a breeder of Samoyeds; however, her kennel has been devoted to Tervuren since 1970. She first bred Tervuren in 1971 but believes that the kennel made its biggest impact in the mid-1980s, primarily because of a remarkable litter of eight puppies born in 1984. Carmen writes, "The litter is every breeder's dream and might come along once in a lifetime." Dam of the litter is Ch. Snowflower Chavon, CD. The sire is Ch. Labelle's A Liberte. Three of the males already have amassed an enviable record: Ch. Snowflower Voila Sharvonne, CD, owned by Sharon Lutz, was the number-one Tervuren in 1987, a Best in Show dog with many Group placings and

Select at the 1988 ABTC National Specialty show, then Best of Breed in 1989; Ch. Snowflower Skyy Chateau, Am., Can. CD, ranks high in breed standings, and also is a multiple Group-placing, Best in Show dog; Ch. Snowflower Trace of Velvet, CD, was Reserve Winners Dog at the 1985 ABTC National Specialty at fourteen months of age and is also a Group winner.

Other top offspring in the litter are OTCH Ch. Snowflower Brady O'Liberte, TDX, and a bitch kept by Snowflower, Ch. Snowflower Deal a Little Magic, already the dam of Group-winning offspring, and of Ch. Snowflower Summer Sun, Best of Winners at the 1989 National Specialty.

LIBERTE KENNELS (1972)

Owned by Cheryl and Bill Hardman, Liberte kennels began in 1969 with the purchase of two female puppies. They were to become Am., Can. Ch. Ravie Ma Fidele Amie, Am., Can. CDX, and Patana's Fame of Georjune, CD.

Ravie was an exceptional obedience worker, proving her desire to please by winning a High in Trial and twice earning a *Dog World* award. Although Ravie was bred, her kennelmate Fame gave Liberte its foundation. A daughter of Am., Can. Ch. Joker of Georjune, Fame produced four litters, cobred with Mary-Jo Oldendick of Carousel kennels. These litters earned Fame both her C-BAR and O-BAR. Among her offspring was OTCH Ch. Liberte's Elixer O'Carousel, TD, one of the breed's earliest OTCH titleholders.

By 1975, a year-old son of Ch. Geronimo de Chateau Blanc came to reside at Liberte. A High in Trial winner, he was known as Ch. KD's Yankee Doodle Dandy, CD. Although he sired a number of litters, few were shown to their championships. In 1979, he was joined by Ch. Liberte's Casino Aty, CD (Ty), a son of Ch. Ovation de Chateau Blanc, CD. Ty proved to be the more dominant sire, producing multiple champions, obedience titleholders and Group placers.

In 1981 a brother/sister team joined Liberte. They were sired by Ch. Nugget de Fauve Charbonne, CDX, TD, out of Ch. Danseuse D'Elegance. The male was to become a Best in Show winner, Ch. La Belle's A Liberte (Grizz). Grizz amassed an outstanding record in the show ring and twice earned a Select at National Specialties. As a sire he proved his worth by producing the outstanding Snowflower dogs mentioned earlier.

Grizz's sister, Ch. Liberte's La Belle Amie (Aby), shown sparingly, also has an outstanding record. At eight and one-half months of age, Aby won Best in Sweepstakes and Reserve Winners Bitch at the 1982 ABTC National Specialty under breeder-judges Marcie Spalding and Lawrence Stanbridge. She has several Group placements and was Select at the 1988 National Specialty under breeder-judge Barbara Krohn. Aby was bred to Ch. Liberte's Casino Aty for her first litter and produced multiple champions and a Group-placing son. Her second litter, by Ch. Snowflower Brady O'Liberte, UDTX, has produced another Group-placing son.

Liberte Tervuren will be found in the background of many outstanding dogs.

MONT-CENIS KENNEL (1972)

Established by Violette (Vi) and Charles Wilson, the kennel's foundation bitch was Ch. Regina's Echo de Bonheur. Gina was a typey, showy, well-balanced bitch and an outstanding mover. Born in October 1969, she accomplished a record in the show ring and as a top producer. She often excelled in the breed ring when the competition was keenest, winning Best of Winners (BOW) at the 1970 ABTC National Supported show from the Puppy Class at seven months of age. She repeated the BOW at the 1971 National to finish her championship and go on to BOS. She again won BOS at the 1972 National. At the age of nine and one-half, Gina came out of retirement to win BOB from the Veterans Class at the ABTC 1978 National Specialty.

Gina had a total of twenty offspring, of which ten finished their championships. She produced the Mont-Cenis "A" litter with Ch. Utrillo de Braise Rouge, CD. Several would become champions. Bred next to Ch. Scorpio de Fauve Charbonne, CD, TD, she produced an all-female litter. Ch. Brillance de Mont-Cenis, CDX, would become the foundation of Sharon Redmer's StarBright kennel, and Ch. Bergere de Mont-Cenis was BOW at the 1976 National Specialty. When Regina's daughter, Ch. Alsace de Mont-Cenis, was bred to Ch. Scorpio de Fauve Charbonne, the kennel retained a male named Ch. Elysee de Mont-Cenis, a Group placer and the only sire to date to produce three Best in Show sons: Ch. Bonheur Ruarri MacTire, Ch. Bonheur Star Treader, CDX, TD, and Ch. Crestar's Bon Dieu, CD.

PINKCLIFF KENNEL (1972)

Owner Pinky Johnson introduced the Belgian Tervuren to Florida when she acquired two littermates from Chateau Blanc kennel. The bitches were to become Ch. Faola de Chateau Blanc and Fauvette de Chateau Blanc. The bitches, out of Ch. Cyrano de Chateau Blanc, CD, and the import Ch. Ouka du Val d'Orge, fulfilled the expectation of both breeder and owner; both were elegant and had good dark masks, good movement and good scissor bites. Pinky based her entire breeding program on the premise of keeping Cyrano's genes alive, and all her dogs go back to those genes. Pinkcliff has produced more than twenty champions and helped the breed to be known in an area devoid of Belgian Tervuren at the time.

At one point, the kennel was almost totally destroyed by fire, but Pinky managed to keep her bloodline intact. In 1981 Ch. Pinkcliff's Lukyna was BOS at the ABTC National Specialty, and her breeding program has produced dogs winning their titles as far north as Canada.

Ch. Chagall du Masque Noir, CDX, BAR winner

Ch. Elysee de Mont-Cenis, BAR, sire of three Best in Show sons, bred and owned by Charles and Violette Wilson

Ch. Pinkcliff's Lukyna of Hi Times, CD, National Specialty Winners Bitch in 1981 and Select in 1988, owned by Donna E. Cole and Cary Rothstein

FROST FIRE KENNEL (1973)

Owned by Judith Lee Smith, this kennel takes its name from Frost, for the Siberian Huskies already in residence when the first Tervuren arrived, and Fire, for the Tervuren.

The kennel acquired its first Tervuren in 1970 with the purchase of a bitch puppy that became Am., Can. Ch. Sabrina de Flambeau Rouge, CD. She was bred by Robert and Elaine Smid. Three years later, a ten-and-one-half-month-old male pup joined the kennel. He would become Am., Can. Ch. Hi Times Kanook of Crocs Blanc, CD. The influence of these two dogs on contemporary American Tervuren cannot be ignored.

It is fair to say that Kanook was one of the breed's most honored males. During his career, he earned Bests in Show, both here and in Canada, and still holds the record for winning the National Specialty show three consecutive times. Number-one Tervuren for many years, he also earned his BAR easily, siring a Best in Show son and has six Best in Show grand-offspring.

At this writing, although Kanook does not hold the record for siring the most champions, he has the greatest number of C-BAR points in the breed—poignant testimony to his strength in producing quality in a limited breeding program. He was Judy's constant companion, and his rare combination of sensitivity and loyalty made him an ideal specimen of our breed.

Sabrina was first bred when she was three and one-half years old. She is the top-producing bitch in the breed's history with twenty-one champions. They include multiple National Specialty BOB and BOS winners, and multiple Group placers. Sabrina's litter by Ch. Chateaubriand, CD, produced the "DW" litter, several of whom would become the foundation stock for new kennels. Among the most prominent were Am., Mex. Ch. Frost Fire's Deuces Wilde, CD, who twice earned BOB at ABTC National Specialties and began the Garritys' Sang Bleu kennel in California. Ch. Frost Fire's Deep Brandywine, CD, started Mary Gay Burr's Atalanta line in Maryland, and Ch. Frost Fire's Daemon Wrum, CDX, went on to become the foundation stud at Nancy Glabicki's Fancrest kennels. Also influential was Frost Fire's Whimsical Damsel, CDX, whose obedience prowess motivated Linda Newsome of Tacara kennels to continue in the breed.

Subsequent breedings of Sabrina were to Kanook and Ch. Lancer de Chateau Blanc. A daughter from the Kanook breeding, Ch. Frost Fire's Ipso Facto, CD, became the kennel's first homebred to be kept; she was to become a winner and have acclaimed offspring in her own right. Ipso was BOS in 1977 at the National Specialty, and Select in 1981. Her littermate, Ch. Frost Fire's Fiery Imprint, became the number-one Tervuren in the United States in 1977. From this breeding another littermate, Frostfire's Innovation, CD, went to Alaska as a foundation for the Bower/Warnes' Esprite de Joie line. The most influential male of the Kanook-Sabrina breeding was Linda Newsome's Ch. Frostfire's Gandalf Xebec, CDX.

Am. & Can. Ch. Sabrina de Flambeau Rouge, CD, BAR, foundation bitch at Frost Fire and a top producer

```
                                    D'Artagnone Du Falaise BAR (Canada)
                          Ch. Mars De Fauve Charbonne UDT BAR
                                    Ch. Jasmine de Cledeville BAR (France)
             Ch. Our Valient Du Garde Roux C-BAR
                                    Ch. Kenny de Cledeville CD BAR (France)
                          Linnette Du Garde Roux
                                    Ch. Kis-Tam's Renee CD TD C-BAR
CH. SABRINA DE FLAMBEAU ROUGE CD BAR, whelped 12/2/69
                                    Hety du Clos Saint Clair (France)
                          Ch. Kis-Tam's Candide Pataud CD C-BAR
                                    Tammi Candide C-BAR
             Ch. Martin's Chris of Sunfire CD BAR
                                    Ch. Topper Candide CD
                          Sunfire Witchcat
                                    Ch. Chatte Brun du Val de Tonnerre CDX
```

From the Lancer-Sabrina breeding, Ch. Frost Fire's Holocaust went to Kathy Miramontes' Bravura kennels and became a Group-placing bitch. Judy kept Ch. Frost Fire Hallelujah, finishing her championship and placing in the Group, in addition to twice winning Select at Nationals, including BOS in 1986 at the age of ten years. The males also finished their championships, with one being repurchased as an adult to finish in seven shows.

SANG BLEU KENNEL (1975)

Sang Bleu was started in 1973 with the acquisition of a seven-week-old puppy that would mature into a two-time National Specialty winner, Am., Can. Ch. Frost Fire's Deuces Wilde, CD (Jack). Jack was purchased to become the foundation stud at Sang Bleu, but early sterility allowed him to sire only the first two litters for Sang Bleu. Both litters were out of Hilton's Wicked Witch and included the breed's first international champion, Am., Mex., Int., World Ch. Hilton's Kadu Chateau Lynn, CDX, owned by Lynn Morgan of California, along with several other champion offspring.

In 1974 Sang Bleu acquired Carousel's Gabrielle in co-ownership with Elizabeth Provis and bred her to Ch. Lancer de Chateau Blanc. This litter had among its members Ch. Chambery Camille de Sang Bleu, CD, PC (Mex. CD), who won Best Puppy in Show in Mexico; Chambery Crystal de Sang Bleu, a High in Trial winner, and Chambery Cameo de Sang Bleu, who was kept by the kennel and bred to Am., Mex. Ch. Hilton's High Horizons to produce the "F" litter, which contained several American and Canadian champions.

One of these, Fandango de Sang Bleu, CD, became a prominent stud for the kennel. He sired the "L" litter out of Ch. Hilton's Joli Fleur de Lis, who produced multi-Group placers, Supported show winners, Mexican champions and a Group-winning bitch in Japan, Ch. Lullaby de Sang Bleu.

The most important bitch of Sang Bleu breeding was Ch. Hilton's Joli Fleur de Lis. Joli has produced eleven champion offspring to date, including Ch. Ish Ka Bibble de Sang Bleu, sired by Daradan's Jovan de Sang Bleu. She also produced five champions in the "L" litter and two champions from the "S" litter, sired by Montre Fou de Sang Bleu. The latter two are BIS, multi-Group placer and 1987 ABTC National Specialty Select winner Am., Mex. Ch. Stormin Norman de Sang Bleu and his brother, multi-Mexican Group placer Mex. Ch. Sterling Silver de Sang Bleu.

Among Joli's other offspring is Am., Can., Mex. Ch. Demon de Sang Bleu, who resides with Sang Bleu. Demon finished his championship in all three countries with breed wins from the classes. In Canada, he finished his championship undefeated, earned Group placings from the breed classes and was ranked number-two Belgian Sheepdog.

As a sire Demon has produced many champions and obedience titleholders, among them the top-producing Canadian bitch, Can. Ch. OTCH Kha de Rio Berger (out of Chambery Bit of Grace) and National Specialty Select winner Ch. Rhyme-n-Reason de Sang Bleu, CD, co-owned by Mike and Eileen Hudak.

Included in the Garritys' alphabetical litter naming system are also a number of Schipperke litters, from which some outstanding show dogs have also resulted.

GLENOAK KENNEL (1975)

Glenoak gradually emerged through owner Joyce McHenry's appreciation of her first Tervuren, Ch. Scorpio de Fauve Charbonne, CD, TD, one of the breed's best-known sires and show dogs.

Before she obtained four-month-old Scor from the Krohns in early 1970, she had been active in Obedience competitions with several different breeds. Looking for "a breed that had a strong devotion to their owners" and could "do it all," she was hooked on Tervuren after seeing Nancy Burka's (Maplewood kennel) Ch. Quinn de Braise Rouge. Scor was everything she had dreamed of, and more. Although breeding had never been in Joyce's original plans, she became interested in producing the best dogs she could.

Her first bitch, Ch. Bichette Sur le Qui-Vive Araby, CD (Julie), was purchased at two years of age with Marguerite Horstman (Echo Hill kennel) as co-owner. After finishing her championship, Julie was bred to Ch. Echo Hill Wizzard of Oz, CD (a Scor son), and produced the first Glenoak litter. Joyce next purchased a co-ownership on Ch. Ingenue de Petite Chalet, CD, with Nancy Burka (Maplewood kennel). Genie, along with Scor and Julie, became the foundation of Glenoak.

Always following a limited breeding program, the kennel has produced thirty-four dogs thus far. Twenty-two are champions, eighteen have CDs, nine have CDXs, eleven have TDs and one has a TDX. Three Glenoak dogs are Group placers, among them Ch. Glenoak Eclair for Maplewood, CD, a multiple Group placer with Group-placing offspring.

LOGJAM KENNEL (1975)

Logjam was born with the marriage of Pauline Logsdon and John A. McClintock. Pauline's first Belgian Tervuren was the multiple Group-placing Ch. Prince Gorgi de Braise Rouge, Am., Can. CD. His daughter, Am., Can. Ch. Uriana de Valkyra, Am., Can. CD (Annie), became the foundation bitch for Logjam.

John co-owned and later owned the magnificent Am., Can. Ch. Crocs Blancs Diablo O'Hi Time, litter brother to Hi Times Kanook of Crocs Blanc. Diablo had over one hundred Best of Breeds and thirty-eight Working Group placements in the United States and Canada. He had two Canadian Bests in Show and was Best of Breed twice at the Belgian Sheepdog Club of Canada

1987 National Specialty Select winner Ch. Rhyme-n-Reason de Sang Bleu, CD, owned by Mike and Eileen Hudak

Ch. Scorpio de Fauve Charbonne, CD, TD, BAR, with owner Joyce McHenry

Am. & Can. Ch. Hi Times Top of the Crop, UDT, BAR, foundation bitch at Winjammer

Specialty shows. Annie and Diablo were bred twice to produce the Logjam "LA" and "MC" litters with five champions and one CDX. Logjam Lil Abner was Reserve Winners Dog at the 1976 Specialty.

Ch. Logjam Moonlight Charmer was leased by John and bred to Ch. Scorpio de Fauve Charbonne, CD, TD. This breeding produced the Logjam "PE" litter of four champions, including the multiple Group-placing Am., Can. Ch. Logjam Pajtas Ember, Am., Can. CDX (Piety). Owned by Bill and Barbara Mair, Piety also is tied for the most number of Selects at ABTC National Specialty shows, with five of these awards.

STARBRIGHT KENNEL (1976)

Sharon Redmer acquired her first Tervuren, Sundancer Bravo, UDT, from Kay Maves in 1972. Bravo won her heart and inspired her to seek an excellent foundation bitch. In 1974 she purchased Ch. Brillance de Mont-Cenis, CDX, (Bria), from the Mont-Cenis kennels.

Bria, a daughter of two well-known Tervuren (Ch. Scorpio de Fauve Charbonne, CD, TD, and Ch. Regina's Echo de Bonheur, CD), possessed structural soundness, elegance of profile and a happy self-confidence that would be passed to her offspring and their offspring in turn. Bred first to Ch. Lancer de Chateau Blanc, she produced Ch. StarBright Allez Bleu, Reserve Winners Bitch at the 1978 National Specialty, and Ch. StarBright Amianne, CDX, a multiple Working Group placer.

Bria's second litter, sired by Ch. Yamin van 'T Hof Melyn, was to have a profound impact on the future direction of StarBright and other kennels. Six of the eight offspring would finish their championships. Two would earn their UD degrees, of whom one, Am., Can. Ch. StarBright Bacho Noire, Am., Can. UDTX, became the first Tervuren to earn all these titles in both the United States and Canada.

The breeding also produced Ch. StarBright Black Brocade, purchased by Laura Barlow's Yessit kennels, and Ch. StarBright Bonne Chance, CDX, TD, foundation stud for the Cachet Noir kennels. Most importantly for StarBright, however, it produced Ch. StarBright Bouquetiere, CD, TD (Boo), who would remain with the kennel and continue the work that Bria had begun. Bria gave Boo elegance of outline, sound structure and solid temperament. Yamin contributed lovely European type. The net result is a bitch highly regarded within the breed as one of the country's best. She was Best of Breed from the classes at the 1980 Canadian National Specialty, defeating many of the best Belgians of all varieties and going on to Working Group 1. Shown as a special at three ABTC National Specialties, she has been awarded Select each time, two of them under breeder-judges. She was BOS at the AKC's Centennial Show under Barbara Krohn and is a multi-Group placer.

Boo was bred four times. Many of her offspring exhibit the same qualities that have made her so valued and loved. They have sweet natures, elegant

Am. & Can. Ch. StarBright Bouquetiere, CD, TD, BAR, outstanding winner and brood bitch for Sharon Redmer's StarBright Kennels. She is by Ch. Yamin van 'T Hof Melyn x Ch. Brillance de Mont-Cenis, CDX, BAR. *K. Maves*

```
                              Ch. Ami De Chateau Blanc CD
                     Ch. Daktary de Chateau Blanc CD BAR
                              Ch. Ouka du Val D'Orge BAR (France)
              Ch. Scorpio de Fauve Charbonne CD TD BAR
                              D'Artagnone Du Falaise BAR (Canada)
                     Ch. Mystique De Fauve Charbonne CD BAR
                              Ch. Jasmine de Cledeville BAR (France)
     CH. BRILLANCE DE MONT-CENIS CDX BAR whelped 1/25/74
                              Ch. Sandy Haze Prince of Hearts UD BAR
                     Ch. Teddy Edouard Ours Val De Echo
                              Filoche Du Val De Tonnerre
              Ch. Regina's Echo de Bonheur CD BAR
                              Ch. Brigadier De Chateau Blanc
                     Renee De Noir Et Or
                              Ch. Omegan De Braise Ardente
```

Pedigree of Ch. Brillance de Mont-Cenis, CDX, BAR

Judge Edeltraud Laurin awarding Ch. Sunwise So Danger Beware, bred by J. Paredes and T. Heath and owned by E. and T. Janssen, first in the Herding Group at the Fort Bend KC. *Carter*

This magnificent antique bronze is by Jules-Edmond Masson, a recognized French sculptor who produced works from 1890 to the late 1920s. The piece was discovered at an antique sale in Utah in March 1989 and purchased by the American Belgian Tervuren Club and friends for placement in the Dog Museum of America.

silhouettes, typey headpieces and sound bodies. To date Boo has produced eighteen champion offspring, a number that places her among the four top-producing bitches in the breed.

Boo was bred twice to Ch. Bonheur Ruarri MacTire, producing nine champions. Her third breeding, to Ch. Yessit C'est Tout, TDX, produced StarBright's "E" litter, which includes two Group-placing champions and a multiple High in Trial winning son. Her final breeding to Ch. Coda's Roadside Escapade, CD, TD, produced the "F" litter, which has six champions to date. Two bitches retained from the last two breedings, Ch. StarBright Effervescence and Ch. StarBright Fait Accompli, TD, should carry on the tradition.

WINJAMMER (1976)

Owner Pat Morgan proves what a good foundation can do for a novice who sets out to find a pet that would make a total dog. After two years of research, Pat chose Am., Can. Ch. Hi Times Top of the Crop, UD (Bumper). As of this writing, no other dog can boast her accomplishments in field, conformation, obedience and herding trial competition combined. Pat, however, finds Bumper's most important qualities to be her character, humor, memory ("akin to an elephant's"), patience ("like a saint") and uncanny ability to size up the people she meets.

Bumper's second litter, bred to Ch. Hi Times Jem O Croc Blanc, CD, produced four champions, among them Ch. Winjammers Hi Time Souvenir, CD (Charlie). Co-owned at the time by Pat with Carol and Tom Murray (Souvenir kennels, which now owns Charlie outright), Charlie produced what probably is the best-known Winjammer litter with Ch. Yamin van 'T Hof Melyn. Out of six puppies, three were destined to make history—Am., Can. Ch. Winjammers One For The Road, CDX, TDX (Ryan, multi-BIS, multi-HIT and 1988 ABTC National Specialty winner); Am., Can. Ch. Winjammers On The Rise, a multi-Group placer and herding trial champion; and the first bitch to win a Best in Show in the United States, Ch. HTCh. Winjammers On The Move, CD (Tommy), who repeated this win in Canada and also won BOB at the ABTC's 1982 National Specialty and BOS at the 1988 National.

CORSAIR KENNELS (1978)

Corsair kennels was established in 1976, when owner Steve Sorenson acquired Ch. Debonair Debra de Vedette Noir. In 1977 he also acquired Ch. Whirlwinds Amber of Frostfire. The two became the foundation of the kennel, and the first litter was whelped in 1978. Steve believes that these two bitches carried the best bloodlines from Belgian Tervuren greats of years gone by and that their winning and producing were meant to be. Their offspring are found

Ch. Corsair's Calypso Beat, multiple Group winning bitch bred and owned by Steve and Jane Sorenson

Ch. Tacara's Soubrette Soignes, WB, at 1987 National Specialty, bred and owned by Linda Newsome

in the winners' circle at many major Tervuren gatherings around the United States and Canada.

The kennel bred its first litter under the Timber Trace name. However, a 1979 breeding of Debby to Ch. Achates Esprit de Joie established the Corsair prefix and produced Ch. Corsair's Beaujangles, retained by the kennel. In 1980 Steve imported Ch. Dali de la Pouroffe from Belgium. Dali and Beau have been the principal stud dogs for the kennel. Other well-known Corsair dogs are Ch. Corsair's Gigolo, Ch. Corsair's Hot Rod, Ch. Frostfire's Chaos of Corsair and Ch. Corsair's Hellon Wheels (BOW at the ABTC's 1984 National Specialty show). Ch. Corsair's Calypso Beat is a multiple Group placer and multiple National Specialty Select winner.

Best known of the Corsair dogs is Beaujangles. The all-time top winner in the breed, during his career he won twenty-three Bests in Show, ninety Group 1s (including a Group 1 at the Westminster Kennel Club show during the first year the Herding Group was available at that show) and BOB at the 1983 ABTC National Specialty. Beau was the top Belgian Tervuren from 1982 through 1985.

TACARA TERVUREN KENNEL (1982)

Owned by Linda Newsome, Tacara bred its first litter after ten years of steady involvement in breed and obedience competition. The dam was Ch. Hi Times OK So Show Me, CDX (Toma). Toma was WB and Select at the 1983 ABTC National Specialty. She was bred to Ch. Bonheur Ruarri MacTire, and the union produced two champions. Toma's second breeding, to Ch. Frostfire's Firebrand, CD, produced Ch. Tacara's Halcyon Hans, CD, WD and Select at the ABTC 1985 National Specialty and a *Dog World* award winner, and Ch. Tacara's Henna Horizon, Group placer and Select at the 1987 ABTC National Specialty.

For her third litter in March 1985, Toma took a trip to Hoeilaart, Belgium, to be bred to Holland, Luxembourg, Belgian, French S.R. Ch. Grimm Van de Hoge Laer. This union produced Ch. Tacara's Sojourn Soignes, CD (Ssken). Linda feels that Ssken combines the best of American bloodlines with European type. Ssken sired the sweepstakes winner and WB at the 1988 ABTC National Specialty.

Tacara's other foundation bitch was Ch. Frostfire's Xit Keetra, a Group-placing and High in Trial dog. Keetra is a large bitch who also was bred three times. Her most famous offspring to date is Ch. Tacara's Galileah GoFrostfire, CD, who was BOS at the 1985 ABTC National Specialty sweepstakes and RWB at the 1987 National.

Keetra's last breeding also involved a trip to Europe, this time to Paris to be bred to the striking French Ch. Ours de Clos du Richaumoine. This union produced Tacara's Soubrette Soignes, WB and Select at the 1987 ABTC National Specialty, as well as Ch. Tacara's Spree Soignes and Tacara's Solo

Soignes. Keetra's offspring are particularly noted for their rich mahogany base color and black faces.

SUMMARY

Tracing the Belgian Tervuren's heritage through the years has been a moving experience for us. We have attempted to highlight the people and dogs who have prominently influenced the breed. However, we realize that a wheel has many spokes. If a single spoke is missing, the entire wheel is weakened.

Thus we regret that we cannot recognize every person, dog and kennel instrumental in the success of the breed. Many dedicated breeders, owners and Tervuren whose contributions are immeasurable have been mentioned little, if at all. Many good people have owned a single dog and showed it proudly. In the early days, when every dog was needed in the ring to gain recognition for the breed, their contributions were vital to the integrity of our "wheel." Others have exhibited and been active in many endeavors of our national club. They, too, are important spokes in the wheel. Many kennels that were active in the past are no longer involved in the breed, but their presence is felt in our history.

Some of these inactive kennels were so important to the progress of Belgian Tervuren, however, that we could not conclude this chapter without recognizing at least some of them, as well as kennels that have been steadfast in their promotion of Tervuren. We also must bow to promising new kennels. They are the wave of the future, and the weight of their influence is yet to come. We attempt to honor these kennels and dogs in the next chapter.

Ch. Winjammers One For The Road, CDX, TDX, owned by Roberta Whitesides, is the first multiple Best in Show winner of any breed to hold a TDX.

Ch. Chateaubriand, CD, BAR, an important producer of the 1970s. Breeders: David and Betsy Kilmartin; owner: Carousel Kennels.

6

More Kennels, Dogs and People

IT IS BASIC to the nature of the dog fancy that there is a constantly changing cast of characters, not only among the dogs that make history, but among the people who help shape it. Some come into dogs and stay for the long term. Others participate for just a few years, but in some cases those who have not remained long with the Tervuren have earned themselves a place in breed history notwithstanding. This chapter will look at some of the efforts that have made their mark and no longer exist and will also review a number of more recent kennels that may write significant chapters in the annals of the Tervuren of the future. Time will inexorably judge the new as it already has judged the old.

INACTIVE KENNELS

Carousel Kennels

This kennel, owned by Mary Jo Oldendick, was active during most of the 1970s. Basing its breeding program on stock from the Georjune kennels, it produced a number of litters and often co-bred with other kennels, including the Iowa-based Liberte kennels. An especially noteworthy fact is that Carousel was the final home of Ch. Chateaubriand, BAR, a dog regarded as one of the most influential in our breed.

Commander Kennels

The Commander kennels of Shirley and Ken Dolezal bred during the mid-1970s. Its contribution to our heritage rests on the dogs who went on to influence other kennels. Ch. Commander's Win de Braise Rouge, BAR, was a major contributor to the Braise Rouge line. Equally important was Ch. Commander's Fire Away, C-BAR, who became a well-known stud and show dog and the foundation sire for Chateau de Vie.

Crocs Blanc Kennels

Danielle Daugherty was active in Tervuren for a number of years and often co-bred with Bernadine Paull of Hi Time kennels. Dogs like Kanook bear both the Hi Time and Crocs Blanc kennel names. Her first loves are the Malinois and Belgian Sheepdogs, however, and she has concentrated on them in recent times.

Esprit de Joie

Between 1975 and 1982, Jackie Warne's and Robert Bower's Alaskan kennel of Esprit de Joie produced a number of influential dogs that can be found in the chronicles of other kennels in this book, including championship and obedience titleholders, BAR winners and national specialty Selects. Its foundation dogs were Ch. Chagall du Masque Noir, CDX, BAR, and the bitches Ch. Estrellita du Masque Noir, CD, and Frostfire's Innovation, CD, BAR. Some of its better known produce include Ch. Achates Esprit de Joie, CD, BAR, and Ch. Excalibur Esprit de Joie.

Hilton

This California-based kennel, owned by John and Betty Hilton and Ann Storniolo, was influential on the West Coast and produced a number of litters. It provided foundation stock for Sang Bleu and other kennels between 1967 and 1975. Two C-BAR bitches carry its name—Ch. Hilton's Joli Fleur de Lis, CD, and Hilton's Wicked Witch.

Kajon Kennels

Based in California, Karen Edwards Gomez's Kajon kennel began breeding about 1973 and continued into the mid-1980s. Especially important among its produce are Ch. Kajon's Slaughter, C-BAR, and Ch. Kajon's Sherry, CD, C-BAR, littermates and offspring of Ch. Geronimo de Chateau Blanc and Ch. Paulmar's Cosmic Agena, BAR.

Int. Ch. Hilton's Kadu Chateau Lynn, CDX, the breed's first international champion with a working certificate (CACIT). Breeders: Greg Garrity and Betty Hilton; owner: Lynn Morgan.

Sweepstakes judge Sharon Redmer presents award to Ch. Atalanta's Dulcimer Windsong, shown with owner-handler Marcie Schubert. Bred by Mary Gaye Durst.

Up Tempo

Up Tempo was established in the East by Carol Butrick, who then moved to California and continued breeding until the late 1980s. The kennel produced a number of champions and obedience dogs, including Ch. Up Tempo Naima, CDX, BAR; Ch. Up Tempo Iliea, CDX (BOW and Select, 1985 National Specialty); and Ch. Up Tempo Intrepid, a multiple Group placer.

ON TO THE FUTURE

The kennels that follow have begun breeding relatively recently or have followed limited breeding programs. Their contribution to the Belgian Tervuren breed cannot be ignored, however, and what they do in the future may have a major impact on the breed.

Anduin

Anduin kennels began in 1979, when owners Rory and Linda Friedow acquired Ch. Aerin of Anduin, CDX, O-BAR. She is a 1986 National Specialty Select and a bitch that can be expected to earn her C-BAR in the near future. The first Anduin litter was produced several years later. To date, the Friedows have bred sparingly, but have produced a number of champions and obedience/tracking titleholders.

Atalanta

Mary Gay Burr bred her first litter in 1976 but became truly active in the 1980s. With Ch. Frostfire's Deep Brandy Wine, CD, as its foundation bitch, the kennel has produced a number of champions, including Ch. Atalanta's Aura of Shilo, Winners Bitch and Select at the 1986 ABTC National Specialty and again Select in 1987, and Ch. Atalanta's Dulcimer Windsong, also Select in 1987.

Bilgay

Bilgay, a Florida-based kennel owned by Bill and Gail Cooper, bred its first litter in 1980. Since then, the kennel has maintained a limited breeding program that has produced fifteen champions, including multi-Group placer Ch. Bilgay's Night Rustler, CD, who was awarded a Select at the 1988 ABTC National Specialty, and multiple High in Trial winner OTCH Ch. Bilgay Spindrifter.

Cachet Noir

Cachet Noir was established by Dana MacKonis in the early 1970s, with Ch. Luba vom Giberge, CDX (a Chateaubriand daughter) as its foundation bitch. The kennel began its career under the name Sunburst, but switched quickly to its present name and acquired Ch. StarBright Bonne Chance, CDX, TD, C-BAR (1986 Select) as a foundation stud. Banner, as he is called, has been prominent during the past decade, producing champion and obedience/tracking offspring of excellent quality. An incredibly responsive, all-round achiever, Banner's accomplishments are detailed further in Chapter 17, "The Versatile Belgian Tervuren."

Camarade

Debby Boehm has been active in Tervuren for a number of years and produced her first litter in 1978, with Ch. Debonnaire Debra Vedette Noir, C-BAR, as her foundation bitch. The kennel has been very active during the 1980s, producing a number of champions. It also owns Ch. Fox Hollow's Lothlorien, a renowned bitch, whose accomplishments are detailed under her breeder's kennel name, Fox Hollow.

Carefree

Carefree began its career as Eclat de Vie, but its owner Merrelyn Clark switched quickly to its present name, which recognizes Ch. Cin-li's Alice P. Livesn Carefree as its foundation bitch. Alice, who is on the verge of her C-BAR award, won the Brood Bitch class at the 1987 National Specialty. The kennel names its litters by a system that combines both American and European habits. The first word after the kennel's prefix follows the American habit of alphabetical names. The second word after the prefix follows the European tradition of naming all litters with the same letter in the year that they were bred.

Among its notable offspring are Ch. Carefree Knight Vision and members of the "GS" litter (Gunner's Skipper, Gypsy Serenade). Four of the five members of this litter were Group placers, including wins from the classes, and the fifth, Gypsy Serenade, also won a High in Trial.

Chateau de Vie

Although Judy Bradley has owned Tervuren for nearly twenty years, she did not begin breeding until 1978, when her first litter was produced from Ch. Lancer de Chateau Blanc, BAR, and Ch. Commander's Dare O'Wanderlord, C-BAR. Since then, the kennel has engaged in a limited breeding program that has produced a number of champions. It also owned Ch. Commander's Fire Away, BAR (Gunner), a well-known show dog and sire. A son of Ch. Scorpio

Ch. StarBright Bonne Chance, CDX, TD, C-BAR, Police Dog I & II, and detector dog. Breeder: S. Redmer; owner: Dana Mackonis.

Ch. Daradan's Liten Brun Nalle, BOS from veterans' class at 1987 National Specialty. Breeders: D. and D. Wilcox and C. Siefert; owner: Debbie Schmidt.

de Fauve Charbonne, Gunner was used successfully by a number of other kennels and will be found behind many of today's Tervuren who are competing successfully in the conformation and obedience rings.

Daradan

The Daradan Kennel of Dan and Dara Wilcox has bred on the West Coast for a number of years and has co-bred with a number of other kennels. With Charlyn du Chalet Belgique, C-BAR, as its foundation bitch, Daradan has produced a number of champion and working dogs, including Ch. Daradan's Brun Varg and Ch. Daradan's Liten Brun Nalle, who won BOS at the 1987 National Specialty.

Fox Hollow

Fox Hollow is a small kennel owned by Phil and Margie Marquez that began breeding in the early 1980s and has litters only occasionally. Nonetheless, it has bred a number of quality dogs, and its foundation bitch, Ch. Hi Times Takeover, has earned her C-BAR. Well known among the kennel's output thus far are Chs. Fox Hollow's Varda and Fox Hollow's KT Darling (both National Specialty Selects); Ch. Fox Hollow's Strider, a Best in Show winner, and Ch. Fox Hollow's Lothlorien. The latter, a bitch who answers to the name Lester, has been a major contender in the breed and Group rings and has amassed an impressive list of wins. She was BOS at the ABTC's 1984 National Specialty show and BOB at the club's 1985 National Specialty.

Jamaica

This kennel of Helen H. Hittesdorf produced its first litter in 1980, with Ch. Chantilly Esprite de Joie, UDT, O-BAR (Tilly) as its foundation bitch. She is still "top dog" in the household. Although Helen reports that Tilly's first role in life is as a house pet, she is an obedience, tracking, conformation house pet. Bred only twice, she has eight champion get. Among them are National Sweepstakes BOS and Supported show winners, High in Trial dogs and a Canadian Group placer. Helen thinks that Tilly's most notable offspring is Ch. Jamaica Nemesis, UDTX. Among Tilly's grandchildren, which carry on her shining style, Helen's personal favorite is Ch. Jamaica Clock of the Heart, CD, TD, a National Specialty Select.

LaBarge

Roger and Shirley La Barge purchased their first Tervuren in 1970, and in 1971 finished the first champion Tervuren in the state of Wisconsin. Since then, they have engaged in a limited but effective breeding program that places equal importance on conformation and working ability. Thus far, the kennel has produced twenty champion, twenty CD, seven CDX and two UD dogs. Their bitch, Bonte Esprit de Joie, CD, has placed well in the Brood Bitch classes at three consecutive national specialties. Two LaBarge dogs have earned national specialty Selects. They are Ch. Hessian Warrior de LaBarge, CD, TT (who also placed third in the Stud Dog class at the 1988 ABTC National), and Ch. Here's Bittersweet de LaBarge, who won the honor at the 1986 National.

Petit Chalet

The Petit Chalet kennel of Lynn Wright Wellman, Carol Wright and Steven Wright provides a link to the breed's past. Its first litter was bred under the Le Parvenu prefix in 1965. At about the same time, Jim Davis, an early breeder (and a president of the ABTC) used the Petit Chalet kennel name. Jim was terminally ill and asked Lynn to carry the name forward.

Since then, the Wright clan has bred in a modest way, producing less than one litter a year. Nonetheless, the kennel has twenty-five champions to its credit. The breeders are proudest of two dogs: Ch. Le Parvenu Licorice Stick (Cori) and Ch. Petit Chalet's O'My Adopha (Stormy). A Group placer, Cori was in the ABTC's ratings for top ten Tervuren for BOBs and among *Kennel Review*'s top ten Tervuren. In addition to maternal duties, Stormy was a successful BOB winner against male specials in a number of shows. Another of its bitches, Ch. Petit Chalet's Touch O'Jasmine (owned by Theresa Hunter of Witchcraft kennels), won a Select at the 1986 National.

Sandyhill

Although Jan Barringer bred Poodles for a number of years, the kennel concentrated on breeding Tervuren in the 1980s, relying almost wholly on imported European stock. Sandyhill was extremely active and sent dogs to a number of other American breeders. During its relatively short life, Sandyhill produced at least nineteen champions. Its foundation stud, Ch. Darass de la Pouroffe, CD, has earned his C-BAR award, and its foundation bitch, Ch. Duchesse de la Belle Edita, has earned both C-BAR and O-BAR.

Seafield

Seafield's first Tervuren was Ch. Kajon's May Wine, who won Winners Bitch at the 1977 National Specialty and whose progeny include regional and National Specialty winners in the United States and Canada. In 1983, owner Judy Specht attended the French National Specialty show and was enormously impressed with the type, style and attitude of the dogs she saw. She returned to the Continent in 1985 with a bitch to be bred to a top European stud and thus became the first American breeder to take a Tervuren bitch "back to its roots." Since then, the kennel has imported several dogs from Europe and plans to continue to combine their lines with those of American dogs.

Starwind

This Montana kennel of Sharon Cochran and Elly Fondren was founded in California and bred its early litters under the High Sierra name. Among its early dogs of note were multiple Group-placing Ch. Brandywine's Hi Sierra Aspen and Ch. Cavlr's High Sierra Mahogany, C-BAR. Basing its foundation on Cavalier and Hilton stock, it began a program to improve type and concentrated its efforts on combining the elegance its owners saw in the influential import Ch. Yamin van 'T Hof Melyn (owned by the Walkers) with their American lines.

The kennel began importing breeding stock from Europe, among whom one, Ch. Starwind (from the Netherlands), was Reserve Winners Bitch at the 1988 ABTC National Specialty show and Best of Opposite Sex at the 1989 National. Its owners have continued to import with the goal of establishing a line that combines the best of European and American Tervuren.

Ch. Windsong Belle Star, CD, by Ch. Crocs Blancs Diablo O'Hi Time, C-BAR x Ch. Hi Times Sweet Polly Purebred, CD, C-BAR. Breeder: Marcie Schubert; owner: Kathy Miramontes.

Ch. Hi Times Kanook of Crocs Blanc, CD, BAR (d), the only Tervuren to have won three consecutive National Specialty shows—1974, 1975 and 1976. Breeders: Danielle Daugherty, Bernadine Paull and Connie Wentling; owner: Judith Lee Smith.

Ch. Flair de Fauve Charbonne C-BAR
Ch. Cyrano de Chateau Blanc CD BAR
Ch. Kandice de Fauve Charbonne CDX BAR
Ch. Chateaubriand CD BAR
Ch. Wayfarers' Pacemaker CD C-BAR
Hi Line Querido BAR
Chamette du Bon Chateau
CH. HI TIMES KANOOK OF CROCS BLANC CD BAR, whelped 8/22/70
Hety du Clos Saint Clair (France)
Ch. Kis Tam's Candide Pataud CD C-BAR
Tammi Candide C-BAR
Ch. Rob-Lyn's Ange Acajou CD BAR
Ch. Tervuren Haven's Kactus
Eau-de-Vie du Val de Tonnerre CD
Bonheur du Val de Tonnerre C-BAR

96

7

A Pictorial of National Specialty Winners

O VER TWENTY-FIVE YEARS of the breed's best is presented to you in this special section on National Specialty show Best of Breed winners. The dog's name is followed by its sex in parentheses, the sire (s:), dam (d:) and owner (o:). Enjoy.

1961—Ch. Jory Candide (d). Sire: Ch. Dandy du Clos Saint Jacques, BAR; dam: Daloue du Clos Saint Clair. Owner: William and Opal McGee.

1962—Ch. Fidelite de Fauve Charbonne, CD (b). Sire: Ch. D'Jimmy du Clos Saint Clair, CD; dam: Chrysis de Clos Saint Jacques, CD. Owner: Dorothy Hollister.

1963—Ch. D'Jimmy du Clos Saint Clair, CD (d), owned by R. Robinson, J. Hinckley and D. Hollister

Left: 1964—Ch. Flair de Fauve Charbonne, C-BAR (d). Sire: Ch. D'Jimmy du Clos Saint Clair, CD; dam: Chrysis du Clos Saint Jacques, CD. Owner: Edeltraud Laurin.

Right: 1967—Ch. Kandice de Fauve Charbonne, CDX, BAR (b). Sire: Ch. Dandy du Clos Saint Jacques, BAR; dam: Ch. Jasmine de Cledeville, BAR. Owner: Edeltraud Laurin.

1965—Ch. Ami de Chateau Blanc, CD (d). Sire: Ch. Flair de Fauve Charbonne, C-BAR; dam: Ch. Kandice de Fauve Charbonne, CDX, BAR. Owner: Edeltraud Laurin.

1966 and 1968—Am. & Can. Ch. Kis Tam's Candide Pataud, CD, C-BAR (d). Sire: Hety du Clos Saint Clair; dam: Tammi Candide, C-BAR. Owners: Karen and Patrick Johnson.

1969—Ch. Mars de Fauve Charbonne, UDT, BAR (d). Sire: D'Artagnone du Falaise, BAR; dam: Ch. Jasmine de Cledeville, BAR. Owners: Jack and Donna Allen.

1970 and 1973—Ch. Bonheur's D'Artagnan, UDT, BAR (d). Sire: Ch. Cyrano de Chateau Blanc, BAR; dam: Bonheur's Bobbins & Pins, BAR. Owner: Bernadine Paull.

1971—Ch. Wayfarer's Pacemaker, CD, C-BAR (d). Sire: Ch. Columbine Nikit, BAR; dam: Wayfarer's Nadia du Rochemont, CD, C-BAR. Owner: Sondra Miller.

1972—Ch. Scorpio de Fauve Charbonne, CD, TD, BAR (d). Sire: Ch. Daktary de Chateau Blanc, CD, BAR; dam: Ch. Mystique de Fauve Charbonne, CD, BAR. Owner: Joyce McHenry.

1977 and 1979—Am. & Mex. Ch. Frost Fire's Deuces Wilde, CD (d). Sire: Ch. Chateaubriand, CD, BAR; dam: Ch. Sabrina de Flambeau Rouge, CD, BAR. Owner: Greg Garrity.

1978—Ch. Regina's Echo de Bonheur, CD, BAR (b). Sire: Ch. Teddy Edouard Ours Val du Echo; dam: Renee de Noir et Or. Owners: Violette and Corinne Wilson.

1980—Ch. Ovation de Chateau Blanc, CD (d). Sire: Ch. Lancer de Chateau Blanc, BAR; dam: Ch. Douceur du Vent de Bayville, CD, C-BAR. Owner: Edeltraud Laurin.

1981—Ch. Hi Times C-Sam O'Crocs Blanc, CD, BAR (d). Sire: Ch. Hi Times Little Leo, CD; dam: Ch. Rob-Lyn's Ange Acajou, CD, BAR. Owners: Bernadine Paull and Joyce Ecker.

1982—Ch. HTCh. Winjammers On The Move, CD, TD (b). Sire: Ch. Yamin van 'T Hof Melyn, BAR; dam: Ch. Winjammers Hi Time Souvenir, CD, BAR. Owners: Becky Burgess and Pat Morgan. Tervuren fanciers are behind this bitch as she goes on to Best in Show.

1983—Ch. Corsair's Beaujangles (d). Sire: Ch. Achates Esprit de Joie, CD, C-BAR; dam: Ch. Debonair Debra de Vedette Noir, CD, C-BAR. Owner: Steve Sorenson.

1984—Ch. Bonheur Ruarri MacTire, BAR (d). Sire: Ch. Elysee De Mont-Cenis, BAR; dam: Kalyn's Zazarac De Bonheur, CD, BAR. Owners: Kay Maves, Sharon Redmer and Faye Dickens.

1985—Ch. Fox Hollow's Lothlorien, TT (b). Sire: Ch. Corsair's Beaujangles; dam: Ch. Hi Time's Take Over, CDX. Owners: Debby Boehm and Margie Marquez.

1986—Ch. Touchstone's Streak of Frostfire (d). Sire: Ch. Corsair's Frost Fire Cyclone, CD, TD, C-BAR; dam: Ch. Arista Achates of Annik's, CD. Owners: Cindy Herfindahl and John Melcher.

1987—Ch. Corbin Toujours Jeune, CDX, TD (d). Sire: Ch. Yamin van 'T Hof Melyn, BAR; dam: Ch. Bronze Bell's Golden Flame, CDX. Owners: Kelly and Lori Keele.

1988—Ch. Winjammers One For The Road, CDX, TDX; Can. CD, TDX (d). Sire: Ch. Yamin van 'T Hof Melyn, BAR; dam: Ch. Winjammers Hi Time Souvenir, CD, BAR. Owner: Roberta J. Whitesides.

1989—Ch. Snowflower Voila Sharvonne, CD (d). Sire: Ch. Labelle's A Liberte; dam: Ch. Snowflower Chavon, CD. Owners: Sharon Lutz and Charles Rogers, M.D.

103

A study in proud carriage

Lovely type in an adult bitch

8

Blueprint of the Belgian Tervuren Standard

BEFORE TERVUREN WERE REGISTERED as a separate breed in the United States, the 1956 Belgian Sheepdog standard (as published in the AKC's *Complete Dog Book*) listed black, fawn or any other color as acceptable under the color description of the long-haired Groenendael. The short-haired Malinois could be brindled fawn, fawn or any other color. The word *Tervuren* did not appear.

The standard briefly addressed size, specifying only that males should be at least twenty-three and one-half inches and females at least twenty-two and one-half inches. No upper limit was given. On the other hand, an ideal weight *was* given. Both dogs and bitches were to be least fifty-three pounds (one can only speculate what a twenty-two-and-one-half-inch, fifty-three-pound bitch would look like—hefty, indeed). A scale of points similar to the present scale for Great Danes and other breeds also was provided. It was meant to weigh the various features of the breed in proportion to their relative importance. Today, the Belgian Tervuren standard (and the other Belgian standards) omits weight limits and point scales, and the size specifications are far more precise.

The AKC first adopted a standard specifically for Belgian Tervuren in 1959, when they were made a separate breed. Written by Bob and Barbara Krohn, it was a close interpretation of the Belgian standard, omitting that standard's references to other coat colors and types.

The standard was revised by the American Belgian Tervuren Club (ABTC) in 1980. The club wished to clarify some of the original wording and

POORLY MARKED **LACK OF MASK**

CORRECT PLANES **FAULTY PLANES**

EARS: IDEAL **GOOD** **TOO LONG** **TOO LARGE, WIDE-SET**

Drawings by Marcia R. Schlehr

106

describe disqualifying faults more specifically, so that greater uniformity of desired breed qualities could be achieved. At the present time, the ABTC is considering further clarifications of its standard.

THE OFFICIAL STANDARD FOR
THE BELGIAN TERVUREN
(JUNE 1, 1980)

General Appearance—The first impression of the Belgian Tervuren is that of a well-balanced medium-size dog, elegant in appearance, standing squarely on all fours, with proud carriage of head and neck. He is strong, agile, well muscled, alert and full of life. He gives the impression of depth and solidity without bulkiness. The male should appear unquestionably masculine; the female should have a distinctly feminine look and be judged equally with the male. The Belgian Tervuren is a *natural* dog and there is no need for excessive posing in the show ring.

Personality—The Belgian Tervuren reflects the qualities of intelligence, courage, alertness and devotion to master. In addition to his inherent ability as a herding dog, he protects his master's person and property without being overtly aggressive. He is watchful, attentive and usually in motion when not under command.

Temperament—In his relationship with humans he is observant and vigilant with strangers, but not apprehensive. He does not show fear or shyness. He does not show viciousness by unwarranted or unprovoked attack. He must be approachable, standing his ground and showing confidence to meet overtures without himself making them. With those he knows well, he is most affectionate and friendly, zealous for their attention and very possessive.

Head—Well chiseled, skin taut, long without exaggeration.

Skull and Muzzle—Measuring from the stop are of equal length. Overall size is in proportion to the body, top of skull flattened rather than rounded, the width approximately the same as, but not wider than the length. The topline of the muzzle is parallel to the topline of the skull when viewed from the side. Muzzle moderately pointed, avoiding any tendency toward snippiness or cheekiness.

Stop—Moderate.

Jaws—Strong and powerful.

Lips—Tight and black, no pink showing on the outside when the mouth is closed.

Nose—Black without spots or discolored areas.

Nostrils—Well defined.

Teeth—Full complement of strong white teeth, evenly set, meeting in a scissors or a level bite. Overshot and undershot teeth are a fault. Undershot teeth such that contact with the upper incisors is lost by two or more of the lower incisors is a disqualification. Loss of contact caused by short center

This bitch is too short in the muzzle and has an undesirable rounded topskull.

Excellent head planes and proportions

Ears too large and light masking on the muzzle

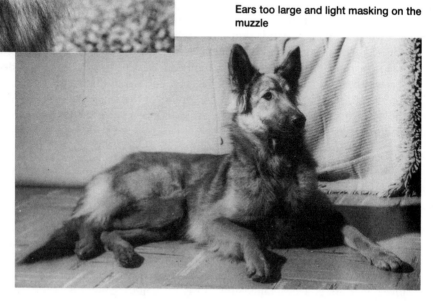

incisors in an otherwise correct bite shall not be judged undershot. Missing teeth are a fault, but teeth broken by accident or discolored should not be penalized.

Eyes—Dark brown, medium size, slightly almond shape, not protruding. Light, yellow, or round eyes are a fault.

Ears—Triangular in shape, well cupped, stiff, erect, height equal to width at base. Set high, the base of the ear does not come below the center of the eye. Hanging ears, as on a hound, are a disqualification.

Expression—Intelligent and questioning, indicating alertness, attention and readiness for action.

Torso—*Neck*—Round, muscular, rather long and elegant, slightly arched and tapered from head to body. Skin well fitting with no loose folds.

Topline—Horizontal, straight and firm from withers to hip. Withers accentuated.

Chest—Not broad without being narrow, but deep; the lowest point of the brisket reaching the elbow, forming a smooth ascendant curve to the abdomen.

Abdomen—Moderately developed, neither tucked up nor paunchy. Ribs well sprung but flat on the sides.

Loin Section—Viewed from above is relatively short, broad and strong, but blending smoothly into the back.

Croup—Medium long, sloping gradually to the base of the tail.

Tail—Strong at the base, the last vertebra to reach at least to the hock. At rest the dog holds it low, the tip bent back level with the hock. When in action, he may raise it to a point level with the topline, giving it a slight curve, but not a hook. Tail is not carried above the backline nor turned to one side. A cropped or stump tail is a disqualification.

Forequarters—*Shoulder*—Long, laid back 45°, flat against the body, forming a right angle with the upper arm. Top of the shoulder blades roughly two thumbs' width apart.

Arms—Should move in a direction exactly parallel to the longitudinal axis of the body.

Forearms—Long and well muscled.

Legs—Straight and parallel, perpendicular to the ground. Bone oval rather than round. Dewclaws may be removed.

Pasterns—Short and strong, slightly sloped.

Feet—Rounded, cat footed, turning neither in nor out, toes curved close together, well padded, strong nails.

Hindquarters—*Thighs*—Broad and heavily muscled.

Stifles—Clearly defined, with upper shank at right angles to hip bones.

Hocks—Moderately bent.

Metatarsi—Short, perpendicular to the ground, parallel to each other when viewed from the rear.

Legs—Powerful without heaviness, moving in the same pattern as the limbs of the forequarters. Dewclaws are removed. Bone oval rather than round.

Feet—Slightly elongated, toes curved close together, heavily padded, strong nails.

Coat—The Belgian Tervuren is particularly adaptable to extremes of temperature or climate. The guard hairs of the coat must be long, close fitting, straight and abundant. The texture is of medium harshness, not silky or wiry. Wavy or curly hair is undesirable. The undercoat is very dense, commensurate, however, with climatic conditions. The hair is short on the head, outside the ears, and on the front part of the legs. The opening of the ear is protected by tufts of hair.

Ornamentation—Consists of especially long and abundant hair, like a colarette around the neck, particularly on the males; fringe of long hair down the back of the forearm; especially long and abundant hair trimming the breeches; long, heavy and abundant hair on the tail.

Color—*Body*—Rich fawn to russet mahogany with black overlay. The coat is characteristically double pigmented, wherein the tip of each fawn hair is blackened. On mature males, this blackening is especially pronounced on the shoulders, back and rib section, but blackening in patches is undesirable. The underparts of the body, tail and breeches are cream, gray or light beige. Belgian Tervuren characteristically become darker with increasing age. Although allowance should be made for females and young males, absence of blackening in mature dogs is a serious fault. Washed-out predominant color, such as cream or gray, is to be severely penalized. Solid black, solid liver or any area of white except as specified on the chest, tips of toes, chin and muzzle are disqualifications.

Face—The face has a black mask and the ears are mostly black. A face with a complete absence of black is a serious fault. Frost or white on chin or muzzle is normal.

Chest—The chest is normally black, but may be a mixture of black and gray. A single white patch is permitted on the chest, not to extend to the neck or breast.

Feet—The tips of the toes may be white. Nail color may vary from black to transparent.

Breeches—Cream, gray or light beige.

Tail—The tail typically has a darker or black tip.

Gait—Lively and graceful, covering the maximum ground with minimum effort. Always in motion, seemingly never tiring, he shows ease of movement rather than a hard driving action. He single tracks at a fast gait, the legs both front and rear converging toward the center line of gravity of the dog. The back line should remain firm and level, parallel to the line of motion; viewed from the side he exhibits full extension of both fore and hindquarters. His natural tendency is to move in a circle, rather than a straight line. Padding, hackneying, weaving, crabbing and similar movement faults are to be penalized according to the degree to which they interfere with the ability of the dog to work.

This headpiece displays excellent mask and eye shape and well-set ears.

An entirely black face can be pleasing and equally acceptable. *K. P. Johnson*

This five-year-old dog has lost pigment on the outside of the lips . . .

. . . while this fourteen-year-old bitch still has good lip pigment. *K. P. Johnson*

Size and Substance—The ideal male is 24 to 26 inches in height and female 22 to 24 inches in height measured at the withers. Dogs are to be penalized in accordance to the degree they deviate from the ideal. The body is square; the length measured from the point of shoulder to the point of the rump approximates the height. Females may be somewhat longer in body. Bone structure is medium in proportion to height, so that he is well balanced throughout and neither spindly or leggy nor cumbersome and bulky. Males under 23 inches and over 26.5 inches or females under 21 inches or over 24.5 inches are to be disqualified.

Faults—The Belgian Tervuren is a herding dog, and faults which affect his ability to herd under all conditions, such as poor gait, bite, coat or temperament, should be particularly penalized.

DISQUALIFICATIONS

Ears hanging as on a hound.

Tail cropped or stump.

Solid black or solid liver or any area of white except as specified on the chest, tips of toes, chin, or muzzle.

Undershot teeth such that contact with the upper incisors is lost by two or more of the lower incisors.

Males under 23 inches or over 26.5 inches; females under 21 inches or over 24.5 inches in height.

DISCUSSION OF THE STANDARD

The standard provides a detailed blueprint of correct breed type. *Type* is the unique combination of distinguishing characteristics that makes a breed unmistakably what it is in appearance, movement and temperament. Read individually, some parts of the standard may be similar to those of another breed's standard (for example, shoulder angulation or single-tracking gait). Taken as a whole, however, the standard's portrait of a Tervuren will resemble no other breed.

It is possible for a Tervuren to be a beautiful animal but a poor breed specimen. Top-winning show Tervuren obviously are attractive dogs. Keep in mind, however, that not *all* of them may have good breed type. The contemporary American show ring tends to recognize showiness, attractiveness and general soundness of structure far more than it does good breed type—a fact true in every breed.

Failure to recognize that one's dog does not have good type can be damaging to the breed. If an untypical Tervuren is bred, its owner, and the owners of resulting offspring, may come to believe that the appearance of their dogs is correct. A similar error occurs when a breeder strives to replicate a beloved dog out of sentiment, without stopping to consider whether or not the animal was worthy of replication.

An eye for correct type is gained by developing a mental portrait of the

An illustration of pleasing movement

perfect dog. The standard must be read and reread. It is useful to observe a number of Tervuren for a period of time and weigh them against the standard. Reviewing photographs of prized contemporary European dogs also is an aid (remembering that there are variances in taste from country to country), as is consulting with respected breeders and long-time fanciers.

Through such study one can then begin to form a solid understanding of the ideal specimen of the breed: proud carriage, square body and correct ratio of leg length to body. An arched neck, high-set ears, dark almond-shaped eyes and black mask are typical of the Tervuren headpiece, with its intelligent, alert expression. To an experienced observer, the required level topline, flowing tail carriage and dense, straight coat of warm color are fixed in the mind's eye. The Belgian Tervuren is quick and agile, its movement is graceful, lively, *easy*. Such observation becomes second nature to the trained eye.

However, a Tervuren whose *appearance* is typey can still lack correct type because of overall *physical* unsoundness. Such an animal should be as unacceptable as one with an incorrect head or profile because one of the breed's most notable assets is its versatility as a herding and working dog.

The standard defines correct Tervuren structure. Structure, in turn, defines movement. Tervuren movement is as unique to the breed as its physical appearance. A Tervuren is not stilted at a trot, nor does it have a hard-driving gait. It is balanced. In this case, "balance" means that the angulation of the front and rear are equal. The front does not drag a straighter rear, nor does a more angulated rear overdrive a weaker front. As in so many parts of the breed standard, "moderate" may be the best way to describe a characteristic Tervuren.

Tervuren Color

Historically, the breed's attractive coloration gathered fanciers to fight for the status of the Tervuren as an individual breed in the United States. A rich fawn to mahogany base coat, with black overlay, always has been the ideal and is considered essential as a breed characteristic. An acceptable overlay may be merely a light blackening on the chest, shoulders and rib section, or it may be quite extensive, so long as it is not in patches. On the face, a black muzzle extends at least to the eyes. Some blackening on the skull, or a fully black head, is normal. The ears are mostly black.

Correct coloration takes time to develop. A puppy may have nothing of the warmth or black overlay it will have as an adult, for both characteristics continue to intensify as the dog ages.

Understanding Correct Temperament

A discussion of breed type must not ignore breed temperament. Some would-be enthusiasts, attracted to Tervuren because of their appearance, want them to be as friendly to strangers as to beloved friends. This is an expectation both misguided and incorrect. Our earliest records confirm the breed's use in herding. Such work requires the dog to be gentle, yet alert and watchful, and capable of aggressiveness in the protection of its flock and master.

A story from the breed's history perhaps best delineates the qualities that have been prized in these dogs. An excellent article on Belgians appearing in the December 31, 1924, issue of the *American Kennel Gazette* ("The Dog That Ouida Wrote About") documents how, in 1909, Consul-General Diederich of Belgium wrote a report on police dogs for the Department of Commerce and Labor. In it he said:

> Great difficulties were at first experienced in selecting the animal best adapted to such service, and it was only after considerable time had been spent in experimenting that a final choice was made of the breed known as the Belgian Shepherd Dog.
>
> This species was found to be the most intelligent, showing at the same time marked qualities of endurance which are considered of great importance when the animal is to be used for police purposes.
>
> The dog is strong and able to withstand the changes of weather. He is an excellent watch dog, active and possessed of dauntless courage, which makes him a faithful protector of his master.
>
> The general appearance of the Belgian sheepdog indicates an intelligent animal used to life in the open air of the country, and built to resist the inclemency of the seasons and the sudden changes of weather so noticeable in the Belgian climate.
>
> To his inborn aptitude as guardian of the flocks, he adds the valuable qualities of the best watch dog; in emergencies he becomes, without any hesitation, the stubborn and spirited defender of his master. He is also watchful and attentive. His questioning look indicates intelligence. Always in motion, he seems to be tireless.

It is rewarding to see that these same qualities remain prized today. The Tervuren remains responsive to training and flexible in what he can be trained to do. He prefers the companionship of his family and is gentle with those he knows. Although watchful of strangers, and normally neither aggressive nor timid, a proper Tervuren accepts advances from strangers but does not exhibit excessive friendliness toward them. "Wary of strangers" does not mean "frightened of strangers" or "aggressive toward strangers" (unless the situation warrants it). When he is handled physically by a stranger (a veterinarian or a judge, for example), he tolerates the imposition confidently.

Thus, many facets contribute to a clear understanding of correct breed type. The standard is open to some degree of interpretation, but individual biases must never extend beyond its definitions. Breeders dream the dream of perfection. Striving for the ideal, one breeder may place more importance on one quality than may another. So long as these qualities remain appropriate within the breed standard, this "human difference" is all to the good. It provides breeders with a broad genetic "shopping bag" of characteristics from which to choose.

Three generations of influential stud dogs, pictured as they placed in the stud dog class at the ABTC National in 1976. *From left:* Ch. Chateaubriand, CD, BAR; his son Ch. Hi Times Kanook of Crocs Blanc, CD, BAR; and Kanook's son Ch. Lancer de Chateau Blanc, BAR. Judge: Joseph Gregory.

Ch. Our Valiant du Sanroyale, Mex. TT, holds championship titles in America, Canada, Mexico, Puerto Rico, the Dominican Republic, Bermuda and South America, and the titles of Ch. of the Americas and Int. Ch. of Beauty.

9

Color Genetics and the Belgian Tervuren

TWO CHARACTERISTICS DISTINGUISH the Tervuren from his other Belgian brethren: his coat *type* differs from that of the Malinois and Laekenois, and his *coat color* differs from that of the Groenendael.

All dog breeds possess the same number of genes that define color. The way in which these genes combine produces a breed's distinctive colors and/or markings. Other genetic "modifiers" play their roles by influencing variations of shadings, hues and relative amounts of color characteristics.

Although its desired base color ranges from warm fawn to rich mahogany, the Tervuren can appear in many other shades. An entire range of gray and gray-beige (sable) tints, liver and what appear to be solid black colors have been produced. Before describing the genes that influence Tervuren color, however, a brief explanation of basic genetic principles may be useful to those unfamiliar with them.

SOME BASICS OF GENETICS

Genes are the fundamental genetic building-blocks. Genes exist in pairs and determine each feature of every living thing, including the dog. One gene in a pair is inherited from the sire, the other is inherited from the dam.

Genes vary in their ability to influence the appearance of a dog. Those with strong influence are called *dominant genes*. Others, whose influence is hidden or weakened when paired with a dominant gene, are called *recessive genes.*

Both genes in a pair can be dominant, one can be dominant and one recessive or both can be recessive. If both genes for a given trait are dominant, the animal possessing that gene pair not only will exhibit that trait in its physical appearance but will pass it to all of its offspring. If one gene is dominant and one is recessive, the animal's appearance will reflect some, or all, of the dominant gene's influence, but it will be capable of passing either the dominant or recessive gene to its offspring.

If an animal possesses two recessive genes for a given trait, it will exhibit that trait. Moreover, like the animal with two dominant genes, it can only pass the recessive gene to its offspring. Because dominant genes generally do a thorough job of hiding or "masking" the presence of a recessive partner, a recessive gene can be passed undetected for generations until it finds an identical partner in a breeding. When that occurs, the recessive trait "pops up" in the affected offspring, leading to the familiar question, "Where on earth did *that* come from?" This is how we get our surprises when dogs of normal coloration produce grays, livers or blacks.

COLOR GENETICS

This chapter is not meant to be an exhaustive study of color genetics. Only those genes critical to Tervuren color will be described. They are grouped by letters to identify them: the *A* gene, the *B* gene and the *C* gene.

The *A* Gene

The *A* gene controls the distribution of dark pigment on a dog's entire body. Note that we say "dark" pigment, not "black pigment," since other genes determine the actual color of the dark pigment. The genes that influence distribution of dark pigmentation are listed here in the order of their relative dominance:

> *As*—dominant to all in the series, the *As* gene dictates that dark pigment is distributed evenly throughout the coat. This gene produces the pigment of the Belgian Sheepdog and all other entirely black dogs.
>
> *ay*—recessive to *As* and dominant to the others, the *ay* gene limits the distribution of dark pigment in the coat. This gene is the basis of Tervuren color.
>
> *at*—the *at* gene produces a "tan-point," which is characteristic of the black-and-tan coloration found in various breeds, such as the Doberman Pinscher. The body is black, with fawn on the muzzle, inside the ears, on the throat and/or chest, under the belly and under the tail. Some Tervuren possess the *at* gene in combination with the *ay* gene, or in double combination—*at-at*—the consequences of which are examined further on.

118

The Belgian Sheepdog must be either *As-As, As-ay* or *As-at*. The Tervuren must be *ay-ay* or *ay-at* to be any of the possible Tervuren colors. In addition, the Groenendael is capable of producing Tervuren (two Groenendael carrying *As-ay* will be black but can produce *ay-ay* offspring), but Tervuren bred to Tervuren can produce only Tervuren of any "other than black" hue (excepting the "recessive black" gene to be addressed later).

The *B* Gene

The *B* gene offers only two options:

B—the dominant gene that dictates that any dark pigment in the coat will be black.

b—the recessive gene that dictates that dark pigment will be liver. Liver Tervuren are the result of this gene occurring in recessive combination.

The *C* Gene

The *C* gene controls the depth, or richness, of basic body color and probably is the most important in explaining the variety of possible base colors in Tervuren. Although there are several genes in the *C* series, two affect Tervuren base color most directly:

C—the dominant gene that ensures that the depth of base color will be rich (with or without lighter shading on the legs). In conjunction with the *ay* and *B* gene pairs, the *C* gene produces the typical Tervuren of desired base color.

Cch—called the chinchilla, or silvering gene, the *Cch* inhibits depth of color in the coat. Depending upon the influence of genetic modifiers, it produces a diluted base color of varying hues that lack richness of color. The color may range from washed-out red to dull yellow, to yellow-gray, to gray, to near-white. This gene has been present in Tervuren from the beginning and probably was prevalent around the turn of the century, which may have led to Tervurens' lack of popularity during the breed's infancy.

So-called gray offspring of Tervuren parents generally exhibit the color in its pure form only as young dogs. As they grow older, fawn tints appear and intensify in the coat, leading some breeders to consider the color acceptable according to the standard, if slow-appearing.

Remember again that the *C* gene is dominant to the *Cch* gene. That is, pure fawn to mahogany base color is dominant to the dilute base colors. Thus, many Tervuren exhibiting desired base color carry the *C-Cch* gene (that is, they are *C-C-Cch*) and produce the other hues so often seen.

One other gene series should be mentioned because of its contribution to Tervuren color. The *E* series is complex and difficult to understand. However, it is important to know that the dominant gene in the series, *Em,* produces the typical black mask on the muzzle. A dog not possessing at least one *Em* gene in the *E* pair will have no mask at all.

A Color Blueprint

A Tervuren pure for correct color under the present standard will possess these genes:

ay-ay—restricts the formation of solid dark pigmentation throughout the coat.

B-B—dictates that the deeply pigmented areas of the body will be black.

C-C—determines depth or "richness" of color. The *C-C* gene produces the mahogany to warm-fawn Tervuren.

Em-Em—produces the black masking required by the breed.

Other Possible Color Combinations

Although the preceding blueprint defines a dog carrying ideal Tervuren color, and capable of passing only that color, the possibilities of each gene pair, combined with the possibilities of the other pairs, can produce an enormous variety of color outcomes. Because space does not permit discussion of all possible results, only the most obvious are mentioned here. The reader wishing more information should consult the references listed at the end of the chapter. The *Em* gene is omitted for simplicity's sake (that is, mask is assumed to be present):

ay-ay, B-B, C-Cch—This dog has correct base color and blackening but carries the gene for diluted base color.

ay-ay, B-B, Cch-Cch—This dog is one of the dilute colors discussed previously, with normal blackening. It cannot pass on the gene for saturated base color.

ay-ay, b-b, C-C—This is the "liver" Tervuren. The dog's base color is ginger, with darker liver coloration at body locations that otherwise would be black. The eyes are generally hazel colored, and the nose and pads are liver. A dog with the gene pair *B-b* will be normal in appearance but capable of producing liver offspring.

The Recessive Black Tervuren

So-called recessive black Belgians are found in all the varieties, and the inheritance pattern has been well established. The culprit is the tan-point *at*

Early American champions Ch. Juin de Lafayette and Imp Rouge de Fauve Charbonne, CD, owned by Barbara Krohn

Ch. Cyrano de Chateau Blanc, CD, owned by Gerlinde Hockla and Edeltraud Laurin, is shown with Janina Laurin in 1966. Cyrano, sire of the breed's first Best in Show winner, helped Janina qualify for Junior Showmanship competition at the Westminster show before his tragic early death.

Ch. Ares du Bois du Tot, a French National Specialty winner born 2-27-85. Breeder: Dr. Yves Surget; owner: Mme. Fouguier. This is a gray Tervuren, called *sable* in Europe.

gene. The genetic makeup of a black Belgian is *at-at, B-B* and one of the *C* gene combinations. A *C-C* or *C-Cch* pair will produce a black animal with traces of fawn or mahogany at the tan points. The *Cch-Cch* pair produces traces of gray. The extent of visible tan or gray points is affected by other genes and modifiers. The dog may appear to be solid black with only hints of "rustiness" or gray at the points, or the points may be entirely obvious. The presence of the *Em* masking gene will further obscure lighter points on the muzzle and head.

A Tervuren carrying the gene pair *ay-at* will appear to be normal, since *ay* is dominant to *at*. However, it is capable of passing either gene to its offspring and, if bred to a dog also carrying the *at* gene, of producing black pups.

SUMMARY

Although the principles of genetics can be difficult to grasp at first, it is important to learn as much as possible about them before beginning to breed. The genetic potential of a dog and bitch to produce any characteristic, including color, can be analyzed and the possible outcomes predicted.

As a concluding comment, it may be useful to dispel some myths regarding the usefulness of intervariety breedings. Some breeders in our country long have held to the premise that it is necessary to interbreed Groenendaels and Tervuren to ensure that the Tervuren maintains its black mask and overlay (as discussion only, because in practice it is not allowed in the United States). It should be obvious to those wishing to study the preceding genetic information that this is not so. Groenendaels may or may not carry the genes necessary for masks and body blackening. The Groenendael can remain black but perpetuate Tervuren offspring lacking either or both mask and body blackening. Intervariety breedings in other countries are done with the recognition that color characteristics may suffer initially in the interest of structure and type, although most breeders believe that such deficiencies can be corrected within a few generations.

The potent combinations of the *As* and *B* genes in the Belgian Sheepdog mask entirely the presence or absence of the *Em* gene necessary for Tervuren mask. Likewise, the factors that control richness of colors, and those governing the presence and amount of body blackening, are hidden in the black Belgian.

For further information on color inheritance patterns, the following works are recommended:

Clarence C. Little, *The Inheritance of Coat Color in Dogs* (Howell Book House, 1967). Although now somewhat outdated, this book remains indispensable to those wishing a thorough introduction to the subject.

F. E. Verbanck, "Type, Robes, et Mariages chez le Chien de Berger Belge," *Le Berger Belge,* February 1972, 21–27. This article discusses the history of color and breeding of the Belgians.

Cl. Burnez, S. Burnez and Y. Surget, DVM, "La Couleur Noir Recessive chez les Bergers Belges," *Le Berger Belge,* April 1972, 61–73 (reprinted in English in *The Berger Belge Anthology, History, Genetics and Varieties,* by Sally Mitchell Perry and Adrienne A. Pagel [private printing, 1981]. *Note:* This book is available through *Tervuren News Tales* and should be part of the library of any serious Tervuren owner. The article analyzes the genetics of recessive black Belgians and traces the history of the *at* gene and its transmission through generations of dogs.

Karen A. Turner, "Tervuren Color Genetics," *Tervuren News Tales,* October 1985, 45–47. Although this article expresses personal viewpoints that do not necessarily reflect the ABTC's current official position on color, it provides an excellent detailed analysis of the possible colors found in Tervuren.

Baby puppies

10

Selecting a Belgian Tervuren

IF YOU ARE CONSIDERING a Belgian Tervuren, think first about what you intend to do with your pet during its lifetime. Because it is not a breed content to be confined to a sedentary life, you should be planning to *do* something with your Tervuren on a regular basis. Of course, many dogs discussed in this book are exceptional and have performed well in their owner's field of interest. Certainly not every Tervuren achieves such distinction, but it should be obvious that these dogs are happiest doing things with their owners. Whether your dog be a show, obedience, working dog or "just a pet," only by enjoying close association and activity with your Tervuren will you be happy together. You should be ready to make a commitment to raise your new friend to be a joy to you and your community.

CHOOSING A BREEDER

Knowing how to find and choose a breeder will help ensure that you bring home a physically and temperamentally healthy animal. We strongly recommend that you contact people who have had a long association with the parent club and continuing involvement with the breed. These members can refer you to reputable breeders and individuals with dogs or litters for sale.

The final choice of a breeder will be yours. Neither the American Kennel Club nor the ABTC will recommend one breeder over another, although both organizations can provide you with a list of breeders in your area. A good breed club will also do its best to provide informative pamphlets and other resources designed to educate new fanciers.

Look for breeders who raise their litters in their homes under good care and who will give you advice and assistance with your new dog. Reputable breeders do not sell to commercial breeders (puppy mills) or resale outlets such as pet shops. Although pet-shop puppies may look appealing, they are produced by breeders whose motive is profit, not the betterment of the breed. Innocent buyers often pay a higher than "show-quality" price for a puppy of inferior breed type. In addition, these unfortunate animals generally have not received the proper socialization they so desperately need as youngsters.

Conscientious breeders attempt to breed dogs free of serious inherited problems and will discuss the background of their dogs with you. Although the Tervuren is a very natural and hardy dog, it (like any other dog) can inherit any number of problems, a fact to which your veterinarian will surely attest. Ask the breeder about any known history of epilepsy, hip dysplasia or eye problems in his stock. If you are able to see one or both parents, do not look lightly on anything that disturbs you. The chances are that the puppies will be much like them.

SALES CONTRACTS

No matter what verbal guarantees or agreements a breeder may give you, it is extremely important to select one who stands behind his or her puppies with a purchase agreement or contract. Such a contract should state purchase conditions clearly, showing concern and protection for you, as a buyer, as well as for the welfare of the dog and the breed. Without a good contract, there is often little the buyer can do if a problem occurs. In general, you can expect that the guarantees for a show prospect are more extensive than those for a dog intended to be strictly a companion. In either case, however, the contract should guarantee good health and temperament.

Some contracts state that the breeder will refund a portion of the purchase price or replace the dog with another puppy if specific problems should arise. In replacement agreements, make sure that you understand whether you would keep or return your original dog, and what its fate might be if it is returned. Often, the breeder absolves further responsibility after a given time, so make sure of the date. Look the agreement over so that there are no surprises.

Occasionally, breeders offer to sell on a co-ownership basis, an arrangement that allows them to remain in partial control of the dog. If you are offered such a contract, find out why and exactly what the conditions of the co-ownership are. Although co-ownerships often allow you to pay a lower price for the dog, commitment to a long-term showing or breeding agreement can be far more costly in the end. Some co-ownerships are mutually desired and friendly, but others can endanger friendships through misunderstandings that surface later on. Be sure you are willing and able to meet the conditions of any co-ownership, and *get it in writing.*

OTHER CONSIDERATIONS

If you have chosen well, you can expect to be subjected to the breeder's scrutiny, as well. Do not be surprised or offended if *you* are questioned in detail about the care you plan to give your puppy. After all, a breeder does not expend the effort to raise a nice litter, only to have the offspring fall into the wrong hands. Whether you buy for show or a pet, you should be willing to have your dog's eyes tested for inherited problems and its hips X-rayed by a veterinarian for possible dysplasia when it reaches the proper age for such diagnoses. Of course, these tests are in addition to appropriate veterinary care that you should provide your dog throughout its life.

Each breeder is entitled to set the price for his or her puppies. If this concerns you, make enough inquiries to know the normal price range for a well-bred, healthy puppy. Some breeders will charge more because of the reputation of their dogs and high demand for their puppies. While the price may be justified, high price does not necessarily ensure high quality.

WHICH ONE TO SELECT?

When it comes to the actual choice of a Tervuren, decide in advance the gender, age and specific qualities you prefer. This will help you narrow down available dogs quickly and help the breeder assist you in your choice.

Knowing the differences between male and female Tervuren is important in making your choice. The male carries more coat, and generally has a major shed about once a year. The female can carry a lovely coat, but it will not be as long as the male's and she will usually shed twice a year before heat periods. During her heat, which lasts about three weeks, it will be necessary to take care to prevent any unwanted matings. If you have an unaltered male and female in the house, the male will become very distracted and an exasperation during the bitch's heats.

Both sexes are sensitive to your moods, highly trainable and eager to please. The male is taller and heavier than the female, usually has a deeper bark and that special carriage that bespeaks confidence and pride. He is in charge of his household and other canine family members. The female is distinctly feminine and knows what she is about. She has a special twinkle to her eye, which often shows a delightful devilishness, and has the final say in all matters.

If you do not intend to breed your Tervuren, or if it develops a serious fault or hereditary disorder that would make it an unwise choice in a breeding program, consider spaying or neutering your dog. This usually eliminates any

Ch. Sunfire Cordon Bleu, CD, with pups. *Kay Maves*

Four and a half weeks old. *K. P. Johnson*

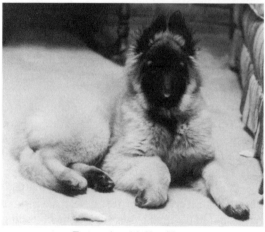

Ten weeks old. *Kay Maves*

inconveniences associated with the sex of your dog; moreover, research indicates that spayed females and neutered males tend to live longer lives than unaltered dogs.

If an older dog or puppy would fit into your lifestyle more easily than a young puppy, you should certainly consider one. You can sometimes find an older dog available from a breeder or an owner who must part with a dog, or even the occasional dog that has been rescued from an unfortunate situation (the ABTC has an active rescue committee working to place such dogs). Be sure to find out the personality of such a dog and acquire it only if you feel it would adapt well to your home. Even an abused Tervuren often adapts quickly to its new owner, once it feels welcome in its new environment.

If you know just what you seek in your new Tervuren, the final choice can be an easy one. If you are picking from a litter of pups, you may prefer to trust the breeder's experience and judgment in selecting a puppy to suit your wishes. It is common for breeders to match puppies to their prospective owner's wishes, since they see the litter constantly and get to know each puppy's unique qualities better than you can in one visit.

Regardless of who selects your puppy, the entire litter should appear healthy and well socialized. Preferably, the litter has been raised with human attention and handling in a normal household with all its noises and activities, rather than isolated in a kennel, with attention only given to feeding and cleaning needs. A well-socialized and rested puppy will usually display the temperament qualities it will have as an adult: it should be willing to play and be alert but not be fearful about normal noises, strangers and activities.

If you want a typey specimen with promising fawn and black coloring, or certain physical characteristics that you do not have the experience to select, it would be wise to ask the breeder for help or to have someone experienced in the breed come along and give advice. Generally speaking, bone (look at the legs) should not look fine and weak, or too heavy. Tervuren puppies are not massive with huge paws and heavy ears, nor should they look like miniature adults with adult proportions. There will be a definite look of "puppy": skin and bone to grow into, but without heaviness. Front and rear legs should be sound and straight, not bowed or crooked. Ears should not be heavy or set low on the head and are normally standing firmly upright between seven and twelve weeks of age. The puppy that prefers to trot, rather than hop from place to place (although all puppies hop and jump!), will most likely be an adult with an easy, correct, trotting gait.

Adult color develops slowly and will not be seen in a young puppy, but clues can be found in its base coloring. Look for rich mahogany behind the ears and overall warm fawn body color, tipped with black. The amount of black overlay a puppy will develop as an adult often is evident shortly after birth. From about seven weeks on, however, the base color may predominate until the coat has a chance to lengthen and mature, at which time the overlay will develop once again. For show or breeding purposes, any white on the body

Four months old. *Sue Morlan*

130

should be confined to the tips of the toes or a small patch on the chest. When present, this is easily seen in puppies.

The muzzle should always be black no matter what the age, and the amount of blackening on the rest of the head (above the eyes) will vary from dog to dog. Light color encircling the eyes usually extends down onto the muzzle with age. In fact, if a puppy does not have a solid, inky-black muzzle to the eyes, consider that as a sign that the mask will recede proportionately as it matures. A face with little or no black on the muzzle is considered untypical for the breed. Frosting on the chin and tip of the muzzle is perfectly normal and can be detected at birth.

It may reassure you to know that selecting your "perfect" puppy is often a difficult and risky task, even for "experts." Although those experienced in the breed will be correct more often than not, top-winning show dogs have been sold as "pet quality," and promising pups have never realized their early potential. Likewise, many top-winning working animals were thought to have incorrect temperaments as puppies.

To sum up, careful research and selection greatly increase your chances of picking a Tervuren that will mature into the dog of your dreams, but there are no iron-clad guarantees. You will only be really satisfied with your choice if you are willing to accept and love your dog despite its shortcomings. Make the most of your relationship, for real enjoyment comes from the mutual love and admiration the two of you share.

Best in Show winners all: Ch. LaBelle's A Liberte and sons Ch. Snowflower Skyy Chateau and Ch. Snowflower Voila Sharvonne

Shoelace succotash

Training on a grooming table increases the puppy's confidence and is often an easier way to begin. *J. L. Smith*

11

Developing Correct Attitude and Behavior

THE BELGIAN TERVUREN has a great desire to learn and work. He is an excellent listener, always alert for instruction or praise. With a little daily time and guidance on your part, he can be a joy to own. How successful your dog becomes at what you wanted him for will depend to a large degree on the training and guidance you give him.

With increasing dog nuisance complaints and publicity over dog bites, the importance of proper training cannot be overemphasized. Lacking training and given the opportunity, a Tervuren may invent his own "work"—which could mean herding cars, the paperboy or joggers, or just making a general nuisance of himself.

Plan to give your Tervuren at least an hour each day for attention and training. This need not be given all at once, but it is the minimum amount of the time he needs to learn with you each day.

Keep in mind that your Tervuren will develop in stages. Young puppies may try anything; they are full of curiosity and energy. Older puppies enter a more cautious stage and may begin questioning your commands. As maturity nears, many Tervuren enter a period of distrust of strangers and of being touched by strangers.

We believe that the right approach to training the Tervuren consists of three levels, none of which is ever dropped completely: (1) socialization and common-sense basics, (2) "conformation" training and (3) formal obedience training.

SOCIALIZATION AND COMMON-SENSE BASICS

After the Puppy Comes Home

It is altogether too easy to fall in love with a Tervuren puppy. With its jaunty little trot, dark face and sooty, woolly coat, it seems to do no wrong. Too many new puppy owners make the mistake of waiting until their puppy is old enough for more formal training, such as obedience school, before they attempt any training. They probably will be facing problems with their dog when that time comes. Young Tervuren puppies learn early, and they learn more than simple ideas. They learn attitudes about life that form lifelong habits.

Early and continued socialization is of particular importance. By this we mean exposure to the world in which we live—with all its sounds, movements, creatures and, most importantly, its people. Proper socialization ensures that you will get the most out of your dog's inborn temperament.

Your Tervuren should be regularly taken outside the confines of its home so it can learn to accept petting by strangers of all ages. It should be exposed regularly to strange noises and a variety of footing from which no harm will result. If it becomes nervous, laugh and tell him it is just a baby who you know will be brave one day soon—but do not coax it or offer "sweet talk." This will only encourage it to continue such behavior.

You also do not wish to push it to the point of terror. Watch closely for reactions and learn to "read" your dog. This is an important asset for you to have throughout its life. Give commands that are reasonable and fair to your dog. Insist that it obey, and be consistent in offering *sincere* praise after it has reacted positively. These methods will build its confidence and trust in you.

As a youngster the dog should be introduced to other dogs, especially puppies and gentle adults. Tervuren generally get along well with dogs they know and other animals they are raised with. If introduced with proper courtesy to strange dogs, they will behave very well. Exposure to a dependable enforcement of reasonable commands, and your warm praise, will enable your dog to make good judgments as an adult about what is safe for it and the people in its life and what is not. A properly socialized Tervuren should become an excellent, sensible watchdog for the home, one who is trustworthy among friends and, especially, children.

Handle Your Puppy

Handle your puppy frequently from the beginning so it accepts the human touch. It will be touched, examined and groomed throughout his life, so early handling is essential.

Begin while grooming your dog. Insist that it remain calm and not object to your efforts. If it struggles, take a firm but calming approach. If it mouths

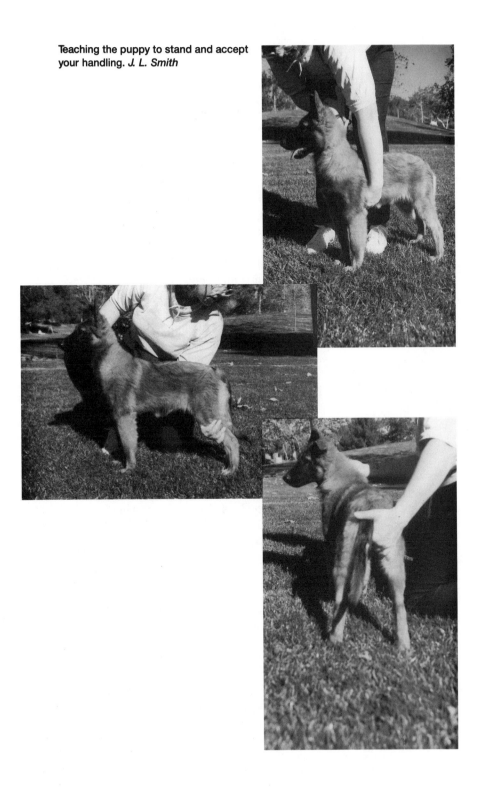

Teaching the puppy to stand and accept your handling. *J. L. Smith*

your hand or the brush, punish it sharply but quickly. Mouthing can become biting, which should never be tolerated, no matter how young the puppy. Continue to groom your pup until it understands that it has no choice except to remain calm, and talk pleasantly to it when it is calm. If it is good, tell him it is good. If it is bad, let it know you do not approve.

Teach the Puppy to Come

We single out this lesson because it is so important. A dog who comes promptly at your call will be a joy to live with and much more easily trained to obey other commands as well.

Teaching your Tervuren to come when called *under all circumstances* should start at once and continue throughout life. Work on this command more than any other. It will provide control and ensure your dog's safety.

Always praise your puppy or dog for coming to your call. Be consistent by only calling your puppy when you are prepared to see that it responds. Never call it to you in order to scold. Go to it. If it is necessary to go to your dog for a correction, always follow this up by calling it to you for praise and love. Rewards (not bribes) of food are very effective in teaching this. No matter how well your dog proceeds, you need to know that *all* dogs will test you at some point, so you should be prepared. Your ultimate aim is that it will always come to your call rather than react by running away!

Teach the Puppy to Stay

This is another important basic command that is good for it to learn. This does not take much instruction, just use common sense and proceed gradually. Do not expect the very young puppy to be able to concentrate for very long. Start with very short periods of time and gradually build up to a few minutes. Be sure to give a clear "release" command with your praise so that it is clear to the puppy when he may move from position.

CONFORMATION TRAINING

Whether or not you plan to show your puppy at dog shows, so-called conformation training is an excellent way to add to a training program. It continues the dog's socialization, teaches manners on the leash and builds confidence, while preparing it for more exacting obedience training later.

Check to see if any of your local kennel clubs offer conformation classes. Some clubs offer puppy kindergarten training classes, which can be a good way to begin early training. Your veterinarian should always be consulted before you take your young puppy out with other dogs.

FORMAL OBEDIENCE TRAINING

Many excellent books are available on this subject and every dog owner should read at least one. The above advice on socialization and training will go far in developing a good attitude in the dog that will encourage acceptance of your more serious training later. Inquire about good obedience classes in your area and be sure to enroll in one when your Tervuren is old enough.

We would like you to be aware of some general training guidelines:

- Keep in mind that there are almost as many *methods* for teaching a dog a particular command as there are trainers giving you advice.
- Find a method for teaching that you are comfortable with, and stick with it. Changing your way of training several times with the same dog, or trying to incorporate several methods to teach the same thing, particularly by the novice, can confuse and discourage the dog.
- The method is not nearly so important as the *philosophy* of training—learn to read your dog so that your timing is appropriate, know when to assist the dog, when a correction is called for and, above all, when to praise.
- Recognize when you are asking too much or too little of your dog. That awareness is essential in becoming a good trainer.

The following are some essential training tips:

- Train with firmness, fairness, kindness and consistency.
- Never give a command you do not mean.
- Never give a command you cannot enforce.
- Never scold or correct the dog unless you are positive he understands.
- Give praise each and every time your dog responds properly, and be sincere!

End all training periods with success. An exercise done correctly one time is better than a thousand corrections for an incorrectly done exercise. And, of course, never lose your temper or train when you are in a bad mood. It should be a happy time of the day for both of you.

Frequent, short "praise breaks" whenever your dog does well will make it feel special and proud. This does not mean "escape" breaks, but breaks with *you*. If you want the dog to feel good about himself (a quality that makes a dog work with a special look of happiness), then treat it as a friend. It will appreciate this attitude and you will become a team.

When a correction is given, do not dwell on it. It should be swift, effective and then forgotten. While the Tervuren can take a correction, its personality will suffer if the dog construes it as punishment.

Training should not be all work and no play. Woe is the poor dog who is not given frequent opportunity to play with its master. Channel this play into the right direction, however. Find an acceptable reward, like a favorite toy. This will form much better habits and attitude than tugging on your pant leg!

SOME TERVUREN TRAINING SPECIFICS

The Tervuren is light on its feet and has fast reactions. It takes notice of all that goes on around it, including sight, sound and touch sensations. It can be distracted by activities around it. This is not a fault but the inherited qualities of a good stock and watchdog. The importance of socialization and exposure to its surroundings has been emphasized. As an intelligent and responsive dog, it can learn to ignore outside activities and concentrate its full attention on you.

Perhaps most importantly, try to keep a smile and understand your dog's dilemma as it learns to control its instincts. Despite your best efforts at training, your Tervuren will go through many stages of mental development. It will take a few years for your dog to settle into your lifestyle, as it learns your vocabulary and expectations. Its nature is to rush to the door, barking when someone arrives, and it is apt to chew on something once in a while, or dig a hole in your lawn. But that's okay, for these are the doggy delights to which even the best-trained companion is entitled every now and then.

12

The Healthy,
Well-Groomed Tervuren

A FRESHLY GROOMED TERVUREN is a lovely sight. Be aware, however, that no amount of grooming can create a beautiful coat on a dog that is malnourished, susceptible to disease or harboring parasites. Nor can such a dog realize its physical, mental and temperamental potential.

HEALTH

Diet

In addition to the physical regimen of preventative inoculations prescribed by your veterinarian, you must be prepared to provide a sensible diet. Dog foods can vary greatly in quality, and you get what you pay for. So avoid cheap brands, even though they may claim nutritional completeness.

Generally, a high-quality brand of kibble that can be fed dry or moistened is a good choice and is favored by many experienced breeders because it is nutritionally balanced and does not require additional supplements to maintain a healthy coat. Consult your veterinarian and your breeder, then select a feeding plan that produces the best results for you.

Parasites

Internal parasites can quickly spell disaster to your dog's health. Even if your dog is seldom exposed to areas soiled by other dogs, it can reinfest itself from previously contaminated areas and can get tapeworms from ingesting fleas, flies and small rodents. Visual examination of the stool must be combined with routine stool examinations by your veterinarian to determine the presence of internal parasites. Almost all worms are detected by microscopic examination of the stool; the major exception, tapeworm, can be visually observed in the stool.

Nearly all dogs occasionally will harbor external parasites, such as fleas or ticks. Depending on your geographic location, these pests may be seasonal or may require constant vigilance. The war against these enemies is important to your dog's health and comfort. Fleas cause great irritation to the animal, spread tapeworm and can trigger allergic reactions in some dogs. Ticks are equally dangerous and can transmit some alarming diseases to your dog, such as Rocky Mountain Spotted Fever and Lyme Disease. Learn to identify these pests on your Tervuren, and the steps necessary to eliminate them. Your veterinarian can recommend safe treatment for your dog and home.

Anal Glands

All dogs have glands known as anal glands that are located not far inside the anus. These glands collect a foul-smelling fluid that should occasionally be expelled for the comfort of your dog. In rare instances, an abscess may form. Often, it is difficult to detect when a problem is developing, but learn to be alert for signs. The dog may show discomfort by "scooting" its rear on the ground, or it may attempt to chew at the anal area. Your veterinarian can show you how to keep these glands emptied, or you may wish to ask him or her to do this for you on occasion. Anal glands are not likely to cause problems in the Tervuren, but an awareness of the possibility can prevent trouble.

GROOMING

The Tervuren Coat

Given a good diet and health, your dog has the prescription for a beautiful coat; grooming simply provides the final polish.

It is surprising how many people believe that dog hair floating about the house is a necessary consequence of owning a dog. If your Tervuren is regularly and properly groomed, vacuuming will be needed no more frequently than in a home without a dog.

The Tervuren has what is known as a double coat—an inner layer of soft, warm insulation (called undercoat), and an outercoat (called guard coat) of long, straight, moderately harsh protective hairs. One of the nice features about the Tervuren is the ease with which you can make their coats glow with a minimum of effort. While routine grooming is essential, constant vigilance is not necessary, as it is with many other coated breeds. Shedding normally occurs in noticeable amounts about once a year in males, and twice a year (before heat periods) in bitches. Neutered Tervuren will experience less frequent major shedding periods but may carry a heavier coat all the time.

The When and Where of Grooming

Begin good grooming practices as soon as you acquire your Tervuren. A young puppy will not require extensive brushing, but you should start its training early through "play grooming" to prepare it for the longer grooming periods it must tolerate as an older puppy and dog.

How often you groom its coat depends upon a number of factors. Under normal circumstances, a thorough weekly brushing should suffice. Of course, if your dog collects burrs or other foreign matter at work or play, its coat should be attended to at once. Before describing the tools and methods, it is important to stress that you should establish a regular and convenient location to groom your dog, where both of you will be comfortable and the lighting is good. Even if you own just one dog, consider investing in a sturdy grooming table. Its folding legs, secure nonslip covering and convenient height ensure that your dog will remain in one place, and your back will be spared from bending.

Grooming should be a pleasant experience for both of you. Insist that your Tervuren behave and firmly correct any misbehavior. In return, you must be fair and treat the dog gently. It will take several grooming sessions before it learns what to expect.

Grooming Tools

Every groomer has his or her set of favorite tools, but these are basic:

1. A large-size, flat, fine "slicker" brush (wooden handle with fine, short, close-set metal brushes, set in a rubber base).
2. A firm boar-bristle brush or "porcupine" (a mixture of natural and nylon bristles) brush set in a cushioned base, with wooden handle.
3. A good metal comb with handle, with teeth set closely enough to remove loose coat, but not so closely that it is difficult to pass through the coat.
4. Blunt-ended sharp scissors.
5. Nail clippers, suitable for a medium-large dog.

The slicker brush is the groomer's workhorse and will do the fastest job of eliminating loose coat and separating the hairs for a nice look. Some show exhibitors seldom use this tool for fear of breaking the coat or taking out too much hair; nonetheless, many a champion has been groomed with this tool.

Grooming tools

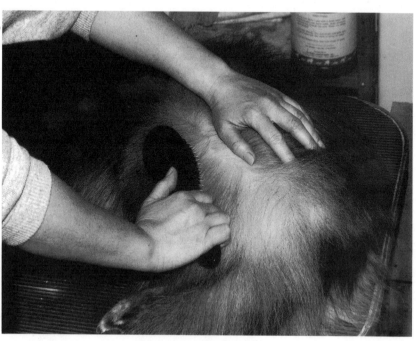

Brush down into the coat.

142

Use care with the slicker so that you do not dig painfully into the dog's skin with the edges of the metal bristles. Use a flat wrist motion in brushing to prevent this possibility.

The boar-bristle brush takes a bit more effort but is gentler on the skin and coat. Because it tends to make the coat appear thicker and will result in less breakage of the hair, it is often preferred for show grooming. You can use considerable wrist motion with this brush, since the edges will not harm the skin.

Use the comb around the ears and anywhere a small mat might be found. If you have the time, an occasional, thorough combing of the entire coat is very effective, giving it a lovely, full look. The comb is also a nice finishing tool to go lightly over the guard coat to put it in place for a photo-finish look.

During a heavy shedding period, the slicker brush is useful because of its effectiveness in removing loose coat; the natural bristle brush is used while the dog is growing and maintaining a nice coat. If you are preparing a shedding dog for show, assess the condition of the coat. Perhaps the coat can be salvaged temporarily by careful, gentle use of the natural bristle brush or a larger "pin" brush, which tends to shape rather than remove coat. If the coat cannot be salvaged, it may be best to use the comb and slicker to remove the dead coat completely.

The scissors are used only to neaten up the hairs about the feet, hocks and pasterns. If you use them properly, your dog will collect less mud, water and snow on its feet.

Grooming Techniques

Whether you are using a slicker brush, boar-bristle brush, comb or a combination, the technique is basically the same. With your dog lying on its side or standing, begin on a lower section of the body, legs or breeches. Hold a section of hair and undercoat open with the flat of your hand, exposing a skin line. Following the grain and lay of the coat, brush (or comb) the section exposed below your hand. Move your hand up a bit and groom the next exposed section. Continue this process until you have gone over the entire coat. Brush to the skin and don't forget the chest, neck, tail and more sensitive belly area. If the dog has been lying down, you may want it to stand when you groom the back, and sit as you work on the neck and chest.

Many owners prefer to groom the feet while the dog is standing. Begin by combing the pastern hairs (behind the front feet) and the hock hair (the longer hair on the back of the lower portion of the hind legs) outward; trim with the scissors to neaten and remove excess length. Brush up the long hairs from between the toes and shape the foot with the scissors by trimming off this excess, cutting the hairs even with the shorter hairs on the toes.

Never cut the hair across the grain, but upward with the contour of the toes. Aim for a natural, rounded "cat-foot" look on the front feet, and a slightly elongated "hare-foot" in the rear. Take care not to cut the hair down between each toe, or the dog will have an unpleasant splay-footed look. Trim excessive hair from underneath the pads and around the bottom outside edges of the foot. The idea is to shape and neaten the foot, cleaning excessive hair without removing it. The result is a neat appearance and a cleaner foot that tracks much less dirt and debris into your home.

Toenails

At this point in the grooming process, use your clippers to trim the nails. Learn from your veterinarian, breeder or groomer how to do this effectively without cutting into the "quick" (or vein), which is painful and causes bleeding. It is important that you gain experience in nail trimming by learning to do it yourself, since your dog's nails should be trimmed regularly. Those who rely on an occasional trip to the veterinarian or groomer for this service usually have dogs with uncomfortably long nails. Long nails can also cause the toes to separate and create a splay foot.

Grooming Tips

Wipe the entire face area with a damp washcloth. Like you, your dog will feel refreshed and look sharper with a clean face. Check your dog's teeth during grooming sessions. You will be able to detect dirty or broken teeth, or a painful abscess long before the trouble gets out of hand. Don't assume that chew-bones will clean your dog's teeth. They are usually not effective in keeping tartar from collecting. Ask your veterinarian for advice on cleaning your dog's teeth.

Use a spray mist bottle filled with clean, clear water. Lightly mist each section of the coat as you part it for brushing. This encourages a healthy coat and skin and aids in keeping your dog spotlessly clean. Before releasing your dog after a grooming session, stand him and lightly mist him again, shaping and brushing the hair into place.

Bathing

You should need to bathe your Tervuren only if it becomes soiled with foreign matter not easily removed by brushing, or because of neglect or dirty kennel conditions. Even if your dog collects mud during an outing, you can let it dry and brush it out. Doggy odor is not normal for Tervuren. Proper brushing will keep the coat clean, huggable and healthy. Dogs sometimes are bathed to relax the coat and speed up a shedding cycle, but use caution in bathing just prior to exhibiting the dog at a show because it will cause the coat to look more "open" and "flyaway" for a day or two.

When you bathe your dog, use warm, never hot, water. Use a shampoo with the correct pH balance for canines. A gentle dishwashing liquid or human

Handle his feet from puppyhood.

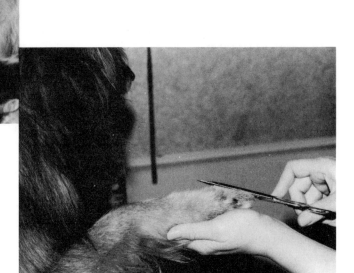

Proper direction of trimming long hair on feet

Inspect teeth and gums during grooming.

shampoo will work in a pinch. Keep the shampoo out of the dog's eyes and be sure to rinse thoroughly to remove all traces of shampoo. Shampoo residue causes a coat to collect dirt quickly and can lead to serious itching. So rinse, rinse and rinse again! Some owners also use a good-quality coat conditioner following the bath. Towel your dog thoroughly and keep it indoors in cold weather until it is *completely* dry.

The Finished Look

When you have finished grooming or wish to take a break, release your dog with a word that will become familiar to it. Tell it that it looks good and that you are pleased with its behavior. It will soon be very proud of itself after each of these sessions.

It probably will shake when it is released, and its coat will fall beautifully into place. No further attention is necessary. You may wish to brush or comb a few hairs into place to improve its silhouette, if you want to take its picture or exhibit it at a show.

The Many Benefits of Good Grooming

If you adhere to a weekly grooming schedule, the process will not be a major project. The rewards of a beautiful and clean coat are well worth the effort. In addition, grooming provides you with the opportunity to inspect your dog closely and assess its health.

Disciplining your dog to accept grooming, nail trimming and your physical handling will teach it patience and respect. The time you spend together in this process will strengthen your bond. Your dog will be a better adjusted, happier animal. In turn, you will be a happier owner.

13

In the Show Ring

E VERYONE INTERESTED IN LEARNING about handling the Tervuren in the conformation ring is well advised to study the breed standard. The standard sets forth guidelines for breeders and judges, and can also be used as a guideline for handling the Tervuren in the show ring.

SHOW GROOMING

Grooming for the show ring is no different from proper grooming for the home. The grooming section in this book will give you a good start in understanding the proper techniques. The standard states that the Belgian Tervuren is a natural dog, and only by abiding to this will our breed remain so! Natural, however, does not mean unkempt or dirty. Any Tervuren shown in the ring should be presented in a clean, properly groomed condition. However, no sculpting or shaping with scissors should ever be done, nor should any foreign grooming material ever be left in the coat. Overgrooming to the point of altering the natural appearance of the dog is greatly discouraged. A spray bottle of clean, clear water should be the Tervuren groomer's mainstay.

As an exhibitor you must learn to honestly access your dog's best (and weakest) qualities, and groom to complement the good points and minimize the others.

Don't trim the hair inside the ears.

Don't scissor the coat anywhere on the body. The feet, pasterns and hocks are the only areas to shape and clean with scissors.

Don't back-comb, tease or groom the coat to stand out from the body. The Tervuren is not a breed shown with an "open" coat (as the Collie, Chow or Keeshond, for example).

Never use coloring on the coat or face (such as to darken the mask). It is strictly prohibited by AKC show rules, and is despised by conscientious fanciers!

Groom thoroughly to obtain a clean, glowing look. The coat must lie flat. Lay the coat down on the back and over the sides, shoulders and hindquarters of the dog.

Use thinning shears sparingly, if at all, to remove excessive undercoat such as in a patch of heavy coat on the top of the rump. (Most often, a thorough *combing* of these areas will remove the excessive undercoat and leave a much more natural look.)

Accentuate the cat-shape of the front feet and the hare-foot shape of the rear feet with proper trimming.

POSING AND THE USE OF BAIT

In the ring the Tervuren should appear alert, intelligent and confident, standing squarely just long enough for assessment by the judge. It should accept the judge's advances without fear or aggressiveness, showing extreme friendliness only to its handler. Excessive posing is frowned upon by the standard because it does not allow the natural, proud carriage or personality qualities to be displayed at their best. Certainly, however, gentle placing of the dog into position for viewing and evaluation by the judge is acceptable. Bait is often used to bring out a nice expression and good carriage.

The use of bait has become an accepted practice in the United States as a result, many years ago, of the AKC prohibiting "double handling" of dogs in the ring. This practice, used frequently in European countries, involves a family member or friend of the dog calling to him from outside the ring. For reasons long forgotten (most likely because of the disruption at ringside, and the unfair advantage given to those with such help available), the AKC strictly prohibits such showing practices.

For training, bait is used to encourage a happy attitude and to teach the dog to stand squarely, alert and confident. In the ring, care should be taken to use the bait properly. Its overuse has caused some judges much annoyance. As courtesy to other exhibitors, do not fling bait around the ring for other dogs to grab at later. Take care not to be feeding your dog constantly, especially

Encourage the puppy to stand happily and look forward. *J. L. Smith*

Looking up at the handler can destroy the look of the neck and top line. *J. L. Smith*

By having the dog look forward rather than up, these lines are improved. *J. L. Smith*

Teach the puppy to gait in a forward line, on a loose lead. *J. L. Smith*

at those times when the judge is trying to evaluate the dog's silhouette or expression. Some exhibitors have also made the mistake of letting their dog grab at bait as the judge examines the dog, making the judge perhaps wonder if the dog just jumped as a result of his touch! Another common mistake is to hold the bait too high, forcing the dog to throw its head back as it looks up at you. While its expression may look very pleasing to you standing in front of it, the dog's neckline and topline can be badly thrown off as seen from the side.

GAITING

The dog should be trained to trot smoothly at the handler's side. It should not be allowed to strain at the leash, bounce about, weave or lag behind. Learn to match your gait to your dog's best stride. If that is a bit faster than the dog's gait in front of you, slow up just a bit as you move around behind the judge, so that you will have ample space ahead of you to move your dog smoothly as you go around before the judge. Never crowd out the dog in front of you as you go around, or attempt to move your dog up alongside of him. These are old and bad tricks. Remember the standard: the judge will be looking for an easy, graceful movement. Racing around the ring is not appropriate for exhibiting the Belgian Tervuren.

EQUIPMENT AND DRESS

A lightweight collar and lead are appropriate for the show ring. Choose a fine slip collar and thin leather lead. Jangling tags are kept on other collars. The less conspicuous the equipment, the more polished and professional the dog will appear.

If you use bait, keep it in a pocket or bag inconspicuously attached at the beltline. Groom *before* you enter the ring, and at the most pocket a small brush or comb to tame a disobedient hair as needed. These are herding and working dogs and they should not be fussed with in the ring.

Dress for the show ring should show respect for the occasion and for the quality of the dog. Dress should be comfortable, neat, clean and pleasant without being a distraction. Shoes need to be appropriate as well, and should have nonskid soles for safety.

Exhibitors in the obedience ring should follow the same grooming practices with themselves and their dogs as do exhibitors in the conformation ring. While skirts are often impractical, neat attire and a well-groomed dog will show respect for the sport and the breed. Also, it is usual that more spectators are watching the obedience ring than the conformation ring!

150

RESPECT THE BREED

The entire breed should be respected in the practices you follow in your individual handling preparations and methods. The future of the breed lies in the hands of those who exhibit. Most Tervuren owners take pride in the inherent beauty and trainability of their breed, and are willing to devote the time and energy necessary to accomplish a natural, honest display in the ring. Elbow work, patience, training and dedication will result in lasting solutions to any breed problems we may face.

Books, videotapes, magazine articles and conformation classes are excellent sources of information. And don't forget the best sources of all—the breeder of your dog, and your fellow exhibitors.

Ch. Kandice de Fauve Charbonne, CDX, BAR, winning BOS at ABTC National in 1964 under judge L. Murr, handled by Gerlinde Hockla, owned by Edeltraud Laurin

OTCH Dusty of Sierra Shadows, TDX, Can. CD

Ch. Javelin of Georjune, UD, was the first UD Tervuren

14

The Belgian Tervuren in Obedience

THE STORY OF BELGIAN TERVUREN in the United States would not be complete without recognition of the breed's accomplishments in obedience. From the beginning, this sport has won more friends for the breed than any other single endeavor.

Breed enthusiasts traditionally have been strong supporters of obedience; a very high proportion of breed champions hold obedience titles as well. At least sixteen of our twenty-four Best in Show winners have obedience titles and some of them have won High in Trial as well. The vast majority of the ABTC's National Specialty BOB winners also hold obedience titles.

THE EARLY YEARS: THE 1950s AND 1960s

When the breed was first introduced into this country, its supporters enjoyed the Tervuren's intelligence and trainability, and used obedience training as an excellent means of attracting public attention. Many new fanciers were won over after seeing a striking, energetic and obedient Tervuren in the ring, at obedience classes or on the streets. It is because of the hard work and devotion of these pioneers that we salute our early obedience winners. What they did for Tervuren had great impact on the initial welfare and growth of the breed in this country.

As has been recorded earlier, the first Tervuren to win points at an AKC breed show was also the first to receive a CD. Chrysis du Clos Saint Jacques earned it in 1954, when Tervuren still were registered as Belgian Sheepdogs, completing her degree in three shows. At her first show she earned a second-place score of 191. Imagine . . . the first placing for a Tervuren in obedience. We wonder if the judge knew what breed of dog was being awarded the ribbon!

As the reader knows, a Canadian Tervuren became the breed's first UDT when Donald and Mollie Hudson's Can. Ch. Nightwatch Russet Chevalier won that honor in 1960. His intelligence and devotion to his owners inspired the entire fancy through warm and delightful accounts told by his owner and published in early *Tervuren News Tales*.

The Hudsons were charter members and later made honorary lifetime members of the ABTC. Mollie now is ninety-eight. After she was contacted for information about her dog Val, she replied in her own handwriting:

> In the years some time ago a little Belgian Sheepdog found its immediate home in Victoria, Canada. He was to be 1st of many things, 1st Champion in the West of Canada, 1st Champion in obedience . . . [he was] Nightwatch Russet Chevalier, a fine specimen and exceedingly intelligent. He and his mistress Mollie Hudson, swiftly moved up the ladder of successes. His master Donald handled his tracking in which he was a natural; wherever he was shown he won.

Many of our earlier club members will remember the homemade movie put together by the Hudsons and distributed among the membership. It was a delightful story of Val's tracking and finding a lost child. It was called "Val Finds His Man."

The 1960s were an exciting time for the breed in obedience as fanciers shared in the discovery of what this trainable "new breed" could accomplish. In 1964, Ch. Javelin of Georjune, UD, became the first UD Tervuren and, in 1965, the first Ch. UD Tervuren in the United States. Javelin earned all three obedience titles in less than one year. In obtaining his CD he became the first of the breed to earn a *Dog World* award by earning all three legs with scores of 195 or above.

Javelin was the first Tervuren to win High in Trial and multiple High in Trial wins in the United States. His owner/trainer Linda Franklin continues to train into the 1980s and has obtained Ch./UD titles on no fewer than seven Tervuren. She began with Javelin and continued with Ch. Oondine of Georjune, UD; their daughter Ch. Javondi's Allure De La Corps, UDT, Sch. III; Ch. Hi Times Let It Be De La Corps, UDT; Ch. Chimina's Etiene De La Corps, UDTX, Sch. III; Ch. HTCh. Chilure's Fiama De La Corps, UDT, Sch. I, AD and Ch. HTCh. Ochiama's Luciana De La Corps, UDT, AD, Sch. I.

In 1966, Tishaminga de Weeping Pines, CDX, became the first Belgian Tervuren to earn a perfect 200 score at an AKC trial. Tish was trained and co-owned by Karen (Droz) Johnson and Eleanor Bennett of Michigan. A number of Karen's Tervuren have won HIT awards, including Tish (above); Ch. Chatte Brun du Val de Tonnerre, CDX (Kit); Ch. Alouette des Rogues Rouges, UD (the breed's first American and Canadian CD and CDX); Ch. Sundancer Day

Breaker, UD, and OTCH Ch. Bilgay Spindrifter, UD. Karen's Tervuren have earned twelve *Dog World* awards, beginning with Kit in 1964 and continuing to 1987 with Drifter. Drifter obtained his OTCH in 1989 and, with several HIT wins, was the top Tervuren in obedience that year (all systems).

In 1966 Ch. Olinda of Georjune (Lindy) became the breed's second UD and the first bitch to earn the champion and UD titles. Lindy was a remarkably consistent winner, showing in seventy-one classes during 1966 and 1967, and placing in the ribbons 82 percent of the time. She earned Top Working breed and seventh all-breed honors in 1966, then rose to third place in the 1967 top ten all-breed listing (*Chips* magazine). In 1967 she beat more dogs in AKC competition than any other dog of *any* breed. Lindy was owned and shown by S. W. "Wally" Kodis of California. Wally has been active in recent years as an AKC obedience field representative.

Jack and Donna Allen's Ch. Mars de Fauve Charbonne, UDT, of Arizona completed his UD and TD in the fall of 1967, becoming our first Ch./UDT winner. Mars was shown in Canada and Mexico as well as in the United States, posting two Canadian High in Trial wins and the titles of Canadian champion and Canadian CDX, TD. He also won the titles of the Mexican PC (similar to CD) and a Mexican tracking title.

Also notable among dogs being shown in the 1960s was Ch. Sandy Haze Prince of Hearts, UD, a High in Trial winner owned by Winford Clifton of Virginia and litter brother to Tishaminga de Weeping Pines. In typical Tervuren fashion, Champ, as he was known, won Best of Breed, fourth in the Working Group and his UD title at the same show.

THE 1970s

In the early 1970s, a remarkable dog appeared who probably "sold" more of the breed to newcomers, particularly obedience fans, than any other single Tervuren of his day. Ch. Bonheur's D'Artagnon, UDT (Dart), and his owner, Bernadine Paull of Michigan, were an outstanding team. Dart's breed accomplishments already have been recognized but the breadth of his achievements deserves special mention. He was the first Ch./UDT/High in Trial dog of any working breed to win an all-breed Best in Show, and the second dog of *any* breed to do so. He earned one HIT en route to each obedience degree, including his Canadian CD. (Dart's kennel mate, Ch. Tanzy De Landas, UDT, also earned a HIT en route to each of her titles.)

Bernadine remembers the April 1973 Sacramento KC show, site of the ABTC National Specialty, as one of the most exciting days in her career. She went directly from giving a demonstration in the ring with her Tanzy (who won HIT at that show as well as RWB in the breed classes) into the Group ring to win a Group 1 with Dart, who had won the specialty Best of Breed. Dart sired at least eight UDT Tervuren, including five in one litter out of Tanzy, all of whom became champions.

Ch. Olinda of Georjune with owner S. W. Kodis (*center*)

Judge Bernie Brown presents High in Trial award to Sunfire Colt Forty Five, CDX, shown by the late Jack Godsil

So enthusiastic and supportive have our owners been about exhibiting in obedience as well as breed that, in 1974, ABTC Vice President Nancie Mages proposed the club's motto:

A well-balanced Belgian Tervuren has a Ch. on one end
and a UDT on the other.

Needless to say, it was adopted at once.

Nancie, a longtime supporter of the breed, saw fit to give the Tervuren good exposure to obedience fans throughout the country in the mid-1970s by placing her Sunfire Colt Forty Five, CDX (Crash), with the late trainer Jack Godsil. Crash was used extensively as a demonstration dog by Jack at the popular training seminars given in cooperation with Bob Self. He also accumulated five High in Trial awards en route to his CDX title, winning the honor of top Tervuren in obedience in 1975 (Delaney system). Unfortunately, Crash was killed in a tragic accident before he achieved his full potential.

The 1970s saw many Tervuren doing exceptionally well in obedience, with no particular dominance being exhibited by any sex, locale or bloodlines. Ch. Kazan of Sierra Shadows, UD, owned and shown by Ken Wilson of California, won High in Trial awards in 1969 and 1970, and was a top Tervuren obedience winner in 1971. In 1972, Ch. Ebony De Chateau Blanc, UDT, owned by Joan Glover of Minnesota, won two High in Trial awards and became the breed's second Ch./UDT and the first bitch to obtain the status of a "well-balanced" Ch./UDT Tervuren.

Ch. Herzog De Chateau Blanc, Am., Can. UD, was the top obedience Tervuren between 1973 and 1975 (Shuman and ABTC systems). Herzog, the first American and Canadian UD Tervuren, was a multiple American and Canadian High in Trial winner, and retired the ABTC club trophy by winning top Tervuren for three consecutive years under the ABTC rating system. He was owned by Jeanne Ohmann and Manetta Tomlison of Kentucky.

The breed's first Obedience Trial Champion (OTCH) was Ch. Hi Times Tops With Theo, owned by the late Lockie Treanor of Tennessee. Theo was top Tervuren (all systems) in 1978, and earned his OTCH on April 4, 1979. Lockie also completed the Ch./UDT titles on Ch. U R Reynard The Fox Of Valkyra, UDT, in 1974 and Ch. Locknor A RePeter, UDT, in 1985.

In August 1979, the breed saw its first OTCH bitch in Ch. Robiel Bridget Fille de Ultra, owned by Larraine and George Thompson of California. This bitch was nine years old when she earned her OTCH, coming out of retirement when the AKC established the title.

The Rogues Rouges dogs, bred by Tom and Sharon Cairns of Oklahoma, have had remarkable success in the obedience ring. OTCH Folie Des Rogues Rouges, owned by Gail Brown, was a consistent winner from 1976 through 1980, placing well in Tervuren ratings and taking a number of High in Trial wins. Karen Johnson's Ch. Alouette Des Rogues Rouges, UD, was another

The breed's first OTCH, Ch. OTCH Hi Times Tops With Theo

Ch. OTCH Robiel Bridget Fille de Ultra

Am. & Can. Ch., Am. & Can. OTCH Liberte's Elixir O'Carousel, Am. & Can. TD, with owner Linda Schaal

multiple HIT winner, as was Don Warner's Briand Des Rogues Rouges, UD, who won nine High in Trial awards from 1971 through 1976. Don has owned several outstanding Tervuren through the years who placed well in the ratings, including Imitator Du Coeur de Leon in 1976, as well as Hera Katty Des Rogues Rouges and Cotes du Rhone De La Zia, both in 1985.

In March 1979, Am., Can. Ch. Hi Times Top Of The Crop, UDT (Bumper), owned by Pat Morgan of Michigan, completed her Canadian UD to become the first Tervuren to obtain Ch./UDT titles in both the United States and Canada. Bumper was a daughter of Ch. Bonheur's D'Artagnon, UDT. The second American and Canadian Ch./UDT, Hi Times Erica O'Crocs Blanc, owned and handled by Jane Eckelman of New York, was also an offspring of Dart. Jane also owned, trained and handled Drifter Esprit De Joie to these same titles. Drifter competed in weight pull events in his spare time.

INTO THE 1980s

The 1970s and early 1980s produced the outstanding team of Ch. OTCH Liberte's Elixir O'Carousel, TD (Brett), and Linda Schaal of Wisconsin. Brett was top Tervuren in 1979 (all systems) and 1980 (Shuman) and the first Tervuren to obtain the titles of Ch./OTCH/TD in both the United States and Canada. (In Canada, a dog achieving a UD degree is designated an OTCH.)

Other of Linda's Tervuren also have excellent records. Her Liberte's Prairie Fire was top Tervuren (Delaney) in 1980, and received a perfect score that year. Liberte's Magnum Force earned his Utility degree in three straight shows and placed high in the ratings in 1981. Her Ch. Snowflower Brady O'Liberte completed his UDT in 1987, his OTCH in 1988 and is a multiple HIT winner.

In Colorado, Ch. OTCH Fern Hill Act One, TD, owned by Barbara Handler, won fourteen High in Trial awards, placing him high in national breed ratings from 1979 through 1983, and earning him number ten of all herding breeds in 1983. He was the first dog of any breed to obtain both Ch. and OTCH titles in the Rocky Mountain area. Barbara also owned and trained Ch. Xquisite de Braise Rouge, UDT, who completed her Ch./UDT titles in 1978.

OTCH Dusty of Sierra Shadows, TDX, owned by Don and Jan Scott of California, was another Tervuren who ranked high in national ratings among Tervuren from 1979 through 1984. In 1988, at ten and one-half years, she became the breed's first OTCH holder to earn the TDX title. Dusty died in the same year. In tribute to her memory, it should be recorded that she earned her TD at one year of age, then passed the test once again at nine after just a short brushup.

The Scotts also owned another notable performer, Ch. Eclipse Esprit De Joie, UDT, who completed his titles in 1985.

OTCH Cin-Li's A'Salem of Sandyhills, TD, PC (*left*), and Ch. Carefree Gypsy Seranade, UD, TT

OTCH Gambiama's Krista De La Corps, TD, Can. UD, AD, TDI, works as a therapy dog. Owner Cynthia Strong with a patient.

Ch. Tacara's Galileah Gofrostfire, CD, a multiple Group placer and multiple High In Trial winner.

Tishaminga de Weeping Pines, CDX, the first Tervuren to receive a perfect 200 score in obedience

P. J. Laursen with Ch. Uptempo's Afternoon Delight, Am. & Can. CDX, and Four Footed Nomad of Chato, Am. & Can. CDX, shown winning the Brace competition at the 1986 ABTC National under judge Linda Scanlon. Each dog is a multiple HIT winner and each has won HIT at a National Specialty.

Another outstanding winner of the 1980s is OTCH Cin Li's A'Salem of Sandyhills, TD, PC, owned by Sandra Hill of El Paso, Texas. Salem was top Tervuren (Shuman system) between 1982 and 1985, accumulating twenty-six High in Trial awards, including one in Mexico. Salem, a therapy dog seen frequently in nursing homes in the El Paso area, earned all his OTCH points in just one year and also placed in the herding breed obedience ratings. Another of Sandra's Tervuren, Ch. Carefree Gypsy Seranade, UD, TT, also won an American and Mexican HIT during 1984.

Helen Hammel Hittesdorf of Colorado has owned and trained three Ch./UDTs: Ch. Fern Hill Knave De Sharvonne, UDT, in 1981; Ch. Chantilly Esprit De Joie, UDT, in 1984, and her daughter, Ch. Jamaica Nemesis, UDTX, in 1987.

Three Tervuren from the Midwest stand out in the mid-1980s: OTCH Gambiama's Krista de la Corps, TD, Can. UD, AD (Jetta), owned by Cindy Strong; Am., Can. Ch., Am., Can. OTCH Hi Times Country Summer (Annie), owned by Bunny Noble and Bernadine Paull, and Am., Can. OTCH Ochiama Legend de la Corps (Lance), owned by Diane Allen.

Cindy Strong's Jetta was a winner both in the obedience rings and in the hearts of many of the less fortunate. Jetta is one of many Tervuren serving as a registered therapy dog. She obtained five *Dog World* awards, and nine American and three Canadian High in Trial wins. Completing her OTCH in just ten shows, Jetta consistently ranked in the obedience ratings from 1983 through 1986. Typical of many well-trained Tervuren, she has been active in community service work promoting responsible dog ownership.

Bunny Noble's Annie earned her Canadian CD during one weekend, with three first places and two HIT wins. She achieved another HIT with a score of 199.5 in Canadian CDX competition. She completed her Canadian UD in 1983 and her American OTCH in the fall of 1984. With a Canadian BIS win in 1982, Annie became the only BIS Tervuren to hold an American and Canadian OTCH.

Diane's Lance accumulated eleven High in Trial Awards and top Tervuren honors during 1986 and 1987, and was tenth in all breeds in 1986 (Shuman system). Lance went on to complete his Canadian UD in 1987, winning the coveted Jake Giacomelli Memorial Trophy for high combined Open and Utility scores.

A unique record was accomplished in 1986 by Tacara's Galileah Gofrostfire, owned and trained by Linda Newsome of Oklahoma. Galileah, who was a winner in the breed and Group rings, received her CD with six High in Trial wins.

Linda was also the owner and trainer of Ch. Frostfire's Gandalf Xebec, CDX (a multiple Group placer and HIT winner in the late seventies), as well as Ch. Frostfire's Outrage, CDX, and Frostfire's Whimsical Damsel, CDX, both multiple High in Trial winners in the mid-1980s. Linda's Tasha (Frostfire's Whimsical Damsel) was a police demonstration dog, and entertained many with her routine of more than thirty-five "amazing tricks." In obtaining

OTCH Brandiwyne's Snooky Bear, the breed's all-time top obedience winner, with owner-handler Gloria McGrath

her Canadian CDX, she received four High in Trial wins, with an average score of 199. Another of Linda's dogs, Ch. Tacara's Sojourn Soignes, went High in Trial at his first show with a score of 199.

In recent years Mary Alice Theriot has been active with her four generations of Ch./UD Tervuren. Theriot's La Fee, Theriot's The Riot, Theriot's The Brat and Theriot's Red Baron earned their titles between 1979 and 1988. Three of these dogs also hold the TD title. These Tervuren had so many other titles that they are discussed more fully in Chapter 17.

The early 1980s saw an impressive obedience winner from California in OTCH Brandiwyne's Lady Mistique, owned by Larry and Gloria McGrath. This bitch was top Tervuren in 1981 (all systems). Soon, however, she would be overshadowed by her housemate and the top-winning obedience Tervuren of all time, OTCH Brandiwyne's Snooky Bear.

Snooky Bear, also owned by the McGraths and shown by Gloria, has demonstrated what an outstanding Tervuren/owner team can accomplish against the best of all breeds. To date, he is the all-time top winning obedience Tervuren. He was Top Tervuren (Delaney and ABTC systems) from 1982 through 1985, third place *all breeds* (Delaney) in 1984 (fourth place Shuman system) and recipient of three perfect scores of 200.

Snooky Bear has accumulated more than fifty High in Trial wins. He earned an even greater number of high-combined scores (highest combined score from both Open B and Utility class at one show), with a score of 197 or *greater* in both classes. He won the most OTCH points of *any breed* in 1984, making him the only breed other than a Golden Retriever (a far more popular breed) to have done this to date. Snooky Bear has amassed an enviable record, in which our early fanciers would take great pride.

See Appendixes A and B for lists of ABTC obedience trial winners, obedience statistics and titleholders.

15

The Herding Dog

HERDING DOG COMPETITIONS have undoubtedly been held as long as shepherds have been using dogs to tend flocks. An organized trial in France was reported in the May 7, 1898, edition of *Scientific American,* in an article entitled, "Competition of Shepherd's Dogs at Angerville." A quote from the publication tells much about the day:

The question of the improvement of the French shepherd's dog was raised two years ago, and, thanks to the initiative of M. Emmanuel, founder and president of the French Shepherd's Dog Club, was made the order of the day. M. Bonlet saw himself at once seconded by the sympathy of the minister of agriculture and supported by the entire agriculture press.

The club now has numerous adherents, and it is with pride that the shepherd and drovers say to you, "We are members of the club."

The dogs that are so useful for guarding and driving flocks were soon submitted to competition, not only from the standpoint of breed and beauty, but also on the grounds in the form of special tests.

The first races, if we may so express ourselves, took place with success in the vicinity of Chartres, last year. The result obtained led the club to organize the Angerville races, which were run on Sunday, May 30. In the land of Beauce, with its immense plains, shepherd's dogs are numerous, and the drovers also have their contingent of very stylish animals.

The train took us at ten minutes to nine to the Angerville station, where the Orphic Society of the place came with great pomp to meet M. Menault, inspector general of agriculture and major of Angerville, surrounded by the organizers of the contest, Messrs. Boulet, Tisserand, Sevrette, Bodmer, Masson and others.

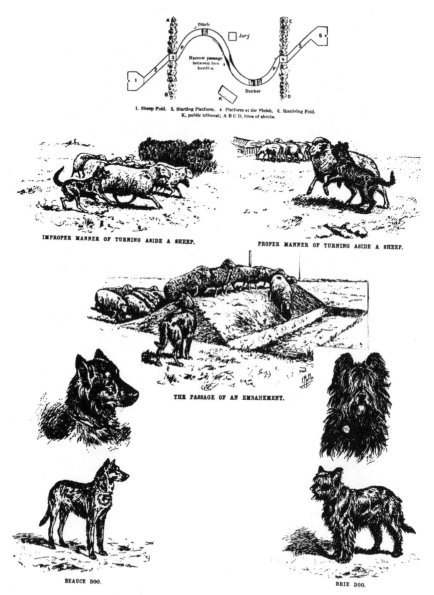

1. Sheep Fold. 3. Starting Platform. 4. Platform at the Finish. 6. Receiving Fold.
K, public tribunal; A B C D, lines of shrubs.

IMPROPER MANNER OF TURNING ASIDE A SHEEP.

PROPER MANNER OF TURNING ASIDE A SHEEP.

THE PASSAGE OF AN EMBANKMENT.

BEAUCE DOG.

BRIE DOG.

Diagrams from the *Scientific American*, 1898

In front of the major's office there was a drawing of numbers by lot, and the number of each dog was carried by the shepherd upon an armlet.

The animals present were judged from the view point of beauty of breed, and then everyone went to breakfast. At half-past twelve a start was made from the major's office for the field of tests, two gendarmes, on horseback, heading the procession, followed by music with a banner at the head. Behind came the spectators and the contestants and their dogs, held by a leash by their owners. The plan of the track will give the aspect of the competition better than words.

The path taken by the sheep was indicated upon the plain only by two furrows made with a plow and staked out by small poles here and there, provided with a tricolored pendant. A strong, cool breeze was blowing that made all the flags and the canvas of the tribunes flap. The weather was splendid and the sun hot.

The competition began. In the stock fold there was a large flock of sheep to be used for the occasion. Each shepherd was to drive a flock of 15 sheep from point 1 to point 6 without allowing the animals to stray from the road between the two furrows. The flock had to surmount obstacles, ascend embankments, re-descend into ditches and pass between hedges that formed a narrow passage, and all this in close groups without any of them separating.

Incidents were not wanting. Out of the 32 dogs registered very few led their sheep from one fold to the other without a hitch. Gallops in disorder across the field and between the legs of spectators made the public merry. More than one shepherd, tired of the obstinate resistance of the sheep to obstacles, seized the leader of the flock from the lot, and, holding him firmly by the nape, dragged him over the embankment and thus made himself followed by the bank of imbeciles.

The good dogs were the ones which, not becoming enervated, led their animals judiciously. They took a little more time for the operation, but prevented disorder in the ranks.

The good shepherd's dog should not seize the sheep by the rump, where a wound by his fangs might spoil a leg of mutton, the essential part in butchery, but rather by the nape.

After the tests in driving, the sheep were placed in hurdles, for the completion in placing and separation of lots.

Although the article did not mention the specific breeds entered in the competition, at this time many identifiable breeds of stock dogs had been developed in Western Europe, such as the Pyrenean Shepherd Dog, the Briard, the Beauceron, the German Shepherd Dog, the Picard and the Belgian Shepherd Dog (Le Berger Belge).

THE BELGIAN TERVUREN AS A HERDING DOG

History

Sheep herding dogs played a vital role in Western Europe, and by the end of the nineteenth century many breeds had been developed, each bred to suit the needs of the region. One of the emerging breeds was the Belgian Shepherd Dog (Le Berger Belge), which came in a variety of coats and colors but had a characteristic build and herding ability.

The Belgian Shepherd Dog at that time was rather small, being about twenty to twenty-four inches high, and rather fine and spare, thus being economical to keep. They were energetic, animated and, adding to their economy, versatile dogs. On small holdings they could work not only small flocks of sheep, but also goats, dairy cattle, swine, geese and ducks. They were expected to be protective of their flock and farm, suspicious of strangers and bold enough to ward off not only predators large and small, but uninvited humans as well. Then as now, the breed was able to cope with many working situations, from small farms to large sheep operations involving hundreds of sheep. Fences were virtually unheard of in many areas of Belgium and France, and the dogs were tireless in their circling of the flock and their vigilance as guardians.

When Belgian Shepherd Dogs were imported to the United States, no doubt several found their way into stock work on farms, ranches and small homesteads. However, the arrival of Tervuren in herding trial competition in the United States is difficult to pinpoint. Certainly, by 1982 there were a few Tervuren regularly competing in trials held by the Australian Shepherd Club of America (ASCA) and other established groups.

Instinct and Style of the Belgian Tervuren

The instinct to herd is derived from the dog's wild canid ancestors. The hunting style was modified through selective breeding to retain the dog's interest in movement of the stock without the single-out-and-kill climax of the hunt. Occasionally, a dog will exhibit the undeniable urge to chase with intent to single out and kill, which is not desirable in a herding dog. Often, however, a potentially excellent young or inexperienced dog will show overaggression or excitement. This instinct should be reduced with training and exposure. It is fairly simple for the experienced eye to tell when the dog's roughness on stock is due to the excitement and inexperience of trying to herd but not to kill prey. For the sake of an all-around stock dog or trial dog, an overaggressive, inexperienced dog is more desirable than a timid or shy one. Sustained interest and assertiveness are necessary components in developing a reliable, virtually inexhaustible, stockdog.

As a general observation, the Tervuren is an upstanding fetching breed, showing moderate to loose "eye." Certainly the fact that so many have passed the herding instinct test demonstrates that an inherited ability remains strong in the breed. This is fortunate, since good herding ability can easily be lost through ignorant breeding. The enthusiastic response of breeders to the ABTC herding program holds good promise for future generations.

"The Belgian Tervuren as a sheepherding dog should have all the virtues

Seven of the breed's early Herding Trial champions. Hi Times Top of the Crop is center. The others carry the Winjammer Kennel names: Spit In Yer Eye, Tuff Act To Follow, On The Move, On The Rise, Top of the Crop Jr. and Snake In The Grass. This group includes 1 multi BIS, 4 multi Group placers, 3 multi HIT obedience winners and 6 champions; 2 are herding trial HIT winners.

Ch. HTCh. Ochiama's Luciana De La Corps, CDX, Sch I, AD, doing an "away to me." *V. Starr*

needed for this work. It is a breed devoted to its family and to its work (Breed Type Manual—ABTC 1983).

The ABTC Herding Program

The American Belgian Tervuren Club (ABTC) put its herding program into effect in 1983, offering Herding Instinct Certificates (HIC) for dogs passing sanctioned instinct tests, and Herding Trial Championships (HTCh.) for dogs excelling in trial competition. The first ABTC herding trial was held in conjunction with the 1985 National Specialty in Sacramento, California, and a herding trial has been held at each National since that time.

The ABTC herding program was designed to provide owners with the opportunity to exhibit the retained herding instinct in their dogs, to provide information to those owners who wish to encourage this instinct in their dogs (whether for practical or competition purposes) and to provide recognition to those dogs who are capably demonstrating herding ability. The ultimate goal expressed by the ABTC herding program is "to encourage, preserve and protect the natural herding abilities of the Belgian Tervuren, and to promote the use of the Belgian Tervuren as a stockdog through competition in herding trials."

HERDING TRIALS

Belgian Tervuren often compete in trials held by the Australian Shepherd Club of America (ASCA), which offers titles to its members regardless of the breed. ASCA trials use ducks, sheep and cattle. The breed is also seen at trials offered by various stockdog associations, including those often referred to as "Border Collie" trials. Most herding trials are open to all breeds. "Border Collie" trials are run on sheep, and titles are not offered. The common classes, in ascending order of difficulty, are Novice, Pro-novice, Open-ranch and Open.

Tervuren herding fanciers are very much indebted to the dedication of these other clubs and to the help and encouragement they have given to our breed.

Outstanding Performers

Pat Morgan's Am., Can. Ch. HTCh. Hi Times Top of the Crop, Am., Can. UDT, STD, OTD, was the breed's first herding trial champion. Pat has been one of the breed's most active supporters and trainers of herding Tervuren, with twenty-four of the breed's first thirty-four herding trial champion dogs either owned and trained by her or carrying her Winjammer kennel prefix. Teamed up with Laurie Thal, owner-trainer of three of these Winjammer HTCh. titleholders, they have tested a large number of the breed's HIC titleholders, as well as offered instruction, assistance and encouragement for untold numbers of owners.

"Eye" is a term meaning an intense, unblinking gaze used by the dog to control the stock, often accompanied by a creeping or crouching approach. Shown is HTCh. Winjammers Spit In Yer Eye, STDdc, OTDs.

HTCh. Ch. Chilure's Fiama De La Corps, UDT, BAR, Sch I, AD. *Fox & Cook*

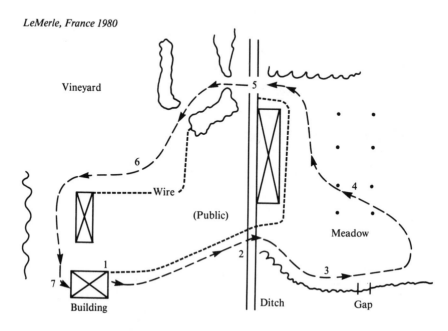

LeMerle, France 1980

Vineyard

Wire

(Public)

Meadow

Building

Ditch

Gap

1. Take sheep out (300 head)
2. Gate (4–5 yards wide)
3. Pass between hedge and "crop" (6–7 yards wide)
4. Graze in square (sheep held calmly enough to graze)
5. Stop
6. Meeting a car (dog stays between car and sheep, keeps sheep on edge in line)
7. Back into shed

[700 yards long—30 minutes to complete]

Trials in France include herds of no less than 100 head per dog. This is a diagram of the course at LaMerle, France, in 1980. *Sue Morlan*

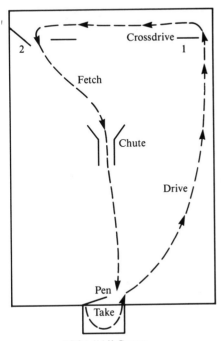

ASCA "A" Course

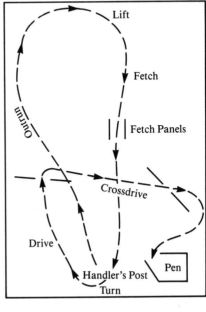

ASCA is developing a "B" course involving an outrun and a free-standing pen. [NOTE: Started class may fetch entire course, no drive is required.] (3–5 head) 8–10 minutes

(Common Course)
"Border Collie Course"
[Shed before and/or after the pen]
(3–5 head) 8–10 minutes

Above, left: diagram of a typical ASCA course (U.S.). *Sue Morlan*
Above, right: diagram of a typical "Border Collie" course (U.S.). *Sue Morlan*

"Go bye" or
"Come bye"

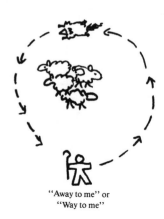

"Away to me" or
"Way to me"

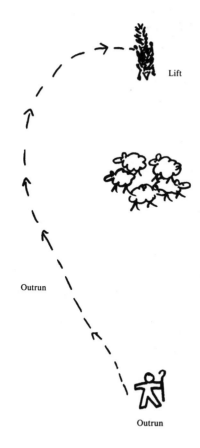

Lift

Outrun

Outrun

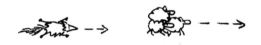

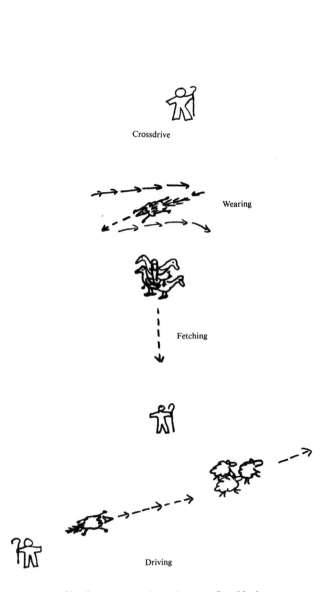

Crossdrive

Wearing

Fetching

Driving

Herding commands and terms. *Sue Morlan*

175

Since the ABTC's inception of the first Specialty-related herding trial in 1985, Linda Franklin's two outstanding bitches remain undefeated as HIT winners. Linda's Ch. HTCh. Chilure's Fiama de la Corps, UTD, Sch.H I, AD, won that first trial and again took the honors in 1987. Her daughter, Ch. HTCh. Ochiama's Luciana de la Corps, UDT, AD, filled in the remaining years by winning in 1986, 1988 and 1989.

Interest in herding continues to grow and enjoys good health across the country. It is a tribute to the breed's versatility, as well as the fancier's devotion to that versatility, that at the 1986 ABTC National Specialty in Flint, Michigan, there was an entry of 129 in the herding trial and HIC events. As of February 1988, nearly 800 Tervuren had passed an HIC test, and there were 26 herding trial champions. This has occurred when the ABTC herding program is still in its infancy.

Herding Terminology (illustrated by Sue Morlan)

Approach—The manner in which a dog comes in to the stock, a "smooth" approach being the most highly prized (that is, a dog moving in very steadily and surely).

Balance—The characteristic of the dog to anticipate movement of the stock from the line he is fetching or driving on, and moving in the direction that the stock are drifting as he keeps them on line. A dog may move to the "balance point" to keep the stock moving to the handler without drifting.

Eye—See photo.

Force Barking—A dog that works quietly, except in situations where the stock challenges the dog, where the dog barks as a precursor to a nip.

Heading—A dog that nips at the heads of livestock to turn them.

Heeling—A dog that nips at the lower part of the hind legs of livestock to move them forward.

Pen—A course term meaning that the dog puts the stock in a small pen.

Power—A dog that, by virtue of its strong self-confidence, can move stubborn or fighting animals, often without nipping.

Shed—A course term meaning that the dog and handler separate the flock as directed, often singling out one head and holding it apart from the flock for a moment.

Take—A course term meaning that the dog removes stock from a small pen.

Weak—A dog lacking the confidence to stand up to stubborn stock.

Wearing, Outrun, Lift, Fetch, Drive, Crossdrive—See illustrations.

Wool-puller—A dog that nips at the bodies of the sheep, marking the flesh by tearing out hunks of wool, called "body biting" on cattle. Biting at the body of stock is a fault.

The breed's first Herding Trial champion, Am. & Can. Ch. Hi Time's Top of the Crop, Am. & Can. UDT, STDc, OTDds, BAR, achieved this distinction as a puppy.

Performing the "fetch" with good eye and approach is HTCh. Winjammers Tuff Act Too, CD, TDX, owned by Barb VanEseltine.

The Guardian, glass sculpture by Warren Hooper donated by Carole Eklund for the 1986 ABTC National Herding Trial winner

Commands Used in Herding

Away to me, or *Way to me*—See illustration.

Down, or *Lie down*—Drop instantly and remain until another direction is given (sit is an option).

Get back—Get behind the stock wherever they are.

Go Bye, or *Come Bye*—See illustration.

Look back, or *Turn back*—Leave the stock and go look for more.

Steady, easy, take time—All mean to slow down but keep moving.

Stop, or *Wait*—Rather than lie down, the dog may stand.

There—Can mean stop but usually means to stop the previously given direction and start in toward the stock.

Walk up—Leave the stop or down and progress toward the stock. (Note: Whistle commands for each of these vary between handlers, but are generally not taught until the verbal commands are mastered).

Often the voice inflection given with these commands has as much meaning as an entire new command. A long drawn-out "a-way-to-o-o-me-e-e" will send the dog far and wide on an outrun, while a quick, emphatic "way to, way to" will send the dog closer and at a run.

See Appendixes A and B for a listing of ABTC herding trial winners and HTCh. titleholders.

16

Tervuren as Trackers

WHAT IS THE FASCINATION so many Tervuren owners have for tracking? It often starts with the owner trying to obtain another title to add to his dog's name, then turns into a bit of an obsession, if you will, with the owner putting the "T" on all the dogs he owns—and sometimes even borrowing other owners' Tervuren to take tracking.

Perhaps it is the enjoyment one discovers in being outdoors, especially at an early hour when the world is quiet. There is sheer pleasure in walking, being one-on-one with your dog, and seeing him have such a good time. Perhaps it is being a part of developing a dog's *natural* ability to scent, a trait that we humans do not share or totally understand. Tracking is unique from so many other dog sports because it puts the dog in charge and forces complete trust by the handler. The bond created through tracking can be something special.

The first Tervuren in the United States to obtain the tracking degree was Ch. Mars de Fauve Charbonne, CDX, who passed the test in Aurora, Illinois, on September 24, 1967. Mars also became the second dog of *any* breed to earn both the American and Mexican tracking titles. The reader can find further mention of this many-titled dog in the chapters on obedience and famous kennels.

Less than two weeks after Mars earned his TD, Ch. Kis Tam's Renee, CD, passed her test, also in Illinois, to become the breed's second TD and first bitch to earn this title. Renee was owned by the late Lou Hawkinson. She was registered with the Warrenville, Illinois, police department and the following

The breed's first AKC tracking dog and first Ch-UDT, Am. Can. Mex. Ch. Mars de Fauve Charbonne, UDT, BAR, Mex. PC, TD

Ch. Kis Tam's Renee, CD, TD, C-BAR

Joyce McHenry with her Ch. Commander Foxfire of Glenoak, CD, TDX

account, once told by Lou's husband, Cliff, is somewhat typical of the situation a good tracking Tervuren might find itself in:

> It came as no surprise to "Renee" when her late hour call to duty came in. In fact, the whole thing seemed a terrible bore to our canine matron. A 100 mph race to the scene gave rise to a few yawns and the threat of two armed and dangerous fugitives seemed of little consequence. Upon arrival, a quick sniff in the narcotic peddler's wrecked car and off she went, through a ditch, down a side road, through the woods. Instead of two or three judges following her with clip boards and a whistle, a large group of stern police, all with shotguns in a very ready position, were there catering to her every whim. If she trotted, they did, if she chose to stroll, they did (this I suspect did please her). A stop at a residence door, and in a few tense moments it was learned the fugitives had indeed been to this house and requested a cab be called. A great deal of search time was eliminated and the police were most appreciative.

The breed's longest active tracking supporter is Joyce McHenry of North Carolina. Starting with her Ch. Scorpio de Fauve Charbonne, CD, who passed the test on April 7, 1974, Joyce has put thirteen Tervuren through to this title to date. Her Ch. Commander Foxfire of Glenoak, CD, also passed the TDX test on February 28, 1982. A daughter of Scorpio, Ch. Glenoak Amanda of Echo Hill, CDX, TD (owned by Randie Meyer), is credited with rescuing a lost child.

One of Joyce's dogs, Ch. Wanderlust of Glenoak, CDX, TD (Rover), was frequently called upon to find articles lost by other tracking dogs (that is, not found by them in training practice or at tests). Rover would simply locate the track that the first dog attempted, follow it along and locate the articles. Rover was helpful in finding a number of other lost items, including a gold watch and a falcon's hood, sometimes finding such items as much as a day or more after they were lost.

Ch. OTCH Hi Times Tops With Theo, owned by Lockie Treanor of Tennessee, was the first Ch. OTCH of *any* breed to hold a TD title (1979).

TRACKING DOG EXCELLENT

The TDX title was initiated in Canada in 1964 and awarded to a dog able to follow a track laid by a stranger over a distance of at least 1,000 yards, at least three hours old, crossed in two places by a more recent track and containing at least five turns. The dog is required to find three articles dropped by the tracklayer along the track.

On September 20, 1964, the remarkable Canadian Ch. Nightwatch Russet Chevalier, UDT, became the first dog of *any* breed to earn the Canadian title of Tracking Dog Excellent. Val, owned by Donald and Mollie Hudson of Victoria, B.C., was an outstanding dog in many areas, and the reader will find further mention of him in the chapters on Canada and obedience.

Val's record did not have its counterpart in the United States for some

Am. & Can. Ch. StarBright
Champignon, Am. & Can UDTX,
owned by Maureen Foley and C.
John Blankley. *Kay Maves*

The glove is found and checked
out with praise. *Kay Maves*

Ch. Coda's Take To The Road,
TD, owned by Randie Meyer

time, since the AKC did not begin holding TDX tests until 1980. On April 5, 1981, Ch. Chimina's Etienne de la Corps, UDT (Alvin), a male owned by Linda Franklin of Illinois, became the first Tervuren to obtain the American TDX title. Alvin also became the first Tervuren in North America to earn the Faehrtenhund (FH), a German advanced tracking title. In doing so, he successfully completed a 2,000-yard track, three hours old, with three diversionary cross tracks, and found four articles.

On September 13, 1981, Ch. Winjammers One For The Road, Am. CDX, TDX, Can. CD, TDX (Ryan), owned by Roberta Whitesides, became the second dog of the breed to pass the TDX test. A multiple Best in Show winner, Ryan is the first dog of any breed to be a TDX and Best in Show winner. He is also a National Specialty BOB winner, demonstrating once again that in Tervuren, beautiful dogs *do* work, and work well. Ryan passed his first tracking test at the age of just six months and one day, and earned a *Dog World* award in achieving each of his obedience titles, both American and Canadian.

On his heels was another record setter, StarBright Bacho Noire (Coco), who became the first Tervuren bitch to earn the TDX, in October 1981. On October 16, 1983, she became the first Tervuren to complete the championship and UDTX titles in both the United States and Canada. Coco is owned by Maureen Foley, who has become our breed's most involved tracking enthusiast of the 1980s. Maureen has completed the TDX on three Tervuren—not only in the United States, but in Canada as well. Additionally, all three are champions, and two have earned both their American and Canadian Utility Dog titles. Maureen has shared her experience in seminars and in the field, assisting many other owners and their dogs in obtaining tracking titles.

James and Donna Rounsaville of Illinois have also been successful with their Tervuren in the tracking field, completing tracking titles on four Tervuren and the TDX on three. Avid trackers, starting with their first tracking title about 1975, the Rounsavilles have also completed the TD on many other breeds. They regard Tervuren as real naturals, feeling that their ability has been largely untapped.

A number of Tervuren fanciers have contributed their talents as AKC tracking judges, with Randie Meyer (N.H.), Maureen Foley (Mich.), Helen H. Hittesdorf (Colo.), David Behrens (Ill.), Bill Cooper (Fla.) and Pat Lawrence (N.C.) being among them.

See Appendixes A and B for tracking statistics and titleholders.

Ch. Javondi's Allure De La Corps, UDT, BAR, Sch III, performing a Schutzhund exercise

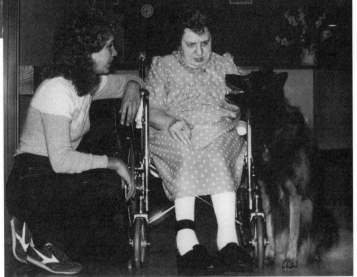

Sharing love

17

The Versatile
Belgian Tervuren

IN ADDITION to their natural good looks, Tervuren are incredibly versatile, serving man in many capacities, some of which are not usually associated with the herding breeds. Its intelligence, trainability, watchfulness and desire to please make this possible. Strong, agile and quick, the Tervuren will give almost any active dog lover an opportunity to "do his own thing" with his dog.

It is impossible to mention everything the Tervuren can be trained to do, and do well, but here are several examples.

SCHUTZHUND

Developed nearly a century ago, Schutzhund training demonstrates the ability of a dog to serve man as companion, protector and tracker—all functions highly regarded as virtues of the dog in its service to mankind. A responsibly trained Schutzhund dog must not be confused with a dog trained to fight other dogs, or with temperamentally unstable dogs.

The Schutzhund sport traditionally has been dominated by breeds such as German Shepherd Dogs, Doberman Pinschers, Bouviers Des Flandres and Rottweilers, with the Belgian Malinois becoming increasingly popular. Tervuren have also made their mark in this sport.

Linda Franklin has been a pioneer in Schutzhund work with Tervuren. Her Ch. Javondi's Allure De La Corps, UDT, SchH.III (called Beauty, and daughter of two Ch./UD parents) is the breed's first homebred Ch./UDT titleholder and the first dog of *any* breed to receive the combined titles of champion, UDT and SchH.III in North America, completing her titles in October 1976.

Linda's Ch. Chimina's Etiene De La Corps, UDTX, SChH.III, AD, FH, Int. (called Alvin) remains the only such titled Tervuren in North America. In September 1979, Linda drove him and his half-sister, BB, from the seat of a dogcart to complete the requirements of the Ausdauer (AD), the German Endurance Test. The two dogs pulled Linda on the cart for twelve and one-half miles in under two hours.

Linda also has trained BB—properly known as Ch./HTCh. Chilure's Fiama De La Corps, UDT, SchH.I, AD—and Ch./HTCh. Ochiama's Luciana De La Corps, UDT, AD, SchH.I (Lucy) for Schutzhund work. In receiving her SchH.I, Lucy won three consecutive Highs in Trial, with two perfect 100-point tracking scores. These two bitches also have competed successfully in ABTC, ASCA and Border Collie herding trials.

Another Schutzhund-titled Tervuren has also been employed in police work, demonstrating one of the breed's original purposes. Ch. StarBright Bonne Chance, CDX, TD, SchH.I, owned by Dana Mackonis, holds the working titles of Police Dog I, Detector Dog I and II, and was used for three years as a narcotics detection dog.

INTERNATIONAL WORKING DOGS

A Tervuren bearing many titles is Mary Alice Theriot's Am., Can., Mex., Puerto Rican (P.R.) Ch. Theriots La Fee, UDT, TT, STDs; Mex. CDX, TD, TT; P.R. TT; Can. UD, TT; SchH.II, FH, AD, VB, WH. This multitalented bitch, known as Nickie, also was winner of three CACIB awards in Mexico, had two legs toward the Mexican Utility title and was the first Tervuren to pass the Temperament Test in the United States (1978). Nickie was sired by Ch. Hilton's Red Fox of Janacque out of J Espere de Fleur de Lis.

Mary also owns Nickie's daughter, Ch. Theriots The Riot, UDT, AD, VB, STDs, TT (sired by Ch. Hiltons Storm Cloud, CD); Riot's daughter, Ch./HTCh. Theriots The Brat, UDT, AD, VB, with six CACIB wins (sired by Am., Can. Ch. Bonheurs Star Treader, CDX, TD); and Brat's son, Ch. HTCh. Theriots Red Baron, UD, AD, VB (sired by Ch. Cachet Noir's Justin, CD). Typical of many Tervuren with multiple titles, Mary's dogs also have been involved in other activities, including movies and television; the bitches have appeared in *First Born* and *Tales of the Darkside*.

Two fit Tervuren can easily pull on the straightaway. Shown are Barb VanEseltine's Apache, CD, and Ch. Winjammers Bound To Be.

Skijoring in Alaska. *Virginia Weed*

Ch. StarBright Cisco Kid, UDTX, shows his winning form in agility competition.

AIDES FOR THE HANDICAPPED

While not seen as frequently as Labradors, Goldens and German Shepherd Dogs, Belgian Tervuren nonetheless have been used with good success as leader dogs for the blind. An article written by Karen Johnson in the January 1972 issue of *Tervuren News Tales* pictorial issue highlighted three Tervuren that had recently graduated from Leader Dogs for the Blind in Rochester, Michigan, and were serving as eyes for their new owners. Eight Tervuren puppies were being raised for the Leader Dog school for its program in the spring of 1988.

Many Tervuren also are used as therapy dogs in hospitals and special "homes." They usually are registered by Therapy Dogs International (TDI) to demonstrate their reliability with the disabled.

Many Tervuren owners also take the time to share their well-trained and gentle dogs with those unable to have their own pet by regularly visiting nursing homes and hospitals.

WINTER SPORTS

Tervuren long have been used in the northern climates for recreational sledding and are increasingly seen competing at racing events. Although not racing specialists (most racers are breeds or crosses with a strong Siberian or Alaskan Husky foundation), Tervuren are fast and responsive, and they love the thrilling competitive spirit that a dog team and its handler share. Since they are almost always someone's pet, instead of belonging to a sledding kennel, Tervuren are much easier to handle than are most sled dogs.

Teams composed of one or more Belgian Tervuren have become a small but active presence in Midwest sled racing. At the Mid-Union Sled Haulers race held in Michigan in early January 1988, with a total of fifty teams competing, eight-year veteran musher Pat Morgan recorded her first win: first place in the five-dog team competition of four and one-half miles, with her four Tervuren and one Belgian Sheepdog. At the same race, Diane Braunschneider also placed first in a three-dog competition with her Tervuren team. Four other Belgian teams also placed well out of thirty teams competing.

Another wintertime activity is skijouring, a recreation that can be shared by one or two dogs and a cross-country skier. Nearly every cross-country enthusiast in our breed has harnessed a Tervuren to a tow-line attached to a belt and allowed the dog to share (and help) in this refreshing outdoor activity. If you haven't tried the sport yet, be aware that the line is attached to a panic-snap on your belt in case of imminent collision. Tervuren are seen competing at skijouring race competitions as well.

Ch. Lancelot de Mont-Cenis, CD, TD, owned by Pam Schultz, steps on the flyball release lever and anticipates the tennis ball before racing back over the hurdles.

In training for agility competition

A happy team. Ch. HTCh. Chilure's Fiama De La Corps, CDX, BAR, AD, Sch I, and Ch. Chimina's Etiene De La Corps, UDTX, Sch III, AD, FH, Int., after completing the AD (endurance test) with owner-trainer Linda Franklin. *Mitzie Breaux*

AGILITY

Originating in England in the mid-1970s, agility competition was developed to entertain spectators between judging events at dog shows. In 1980, the Kennel Club (Great Britain) gave agility competition official status and granted permission to hold an official test at Crufts that same year. Described as an obstacle course run against time, agility has proven to be great fun for dog, handler and spectator alike, and is fast becoming popular in the United States.

Herb Williams of Williams-Petty Productions of Toronto, Ontario, dreamed up an international agility competition for America, known as the Grand Prix. It consists of a 500-foot course over twelve jumps, through six- and twelve-foot tunnels, and up and over a five-and-one-half-foot scaling wall.

The first contest in the United States was held at the Detroit Kennel Club show in March 1987, with forty entrants. The winner was a Belgian Tervuren, Ch. StarBright Cisco Kid, UDTX, owned by Pam Schultz. Cisco, who is also a flyball star (see below), repeated this win in 1988. This competition boosts a dog's self-confidence. He not only loves it—he becomes a big ham!

SCENT HURDLE RACES

A fast and exciting game for spectators, handlers and dogs, scent hurdle competition consists of two dog teams racing against each other. A whistle signals the start of each race. The first dog of each team is released, quickly hurdling its team's set of four jumps, set ten feet apart. In a box at the far end, it quickly finds its owner's scent on a dumbbell placed among the entire team's set of dumbbells, and returns with it back over the jumps. As each dog returns over the starting/finish line, another dog is released in relay fashion, until all dogs have successfully completed a run. The fastest team emerges as the winner.

One top scent hurdle racer is a Tervuren, Sunwise Sheer Energy, CDX, who gained considerable acclaim during the late 1980s as anchor dog for the Greater Houston Occasional Scent Team. Sunnie is owned by Joan Miller.

FLYBALL

A newer game than scent racing, flyball originated in 1970. Like the scent relay, it is also a race over four hurdles. Rather than retrieving a dumbbell, the dog returns with a tennis ball that it extracts from a box placed at the end of its set of hurdles, by stepping on a spring-release pedal. The dog retrieves the flying ball, then returns over all four jumps in relay fashion.

A top flyball competitor, and the first dog of any breed to be inducted into the North American Flyball Association (NAFA) Hall of Fame, was Ch. StarBright Cisco Kid, UDTX, who received the honor in May 1986. (Cisco is the agility star we spoke of earlier.) The NAFA Hall of Fame was introduced to promote the usefulness of top flyball dogs in other activities, such as obedience, tracking, conformation, herding and field work. This versatile dog, who also has participated in Schutzhund work, has proven to be a gentle dog with children and the elderly. Cisco often is called upon to visit area schools, hospitals and nursing homes so that others might enjoy what many of us have taken for granted—the company of a dog.

Am. & Can. Ch. Bonheur's D'Artagnan, UDT, Can. CDX, BAR (d), the breed's first Best in Show winner (6-5-71, at Fox River Valley KC), repeated the win in 1972. Sire: Ch. Cyrano de Chateau Blanc, CD, BAR; dam: Bonheur's Bobbins and Pins, BAR. Breeder: Faye C. Dickens; owner: Bernadine Paull.

```
                              Am. Can. Ch. D'Jimmy du Clos Saint Clair CD (France)
                    Ch. Flair de Fauve Charbonne C-BAR
                              Chrysis du Clos Saint Jacques CD (France)
          Ch. Cyrano de Chateau Blanc CD BAR
                              Ch. Dandy du Clos Saint Jacques BAR (France)
                    Ch. Kandice de Fauve Charbonne CDX BAR
                              Ch. Jasmine de Cledeville BAR (France)
CH. BONHEUR'S D'ARTAGNAN UDT BAR whelped 5-24-67
                              Ch. Gironde de Lafayette
                    Ch. Sandy Haze Prince of Hearts UD BAR
                              Ch. Kriquette de Fauve Charbonne BAR
          Bonheur's Bobbins and Pins BAR
                              Kurt de Fauve Charbonne
                    Dentelle du Val de Tonnerre CD BAR
                              Bonheur du Val de Tonnerre C-BAR
```

18

Honor Roll of Best in Show Dogs

$\mathbf{R}$EADING THE NAMES of the Best in Show Tervuren, and knowing their pedigrees, is like walking down Memory Lane. One needs to recognize that it was the quality transmitted through the genes of the forebears of these great winners that produced their beauty. The breed was recognized by the American Kennel Club in 1959, and the first Best in Show by a Tervuren was achieved twelve years later, in 1971. Through the foresight of the breeders, and through the care, loving and determination of the owners of a breed new in the United States, these dogs were able to reach such heights.

The pedigrees of these Best in Show winners are still strongly embedded in today's Tervuren. If we have one piece of advice, and one wish to leave with the new and young breeders of today, it is: Take the torch that is handed to you, and carry and nurture it for the good of the breed, not just for your own glory.

If you follow this creed, you will find satisfaction in building on the foundations laid by the early breeders.

1972—Ch. Quincy du Garde Roux, CD (d). Sire: Ch. Our Valient du Garde Roux, C-BAR; dam: Orales du Garde Roux. Breeder: Lou Hawkinson; owner: Robert and Elaine Smid.

1973, 1975 twice, and 1976 (also first and second Can. BIS for breed in 1972 and 1974)—Am. & Can. Ch. Hi Times Kanook of Crocs Blanc, CD, BAR (d). Sire: Ch. Chateaubriand, CD, BAR; dam: Ch. Rob-Lyn's Ange Acajou, CD, BAR. Breeders: Danielle Daugherty, Bernadine Paull and Connie Wentling; owner: Judith Lee Smith.

1974—Am. & Can. Ch. Rajah D'Antre Du Louve, CD, BAR (d). Sire: Ch. Kenny de Cledeville, CD, BAR; dam: Ch. Rob-Lyn's Ange Acajou, CD, BAR. Breeders: Connie Wentling and Brenda Leedy; owner: Sallyann Comstock.

1978—Am. & Can. Ch. Paulmars Cosmic Vanguard (d). Sire: Ch. Bonheur's D'Artagnan, UDT, BAR; dam: Ch. Wallendale's Tabatha, CD, C-BAR. Breeders: H. P. and Marra R. Zieler; owner: Lance Wilson.

1980—Ch. Ovation de Chateau Blanc, CD (d). Sire: Ch. Lancer de Chateau Blanc, BAR; dam: Ch. Douceur du Vent de Bayville, CD, C-BAR. Breeder-owner: Edeltraud Laurin.

1982—Ch. Bonheur Ruarri MacTire, BAR (d) (he also won Canadian BIS in 1984). Sire: Ch. Elysee de Mont-Cenis, BAR; dam: Kalyn's Zazarac de Bonheur, CD, BAR. Breeders: Faye and Carrole Dickens; owners: Kay Maves, Sharon Redmer and Faye Dickens.

1982—Ch. Fox Hollow's Strider, CD (d). Sire: Ch. Corsair's Beaujangles; dam: Ch. Hi Times Take Over, CDX. Breeder: Margie Marquez; owner: Linda Peterson.

1982—Ch. Sanroyale's The Hustler, CD, C-BAR (d). Sire: Am. & Can Ch. Rajah D-Antre du Louve, CD, BAR; dam: Ch. La Mariee du Val de Tonnerre, CD, C-BAR. Breeder: Sallyann Comstock; owner: Darell Lee Arelt.

Ch. Corsair's Beaujangles—all-time top winning Belgian Tervuren, winner of twenty American and three Canadian Bests in Show (1982–1986) (d). Sire: Am. & Can. Ch. Achates Esprit de Joie, CD, C-BAR; dam: Ch. Debonair Debra de Vedette Noir, CD, C-BAR. Breeder-owner: Steve Sorenson.

```
                            Ch. Heureux de Chateau Blanc
                    Ch. Chagall du Masque Noir CDX BAR
                            Ch. Satin de Fauve Charbonne CDX BAR
            Ch. Achates Esprit De Joie CD C-BAR
                            Ch. Hi Times Kanook of Crocs Blanc CD BAR
                    Frost Fire's Innovation CD BAR
                            Ch. Sabrina de Flambeau Rouge CD BAR
    CH. CORSAIRS BEAUJANGLES whelped 5/20/79
                            Ch. Chateaubriand CD BAR
                    Ch. Hi Times Kanook of Crocs Blanc CD BAR
                            Ch. Rob-Lyn's Ange Acajou CD BAR
            Ch. Debonair Debra de Vedette Noir CD C-BAR
                            Ch. Rageera Viser At Larj CD
                    Ch. Solar Flash C-BAR
                            Sachet de Flambeau Rouge C-BAR
```

The first bitch in the breed to win American BIS in 1982 (twice) and Canadian BIS in 1981, 1984 (twice) and 1985—Ch. HTCh. Winjammers On The Move, CD, TD (b). Sire: Ch. Yamin van 'T Hof Melyn, BAR; dam: Ch. Winjammers Hi Time Souvenir, CD, BAR. Breeders: Carol Murray, Tom Murray and Pat Morgan; owners: Becky Burgess and Pat Morgan.

1983 and twice in 1986 (back to back)—Am. & Can. Ch. Bonheur Star Treader, CDX, TD (d). Sire: Ch. Elysee de Mont-Cenis, BAR; dam: Kalyn's Zazarac De Bonheur, CD, BAR. Breeders: Faye and Carole Dickens; owner: Natalie S. Rose.

1983 and 1986 (twice)—Ch. Winjammers One For The Road, CDX, TDX (d). Sire: Ch. Yamin van 'T Hof Melyn, BAR; dam: Ch. Winjammers Hi Time Souvenir, CD, BAR. Breeders: Carol Murray, Tom Murray and Pat Morgan; owner: Roberta Whitesides.

1986—Ch. LaBelle's A Liberte (d). Sire: Ch. Nugget de Fauve Charbonne, CDX, TD, C-BAR; dam: Ch. Danseuse D'Elegance. Breeders: June and Debby Fitch; owner: Cheryl J. Hardman.

1987 (back to back)—Am., Can. & Mex. Ch. Crestar's Bon Dieu, Am., Can. & Mex. CD, TT (d). Sire: Ch. Elysee De Mont-Cenis, BAR; dam: Ch. Hossana Du Masque Noir, CD. Breeders: Neale and Becky Steiner; owners: Becky Steiner and Joyce Standish.

1987 and twice in 1988 (also Can. BIS in 1988)—Am. & Can. Ch. Snowflower Skyy Chateau, CDX, Can. CD (d). Sire: Ch. Labelle's A Liberte; dam: Ch. Snowflower Chavon, CD, BAR. Breeder: Carmen Helgesen; owner: Michelle Edling.

1988—Am. & Can. Ch. Sanroyale's Ruff Diamond (d). Sire: Ch. Wysteria's Le Baron, CD, TT; dam: Ch. Kajon's Kashmier of Sanroyale, C-BAR. Breeder: Sallyann Comstock; owners: Frank Morris and Sandra Conner.

1988—Am. & Mex. Ch. Stormin Norman de Sang Bleu (d). Sire: Montre Fou de Sang Bleu; dam: Am. & Mex. Ch. Hilton's Joli Fleur de Lis, CD, C-BAR. Breeders: Greg and Paul Garrity; owner: David Bactzel.

1988—Ch. Snowflower Voila Sharvonne, CD (d). Sire: Ch. LaBelle's A Liberte; dam: Ch. Snowflower Chavon, CD, BAR. Breeder: Carmen Helgesen; owners: Sharon Y. Lutz and Charles M. Rogers, M.D.

1972 photo of Barbara Krohn with Rudy Robinson

Breeder-judge Kay Maves awards a 5-point major to Tacara's Henna Horizon at the Midwest regional Specialty; handler, Tom Traugott.

19

The American Belgian
Tervuren Club

FORMED TO ENSURE THE SURVIVAL of the breed, the
American Belgian Tervuren Club (ABTC) had great purpose from its beginning. It had to prove to the American Kennel Club (AKC) that the breed was
worthy of its status in the Working Group. The efforts of the early breed
supporters have resulted in a true success story, for the breed is now firmly
established and comfortably popular in the United States.

The spirit of supporting this unique and beautiful dog has remained
strong through the years. Today, club membership remains a healthy crosssec-
tion of new pet and show owners, long-established breeders and fanciers and
others involved in a variety of pursuits with their favorite breed.

EARLY CORRESPONDENCE

Early letters tell the story of the club's founding. When the Belgian
Tervuren became registerable as a separate breed in 1958, John Brownell,
assistant to the vice president of the AKC, sent a letter to Bob Krohn in
which he gave general information on the breed and suggestions on forming
a club. Having just helped to convince the AKC not to put the Tervuren in
the Miscellaneous Class and to allow them in the Working Group, Bob
wasted no time in organizing a club. A letter was sent out, dated November
28, 1958:

Dear Tervueren Owner,

The enclosed copy of a letter to me from the AKC will explain the purpose
of this letter to you. I think you will agree that we should start at once to form
a Tervueren Club.

Therefore, I suggest that you let me know at once if you are interested in being
a charter member of such an organization. . . .

So, let's get behind our own "breed" with a lot of enthusiasm. . . . Let's go,
and have both husbands and wives join. When I hear from you, tell me three
people you want on the organization committee at the same time and don't be
bashful about naming yourself.

Bob Krohn

The letter, together with a copy of Brownell's letter, was sent to all known
Tervuren fanciers. You may have noticed the odd spelling of the breed name
in Bob's letter. The name was then spelled "Tervueren," as was the name of
the breed's Belgian birthplace. At the time the new breed did not yet have an
official name in the United States. So another letter from Bob, dated January
4, 1959, read, in part:

Dear Tervueren Supporter,

3. What about breed name? Do you want to
   a. accept the AKC designation—Belgian Tervueren
   b. prefer "Tervueren"
   c. other (you name it)
4. Do you agree to calling the club "Tervueren Club"?

Bob Krohn

A letter sent on February 12, 1959, explains the final choice of the breed
name, and further deals with the name of the club:

To Belgian Tervuren Enthusiasts:

. . . First and foremost, most of you have noticed that the spelling of Tervuren
is changed. One of the "e"s has been left out. The reason is due to the receipt
of a letter last week from Monsieur F. E. Verbanck, Ghent, Belgium. This
gentleman is a judge, long-time breeder of Belgians and accepted authority in
Europe on the Belgian Sheepdog breed. . . . He wrote a very fine letter and I will
quote a part of it. . . .

I have written about the history of the Belgian Sheepdog in the April 1948
issue of *L'ABOI*. . . . I have written about the Tervuren (it is Tervuren now,
since the official name of the borough has been altered).

As for the name of the breed, most persons favored Belgian Tervuren. There
were other suggestions . . . Tervuren Sheepdog, Flemish Stockdog, Belgian
Shepherd, Belgian Police Dog. From Bob's talk with the AKC you have noticed

that certain of these names automatically were eliminated. Therefore, it appears it is settled on the one suggested by the AKC [Belgian Tervuren].

Many of you were entirely neutral as to the Club name. How about keeping it simple? TERVUREN CLUB (The use of the word "Belgian" here might imply to the public that the breed was located in Belgium). . . .

Barbara Krohn

Later that year the group chose the club name, Belgian Tervuren Club. An interesting side note is that the charter members wanted to be sure that Canadians could join, so they left out the word "American," which they felt might give the impression of meaning the United States only. Years later it became necessary to *add* "American" to our club name in preparation for AKC recognition and approval to hold AKC-sanctioned A matches and, ultimately, Specialty shows.

Thus the Belgian Tervuren Club (BTC) and its breed was officially named, and, on January 1, 1960, listed the following charter members: Riccardo Alvino (San Francisco), C. W. Bliss (Cleveland), Edward Charron (Taftville, Connecticut), John and Anne Harris (Scottsdale, Arizona), Donald and Mollie Hudson (Victoria, British Columbia), Robert and Barbara Krohn (Los Alamos, New Mexico), Dr. Arthur Lietze (Corvallis, Oregon) and William and Opal McGee (Temperance, Michigan).

The BTC held its first election in 1960. Donald Hudson was the candidate for president for the 1960–1961 year but withdrew midway in the election process as he felt it would not be appropriate for a Canadian to serve as president. So Bob Krohn, who had previously declined to serve because his wife was a candidate for secretary-treasurer, reluctantly stepped into the presidency.

TODAY'S MEMBERSHIP

The club has experienced a slow but healthy growth since those early times, with the roster showing 715 active voting members for the 1988–1989 club year, with an additional fifty nonmembers subscribing to the *TNT* newsletter. The club has advanced from holding its first sanctioned matches for the breed, to today's independent AKC-licensed specialty shows, which usually include obedience, tracking and herding trial events.

This growth and development has been directly related to the efforts and enthusiasm of the club's membership—not only its officers and directors, but most certainly many selfless and dedicated committee workers. The number of active committees is impressive for a club of this size, and their work has resulted in many benefits for the breed.

Sweepstakes judge Nancie Mages awards win to Symon's Treasure Dixxi.

Am & Can Ch. Logjam Pajta's Ember, Am & Can CDX, is the first Tervuren to have won five consecutive Selects at ABTC National Specialties. Owned and handled by Bill and Barbara Mair; breeder: John A. McClintock.

CLUB ACTIVITIES

Select Designation at Specialties

Early in the 1980s the club introduced the award of "Select," a ribbon that can be given by its National Specialty breed judge to any Tervuren in the Specials Class that the judge believes to be of exceptional quality. This has made the Specialty shows very popular, with a large number of champion entries and top-notch competition. The Select award is highly valued by its winners and respected by all.

Archives

The club has an excellent archives of photographs and historical documents about dogs past and present. Photo albums and presentations are available at Specialty shows and other important events.

Education

The board has given strong support to providing education on the breed to its membership, judges and the general public. It was one of the first clubs to assist the AKC in their production of breed-specific slide shows and videos. In addition to holding regularly scheduled educational judges' seminars, the club's education committee published an illustrated guide for breed judges in 1983. Then, in 1987, it won the prestigious Dog Writer's Association of America award for the best breed club publication of the year for its booklet, *Your New Belgian Tervuren.* The club also sees that the *AKC Gazette* and *Dog World* are provided with monthly columnists writing on the breed.

Breed Records

The ABTC is proud of its dogs and its history, and keeps meticulous records. A pedigree custodian attempts to keep a pedigree on every Tervuren in the United States, and the club has made many Tervuren pedigrees available through publication of its genealogy books. Show and obedience records kept by club members were utilized in the statistics presented in Appendix B of this book.

Breed Health and Welfare

The club appoints health committees that actively study health concerns in the breed, such as seizures and eye problems, and supports related research projects conducted by major university veterinary schools. It has long maintained a hip dysplasia control program. All owners are encouraged to have

Gracing the cover of the *American Kennel Gazette* in 1962: Ch. Jasmine De Cledeville, BAR, and Ch. Imp Rouge De Fauve Charbonne, CD

1982 *American Kennel Gazette* cover features Ch. Ovation De Chateau Blanc

1965 *American Kennel Gazette* cover features Chs. Flair, C-BAR, and Kandice de Fauve Charbonne, CDX, BAR.

Judge Robert Krohn presents award to Vanguard de Braise Rouge, CD, in 1974. Owned and handled by Merrelyn Clark.

their dogs' hips X-rayed and evaluated by the Orthopedic Foundation for Animals (OFA) or a certified veterinary radiologist, then submit the reports to the club registry. In fact, the club will not list the hip X-ray status on any Tervuren in its genealogy books unless they are listed in the club registry.

Additionally, the club is active in improving breeder contracts, watching and discouraging the sales of its dogs to pet shops and other retail outlets. It has an active rescue committee that attempts to see that no unwanted Tervuren is left without a chance to have a good home.

Tervuren News Tales

The real lifeblood of the club, and the vehicle most responsible for the steady growth and popularity of the breed, has been the excellent club magazine, *Tervuren News Tales,* generally referred to as *TNT.* Through the *TNT,* members are kept informed of all events and news of the breed and its membership. It began as a ditto newsletter, then graduated to mimeo reproduction. About 1970, editor Donna Allen initiated an annual "pictorial" issue that was professionally printed and included photos. Eventually, the membership felt that each issue should be of the same professional quality and include photos; thus the present *TNT* came to be. The efforts of an informed and enthusiastic membership have made the effort and expense worthwhile. Editing the magazine and meeting deadlines are monumental tasks, and with deep appreciation we list its editors:

EDITORS OF *TERVUREN NEWS TALES (TNT)*

March 1960–August 1965	Barbara Krohn
October 1965–October 1975	Donna Allen
November 1975–June 1978	Adrienne Pagel
July 1978–February 1980	Sandy Hoffman
March 1980–Winter 1982	Diane Webb
Spring 1983–February 1985	Mary Courter
April 1985–June 1985	Becky Steiner
August 1985–November 1986	Toni Zahm
January 1987–present	Helen Hittesdorf

This is but a summary of the many committees and activities of the American Belgian Tervuren Club.

See Appendix A for a historical list of the club's important events, officers and National Specialty event winners.

20

Breeder's Achievement Awards

$\mathbf{F}$AMILIARLY KNOWN AS "BARs," the Breeder's Achievement Awards are the most prestigious in our breed. They honor the dogs and bitches who have made a significant contribution as producers of champion and obedience/tracking titleholders. The C-BAR title recognizes the animals producing enough champion and grandchampion offspring to earn the title. The O-BAR title recognizes the producers of obedience and tracking titleholders. Dogs earning both awards carry the simple but significant title of BAR. These so-called "Double-BAR" dogs have achieved the highest level of accomplishment for Tervuren used for breeding.

The method by which C-BAR and O-BAR points are calculated is too complex to explain here; however, the total number of points required for each award recognizes that a dog's capacity to produce offspring is greater than a bitch's. Thus, a dog must earn one hundred points to receive either award. A bitch must earn fifty points.

Points are awarded without regard to the identity of the breeder, owner or numbers of litters produced. Only the quality of production is honored. It is possible for a bitch to have one or two splendid litters and achieve a BAR award, or for a dog to sire a small number of superior offspring and still earn his BAR.

Today, eighteen dogs and forty-two bitches are C-BARs. One dog and four bitches are O-BAR. The doubly prestigious BAR has been earned by twenty-one dogs and forty-one bitches.

Ch. Jasmine de Cledeville, BAR

```
                        ┌─ Willy de la Garde Noire (T)
              ┌─ D'Jinn du Clos Saint Clair (T)
              │         └─ Youpette du Clos Saint Clair (T)
     ┌─ Eros de Cledeville (T)
     │        │         ┌─ Xylander de la Brigade (T)
     │        └─ Berengere de Cledeville (T)
     │                  └─ Yvraie de Sang Bleu (T)
CH. JASMINE DE CLEDEVILLE BAR (France) whelped 4/12/60, breeder Mme. LeMoro
     │                  ┌─ Tjop de la Brigade (T)
     │        ┌─ Xylander de la Brigade (T)
     │        │         └─ Tosca du Bon Flair (T)
     └─ Berengere de Cledeville (T)
              │         ┌─ Willy (T)
              └─ Yvraie de Sang Bleu (T)
                        └─ Vedette de la Brigade (T)
```

Ch. Yamin van 'T Hof Melyn (Koning) is a Belgian import. Breeder: L. Viaene; owners; Thomas and Katherine Walker.

```
                          Ogam de d'Artamas (G)
                  Quowboy du Long Spinoy (T)
                          Kinnie de la Ferme Termunt (T)
            Tarass de la Pouroffe (T)
                          Pacha de Landas (T)
                  Riquitta du Val des Aubepines (T)
                          Nitta du Val des Aubepines
CH. YAMIN VAN 'T HOF MELYN BAR (Belgium) whelped 1-13-74, breeder L. Viaene
                          Jimmy de l'Assa (T)
                  Kabyl du Clos Saint Clair (T)
                          Iette du Clos Saint Clair (T)
            Vallia de Colla Dona (T)
                          Kactus du Clos Saint Clair (T)
                  Nouchka de la Dune Aux Loups (T)
                          Iris de la Dune Aux Loups (T)
```

211

```
                    Ch. Flair de Fauve Charbonne C-BAR
          Ch. Ami de Chateau Blanc CD
                    Ch. Kandice de Fauve Charbonne CDX BAR
     Ch. Daktary de Chateau Blanc CD BAR
                    Milord des Masques de Sable
          Ch. Ouka du Val d'Orge Bar (France)
                    Magda du Val d'Orge
CH. SCORPIO DE FAUVE CHARBONNE CD TD BAR
and CH. SATIN DE FAUVE CHARBONNE CDX BAR    (littermates), whelped 11/2/69
                    Ch. Dandy du Clos Saint Jacques BAR (France)
          D'Artagnone du Falaise BAR (Canada)
                    Nightwatch Russet Rondo
     Ch. Mystique de Fauve Charbonne CD BAR
                    Eros de Cledeville
          Ch. Jasmine de Cledeville BAR (France)
                    Berengere de Cledeville
```

Pedigrees of Ch. Scorpio de Fauve Charbonne, CD, TD, and Ch. Satin de Fauve Charbonne, CDX

BAR points are updated perpetually, allowing the ABTC to identify and track Tervuren whose achievements as breeding animals have placed them at the top of the point list. Their records can be staggering. It is not unusual for dogs of either sex to accrue far more than the number of minimum required points for a title. Some have doubled, tripled and even quadrupled the minimum point requirements.

THE TOP PRODUCERS

A complete listing of BAR titlists can be found in Appendix B of this book. A small handful of dogs should be mentioned here, however, to recognize their outstanding achievements. Because points can be extremely close between dogs, and ratings can change with each new issue of the AKC's *Awards* magazine, their names are presented in alphabetical order and not in order of total points earned. The following BAR dogs have earned more than two hundred C-BAR points *and* more than two hundred O-BAR points:

Ch. Bonheur's D'Artagnon, UDT
Ch. Hi Times Kanook of Crocs Blanc, CD
Ch. Scorpio de Fauve Charbonne, CD, TD
Ch. Yamin van 'T Hof Melyn

The following BAR bitches have earned more than one hundred C-BAR points *and* more than one hundred O-BAR points:

Bonheur's Bobbins and Pins
Ch. Brillance de Mont-Cenis, CDX
Ch. Jasmine de Cledeville
Kalyn's Zazarac de Bonheur
Ch. Mystique de Fauve Charbonne
Ch. Rob-Lyn's Ange Acajou
Ch. Sabrina de Flambeau Rouge
Ch. Satin de Fauve Charbonne, CDX
Ch. Tanzy de Landas, UDT
Ch. Winjammers Hi Time Souvenir, CD
Ch. StarBright Bouquetiere, CD, TD

Most of the top producers were owned by major kennels, and the reader will find their achievements detailed elsewhere. However, two mentioned only in passing are entitled here to the tributes they deserve.

Ch. Yamin van 'T Hof Melyn

Koning, as he is called, came to the United States from Belgium in the 1970s with his owners Vice Admiral Thomas and Frances Walker. Already a dog "recommended for breeding" in his native country when he arrived

Ch. Rob-Lyn's Ange Acajou, CD, BAR, with Bernadine Paull, shown winning the Brood Bitch class at the ABTC 1976 National Specialty with her three Best in Show sons: Ch. Crocs Blanc's Diable O'Hi Time, C-BAR, with John McClintock; Ch. Rajah D'Antre du Louve, CD, BAR, with Sallyann Comstock; and Ch. Hi Time's Kanook of Crocs Blanc, CD, BAR, with Judith Lee Smith. All dogs were owner-handled.

Ch. Lancer de Chateau Blanc, BAR, combined many excellent early bloodlines and was an influential stud during the 1970s.

here, his beauty and value to American breeding efforts were recognized at once.

Although his owners regard him primarily as a beloved companion, Koning's influence on American Tervuren has been profound, literally changing the attitude of many breeders toward type and style. He has produced thirty-five American champions and more than one hundred grandchampion offspring, a record that is all the more remarkable if one considers that he did not begin to be used here until he was a fully mature dog. Koning has nearly four hundred C-BAR points and more than three hundred O-BAR points, and may well become the top male producer of all time.

Ch. Rob-Lyn's Ange Acajou, CD

Misha, as she is known, was bred by Dorothy Hollister and Brenda Leedy and owned first by Connie Wentling and Brenda. Later, Bernadine Paull (Hi Times) became a third co-owner.

Although she cannot boast the most direct champion offspring (she has seventeen), Misha has ninety-six champion grandoffspring and is the top-producing conformation bitch of all time, with more than 275 C-BAR points. She also is the only bitch to be credited with three Best in Show offspring: Ch. Hi Times Kanook of Crocs Blanc, CD, Ch. Crocs Blancs Diablo O'Hi Time and Ch. Rajah d'Antre du Louve, CD. (Misha's pedigree appears as dam of Kanook, elsewhere.)

Although many other dogs have contributed to the future of American Tervuren and new influences are felt regularly, the dogs recognized in the preceding paragraphs have left their indelible mark. They have set us on our way, and their names must never be forgotten.

THE POWER OF BAR

Every dog in the two charts that follow has earned both the C-BAR and O-BAR awards. Moreover, each is a *direct* offspring of the dog preceding it, thus affirming the remark that BAR begets BAR. The charts also demonstrate the influence of Ch. Dandy du Clos Saint Jacques and Ch. Jasmine de Clede-ville on the history of American Tervuren.

A closer examination of the descendants of these dogs will reveal many other dogs that have earned their C-BAR or O-BAR awards; however, these charts dramatize the linkages of dogs who have won both.

To simplify the diagram, championship and obedience are omitted.

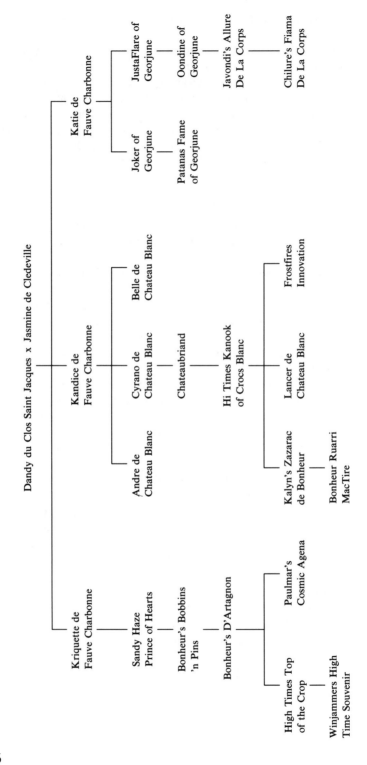

Dandy du Clos Saint Jacques x Jasmine de Cledeville

Kriquette de
Fauve Charbonne

Sandy Haze
Prince of Hearts

Bonheur's Bobbins
'n Pins

Bonheur's D'Artagnon

Paulmar's
Cosmic Agena

High Times Top
of the Crop

Winjammers High
Time Souvenir

Kandice de
Fauve Charbonne

Andre de
Chateau Blanc

Cyrano de
Chateau Blanc

Belle de
Chateau Blanc

Chateaubriand

Hi Times Kanook
of Crocs Blanc

Lancer de
Chateau Blanc

Frostfires
Innovation

Kalyn's Zazarac
de Bonheur

Bonheur Ruarri
MacTire

Katie de
Fauve Charbonne

Joker of
Georjune

Patanas Fame
of Georjune

JustaFlare of
Georjune

Oondine of
Georjune

Javondi's Allure
De La Corps

Chilure's Fiama
De La Corps

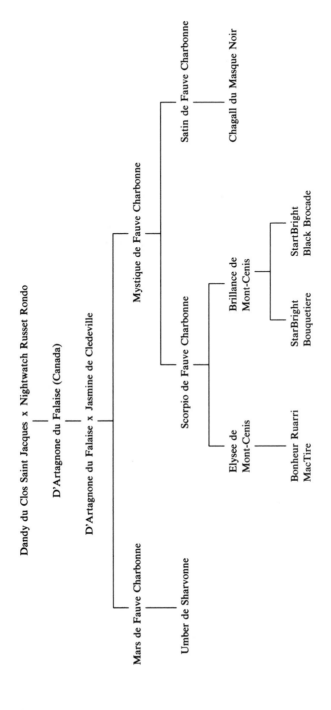

Dandy du Clos Saint Jacques x Nightwatch Russet Rondo

D'Artagnone du Falaise (Canada)

D'Artagnone du Falaise x Jasmine de Cledeville

Mystique de Fauve Charbonne

Satin de Fauve Charbonne

Chagall du Masque Noir

Scorpio de Fauve Charbonne

Brillance de Mont-Cenis

StartBright Black Brocade

StarBright Bouquetiere

Elysee de Mont-Cenis

Bonheur Ruarri MacTire

Mars de Fauve Charbonne

Umber de Sharvonne

Appendix A
ABTC History

The following is a list of important events for the American Belgian Tervuren Club, a chronology of its officers and a list of the winners at ABTC National Specialty events.

Chronological Dates of Important Events for the ABTC

1961: First Supported show, held at International Kennel Club of Chicago, with an entry of thirteen (6 dogs, 5 bitches, 2 specials)

Qualifying sanctioned matches held prior to holding of first licensed Specialty point show (B = B match breed, OB = B match obedience; A/OA = sanctioned A matches):

4-20-1963	Glen Ellyn, Illinois (B)
5-3-1964	Warrenville, Illinois (B)
4-24-1965	Hillside, Illinois (B)
4-16-1966	Hillside, Illinois (B)—20 entries, 1 absent
6-10-1967	Akron, Ohio (B-OB)—7 dogs, 10 bitches, 11 obedience
4-5-1968	Hutchinson, Kansas (B-OB)
6-7-1969	Akron, Ohio (B-OB)—9 dogs, 10 bitches, 10 obedience
4-1-1970	Club changed its name to American Belgian Tervuren Club

6-5-1970	Canfield, Ohio (A-OA)—9 dogs, 22 bitches, 9 obedience
8-2-1970	Southfield, Michigan (B-OB)—10 dogs, 13 bitches, 6 obedience
12-6-1970	Westland, Michigan (A-OA)—16 dogs, 19 bitches, 8 obedience
11-20-1971	Los Gatos, California (A-OA)—7 dogs, 10 bitches, 4 obedience
4-22-1972	First Licensed ABTC Specialty show: Old Dominion Kennel Club of Northern Virginia—17 dogs, 22 bitches, 16 specials (9 dogs, 7 bitches)
6-11-1978	First independent Specialty show, Ann Arbor, Michigan—49 obedience, 159 breed (49 dogs, 51 bitches, 48 specials, 8 stud, 2 brood, 51 sweepstakes)
12-9-1980	ABTC becomes a member club of the American Kennel Club
5-27-1983	First tracking test held by club for Tervuren at its Specialty in Brighton, Colorado (6 dogs)
1985	ABTC holds first herding trial in conjunction with National Specialty show, Sacramento, California.

ABTC Club Officers

1960–1961
P.: Robert Krohn
V.P.: Opal McGee
Secy.-Treas.: Barbara Krohn

1961–1962
P.: John L. Harris
V.P.: Opal McGee
Secy.-Treas.: Barbara Krohn

1962–1963
P.: Cliff Hawkinson
V.P.: Opal McGee
Secy.-Treas.: Barbara Krohn

1963–1964
P.: Cliff Hawkinson
V.P.: Dale Potter
Secy.-Treas.: Barbara Krohn

1964–1965
P.: Rev. T. E. Badger
V.P.: John L. Harris
Secy.-Treas.: David E. Liska

1965–1966
P.: Edeltraud Laurin
V.P.: George McElhany
Secy.-Treas.: Donna Allen

1966–1967
P.: Edeltraud Laurin
V.P.: Faye Dickens
Secy.-Treas.: Donna Allen

1967–1968
P.: Gene Garrett
V.P.: Mariette Francillon
Secy.-Treas.: Donna Allen

1968–1969
P.: Jim Davis
V.P.: Donald Baxter
Secy.-Treas.: Donna Allen

1969–1970
P.: Jack Allen
V.P.: Bill Kennedy
Secy.-Treas.: Karen Johnson

1970–1971
    P.: Jack Allen
    V.P.: Kay Maves
    Secy.-Treas.: Karen Johnson

1971–1972
    P.: Robert Smid
    V.P.: Kay Maves
    Secy.: Nancie Mages
    Treas.: Karen Johnson

1972–1973
    P.: Robert Smid
    V.P.: Faye Dickens
    Secy.: Nancie Mages
    Treas.: Leslie Earl

1973–1974
    P.: Robert Smid
    V.P.: Faye Dickens
    Secy.: Joyce McHenry
    Treas.: Leslie Earl

1974–1975
    P.: Robert Farkas
    V.P.: Nancie Mages
    Secy.: Joyce McHenry
    Treas.: JoAnne DeFrane

1975–1976
    P.: Robert Farkas
    V.P.: Robert VanderCook
    Secy.: Eileen Michals
    Treas.: JoAnne DeFrane

1976–1977
    P.: Nancie Mages
    V.P.: Donna Allen
    Secy.: Eileen Michals
    Treas.: Lee Slorah

1977–1978
    P.: Ken Wilson
    V.P.: Sharon Redmer
    Secy.: Pat Taylor
    Treas.: Lee Slorah

1978–1979
    P.: Jack Gilbert
    V.P.: Donna Allen
    Secy.: Dana Plaskowitz Mackonis
    Treas.: Lee Slorah

1979–1980
    P.: Jack Gilbert
    V.P.: Sharon Redmer
    Secy.: Dana Plaskowitz
    Treas.: Lee Slorah

1980–1981
    P.: Sharon Redmer
    V.P.: Becky Steiner
    Secy.: Karen Johnson
    Treas.: Judith Lee Smith

1981–1982
    P.: Sharon Redmer
    V.P.: Libby Lewitt
    Secy.: Karen Johnson
    Treas.: Joyce McHenry
    AKC Del.: Robert Krohn

1982–1983
    P.: Becky Steiner
    V.P.: Libby Lewitt
    Secy.: Janina Laurin
    Treas.: Jim Jones
    AKC Del.: Robert Krohn

1983–1984
    P.: Becky Steiner
    V.P.: Violette Wilson
    Secy.: Janina Laurin
    Treas.: Jim Jones
    AKC Del.: Robert Smid

1984–1985
    P.: Becky Steiner
    V.P.: Violette Wilson
    Secy.: Eileen Hudak
    Treas.: James Jones
    AKC Del.: Robert Smid

1985–1986
    P.: Janina Laurin
    V.P.: Dana Mackonis
    Secy.: Eileen Hudak
    Treas.: Helen Hammel Hittesdorf
    AKC Del.: Sharon Redmer

1986–1987
    P.: Janina Laurin
    V.P.: Dana Mackonis
    Secy.: Eileen Hudak
    Treas.: Helen Hittesdorf
    AKC Del.: Sharon Redmer

1987–1988
    P.: Janina Laurin
    V.P.: Lee Slorah
    Recording Secy.: Eileen Hudak
    Corres. Secy.: Randie Meyer
    Treas.: Helen Hittesdorf
    AKC Del.: Sharon Redmer

1988–1989 and 1989–1990
    P.: Janina Laurin
    V.P.: Lee Slorah
    Recording Secy.: Eileen Hudak
    Corres. Secy.: P. J. Laursen
    Treas.: Bill Mair
    AKC Del.: Sharon Redmer

ABTC Annual Best of Opposite Sex Winners

The Best of Breed winners are featured in a special pictorial section of this book. The list and information on the BOS winners is provided here (d=dog, b=bitch, s=sire, d=dam, br=breeder, o=owner):

1961　Ch. Fidelite de Fauve Charbonne, CD (b)
    s: Ch. D'Jimmy du Clos Saint Clair, CD   d: Chrysis du Clos Saint Jacques, CD   br: B. Krohn   o: Dorothy B. Hollister

1962　Ch. D'Jimmy du Clos Saint Clair, CD (d)
    s: Boy de L'Athenes du Nord   d: Xala du Clos Saint Clair   br: G. Fontaine   o: Dorothy Hollister

1963　Ch. Nightwatch Tawny Theresa (b)
    s: Ch. Dandy du Clos St. Jacques, BAR   d: Nightwatch Charm (Groenendael)   br: M. Glover   o: Dorothy Hollister

1964　Ch. Charme du Val de Tonnerre, CD (b)
    s: Ch. Kis Tam's Candide Pataud, CD, BAR   d: Ch. Nightwatch Tawny Theresa   br: D. Hollister   o: Jack Allen and Donna Allen

1965　Maylene du Garde Roux (b)
    s: Ch. Kenny de Cledeville, CD, BAR   d: Ch. Kis Tam's Renee, CD, TD, C-BAR   br: L. Hawkinson   o: P. Dodl

1966　Ch. Thistle Candide (b)
    s: Ch. Jory Candide   d: Hiarka du Clos Saint Clair   br: B. Robinson   o: Wm. and Opal McGee

1967　Ch. Monsieur Prince du Garde Roux, CD (d)
    s: Ch. Kenny de Cledeville, CD, BAR   d: Ch. Kis Tam's Renee, CD, TD, C-BAR   br-o: Lou Hawkinson

1968   Ch. Wayfarer's Placide, CD (b)
s: Ch. Columbine Nikit, BAR   d: Wayfarer's Nadia du Rochemont,
CD   br-o: Sondra and Jay Miller

1969   Javondis Allure De La Corps, UDT, BAR (b)
s: Ch. Javelin of Georjune, UD   d: Ch. Oondine of Georjune, UD,
BAR   br-o: Linda Franklin

1970   Ch. Qandi de Petite Chalet, CD (b)
s: Ch. Mars de Fauve Charbonne, UDT, BAR   d: Ch. Orellana de
Braise Ardente, CD, BAR   br: Davis and Harvey   o: Pauline
McClintock and Carol Schnur

1971   Ch. Regina's Echo de Bonheur, CD, BAR (b)
and   s: Ch. Teddy Edouard Ours Val du Echo   d: Renee de Noir et
1972   Or   br: P and S. Festa   o: Violette and Corrine Wilson

1973   Ch. Satin de Fauve Charbonne, CDX, BAR (b)
s: Ch. Daktary de Chateau Blanc, CD, BAR   d: Ch. Mystique de
Fauve Charbonne, CD, BAR   br: B. Krohn   o: Lynn Marie and
Luther E. Sturtevant

1974   Ch. Ebony de Chateau Blanc, UDT (b)
s: Ch. Columbine Nikit, BAR   d: Ch. Kandice de Fauve Charbonne, CDX, BAR   br: E. Laurin   o: Joan Glover

1975   Ch. Hi Times Sweet Polly Purebred, CD, C-BAR (b)
and   s: Ch. Bonheur's D'Artagnan, UDT, BAR   d: Ch. Leistraum's Au-
1976   burn   br: P. and B. Reckenbeil   o: Marjorie M. Schubert

1977   Ch. Frost Fire's Ipso Facto, C-BAR (b)
s: Ch. Hi Times Kanook of Crocs Blanc, CD, BAR   d: Ch. Sabrina
de Flambeau Rouge, CD, BAR   br-o: Judith Lee Smith

1978   Ch. Ovation de Chateau Blanc, CD (d)
s: Ch. Lancer de Chateau Blanc, BAR   d: Ch. Douceur du Vent de
Bayville, CD, C-BAR   br-o: Edeltraud Laurin

1979   Ch. Whirlwind's Amber of Frostfire, CD, TD, BAR (b)
and   s: Ch. Frost Fires Jasper of Bobkat, CDX   d: Ch. Frost Fires Cher
1981   O'Vedette Noir, C-BAR   br: S. Kiley and J. L. Smith   o: Steve
Sorenson

1980   Ch. Pinkcliffs Lukyna of Hi Times, CD (b)
s: Ch. Hi Times Jem O'Crocs Blancs, CD   d: Pinkcliffs Bari de
Fleuryda   br: P. Johnson and B. Paull   o: Donna Cole and Cary
Rothstein

1982   Ch. Winjammer's Prime Time, CD, TD (d)
s: Ch. Bonheur's D'Artagnan, UDT, BAR   d: Winjammer's I'ma
Hi Timer, CDX, O-BAR   br: W. Brewer and P. Morgan   o:
Chris Rebescher

1983   Ch. Fox Hollow's Lothlorien (b)
and   s: Ch. Corsairs Beaujangles   d: Ch. Hi Times Take Over,
1984   CDX   br: M. Marquez   o: Debby Boehm and Margie Marquez

1985   Ch. Corsairs Beaujangles (d)
s: Ch. Achates Esprit de Joie, CD, C-BAR   d: Ch. Debonair Debra
De Vedette Noir, CD, C-BAR   br-o: Steve Sorenson

1986   Ch. Frostfire's Hallelujah (b)
s: Ch. Lancer de Chateau Blanc, BAR   d: Ch. Sabrina de Flambeau
Rouge, CD, BAR   br-o: Judith Lee Smith

1987   Ch. Daradans Liten Brun Nalle (b)
s: Ch. Frost Fires Jasper of Bobkat, CDX   d: Charlyn du Chalet
Belgique, CD, C-BAR   br: D. and D. Wilcox and C. Siefert   o:
Debra Schmidt

1988   Ch. HTCh. Winjammers on the Move, CD, TD (b)
s: Ch. Yamin van'T Hof Melyn, BAR   d: Ch. Winjammers Hi Time
Souvenir, CD, BAR   br: C. Murray, T. Murray and P. Morgan   o: Becky Burgess and Pat Morgan

ABTC Annual National Sweepstakes Winners

Classes are held at annual Specialty shows for Tervuren six to eighteen months of age. The first annual Sweepstakes was held in conjunction with the 1978 National Specialty show. Listed are the Best in Sweeps, sex (d=dog, b=bitch), owner, followed by the BOS winner and owner:

1978   Whirlwind's Amber of Frostfire, (b), Sorenson
HiTimes Liver Lover, Morgan/Murray

1979   Ch. StarBright Black Brocade, (b), Deckert
Our Valiant du Sanroyale, Comstock

1980   Up Tempo Enchantress, (b), Foy
(BOS not offered)

1981   Corsair's Calypso Beat, (b), Sorenson/George
Ajamais Antares, Faldmo/Crawford

1982   Liberte's La Belle Amie, (b), Hardman
Frostfire's Jamaica Twister, Smith

1983 Corsair's Gigolo, (d), Sorenson/Hittesdorf
     Atalanta's Dulcimer Windsong, Schubert/Durst

1984 Sandyhill's Zette de Loup Noir, (b), Thal
     Winjammers Sequel, Morlan

1985 Fox Hollow's Black Hawk, (d), Donovan
     Tacara's Galileah Go Frostfire, Newsome

1986 Coda's Roadside Escapade, (d), Whitesides
     StarBright Effervescence, Redmer

1987 Symon's Treasure Dixxi, (b), Symons
     Tacara's Esoteric Epris, Willig

1988 Tacara's Czarka de Epris, (d), Newsome
     Liberte's Head of the Class, Cawell

ABTC National Specialty High in Trial Winners

The showing class entered is at right (NB = Novice B, OA = Open A, OB = Open B, UT = Utility).

Year	Winner	Class
1978	Uptempos Afternoon Delight, CD (Laursen)	NB
1979	Dusty of Sierra Shadows, CD (Scott)	NB
1980	Ch. Hi Time's Exact Combination, CDX (Wisner)	OB
1981	Ch. Bronze Bell's Golden Flame, CD (Young)	OA
1982	Gambiama's Kyla De La Corps, CD (Coen)	NB
1983	Ch. OTCH Fern Hill Act One, TD (Handler)	UT
1984	Foor Footed Nomad of Chato, CDX (Laursen)	OB
1985	OTCH Brandiwyne's Snooky Bear (McGrath)	OB
1986	Ch. Carousel's Pied Piper, CDX (Janek)	OB
1987	Bilgay Spindrifter, CD (Johnson)	OA
1988	Ch. StarBright Enchanter, (Ledbetter/Redmer)	NB

ABTC National Specialty Herding High in Trial Winners

1985 (1st Open)—Ch. HTCh. Chilure's Fiama De La Corps, UDT, SCH.I (Linda Franklin)

1986 (1st Open)—Ch. HTCh. Ochiama's Luciana De La Corps, CDX, SCH.I, AD (Linda Franklin)

1987 (1st Open—Ducks)—Ch. HTCh. Chilure's Fiama De La Corps, UDT, SCH.I, AD (Linda Franklin)

1988 (1st Open—Sheep)—Ch. HTCh. Ochiama's Luciana De La Corps, CDX, AD, SCH.I, OTDsd (Linda Franklin)

Appendix B

BELGIAN TERVUREN STATISTICS AND TITLEHOLDERS

REGISTRATION STATISTICS

Year	No. Tervuren Registered with AKC	Rank, All Breeds	No. of Breeds
1959	26	98	106
1960	8	103	109
1961	20	100	111
1962	21	100	115
1963	46	94	115
1964	69	93	115
1965	103	91	115
1966	117	91	115
1967	141	92	115
1968	195	92	115
1969	191	90	116
1970	253	90	116
1971	319	88	116
1972	358	84	118
1973	357	88	120
1974	467	82	121
1975	397	85	121
1976	430	85	122
1977	397	85	122

Year	No. Tervuren Registered with AKC	Rank, All Breeds	No. of Breeds
1978	445	84	123
1979	452	83	124
1980	422	85	125
1981	405	87	125
1982	446	85	125
1983	501	88	128
1984	422	87	128
1985	500	86	129
1986	457	87	129
1987	539	88	130
1988	499	87	130

BREED, OBEDIENCE AND TRACKING STATISTICS

Year	Champions	CD	CDX	UD	TD	TDX	OTCH	Best in Show	High in Trial	Shows W/ Entries	Majors
1959						—	—		NA	7	0
1960	2	1				—	—		NA	40	7
1961	0	2				—	—		NA	31	4
1962	5	1				—	—		NA	52	9
1963	6	3	1			—	—		NA	82	20
1964	11	6	2	1		—	—		NA	83	23
1965	11	13	2	1		—	—		NA	133	43
1966	22	20	4	2	2	—	—		NA	185	57
1967	24	10	3	1	1	—	—		NA	183	39
1968	24	13	5	2	0	—	—		NA	245	60
1969	29	26	0	1	1	—	—		NA	287	76
1970	37	30	9	3	3	—	—		NA	307	97
1971	34	39	3	3	3	—	—	1	NA	NA	
1972	45	33	12	0	2	—	—	2	NA	NA	
1973	57	41	13	5	2	—	—	1	NA	NA	
1974	66	54	14	6	5	—	—	1	NA	NA	
1975	43	38	11	2	8	—	—	2	12	NA	
1976	73	63	18	8	10	—	—	1	17	NA	
1977	90	81	12	5	9	—	—	0	15	NA	
1978	79	66	17	9	7	—	0	1	16	NA	
1979	74	69	26	4	12	—	4	0	16	NA	
1980	86	84	24	6	13	0	0	1	16	NA	
1981	94	91	33	12	17	3	0	0	24	NA	
1982	96	81	35	7	15	3	2	9	18	NA	
1983	122	106	26	13	16	1	3	13	32	NA	
1984	104	96	24	9	8	6	2	3	34	NA	
1985	129	103	28	11	19	0	0	1	19	NA	
1986	105	116	25	8	18	0	0	4	18	NA	
1987	132	98	33	7	17	3	2	3	30	NA	
1988	92	93	29	9	24	7	1	5	20	NA	

Note: The TDX degree was not offered until 1980. The OTCH degree was not offered until 1977. NA=records not available.

227

CH/UDT TITLEHOLDERS

*"A well balanced Tervuren has a Ch. at one end
and a UDT at the other"* (Club motto)

	Year	Name of Dog	Sex	Owner(s)
1.	1967	Ch. Mars De Fauve Charbonne, UDT, BAR	m	Allen
2.	1973	Ch. Ebony De Chateau Blanc, UDT	f	Glover
3.	1974	Ch. Tanzy De Landas, UDT, BAR	f	Paull
4.	1974	Ch. Javondi's Allure De La Corps, UDT, BAR	f	Franklin
5.	1974	Ch. U R Reynard The Fox of Valkyra, UDT	m	Treanor
6.	1974	Ch. Bonheur's D'Artagnan, UDT, BAR	m	Paull
7.	1974	Ch. Hi Time's Let It Be De La Corps, UDT, O-BAR	m	Franklin
8.	1976	Ch. Kalyns Whiskey Sour, UDT	m	Dalton
9.	1977	Ch. Walendales Titan Mist, UDT	f	Farkas
10.	1977	Ch. Chimina's Etiene De La Corps, UDTX	m	Franklin
11.	1977	Ch. Chimina's Exquisite Lil Faun, UDT	f	Powers
12.	1978	Ch. OTCH Hi Time's Tops With Theo, TD	m	Treanor
13.	1978	Ch. Grenoble De L'Elite, UDT	m	Van der Cook
14.	1978	Ch. Xquisite De Braise Rouge, UDT	f	Handler
15.	1978	Ch. Hi Time's Top of The Crop, UDT, BAR	f	Morgan, Paull, Grizzle

	Year	Name of Dog	Sex	Owner(s)
16.	1978	Ch. Hi Times Tough Guy, UDT	m	Herman
17.	1979	Ch. Hi Time's Erica De Crocs Blanc, UDT	f	Eckelman
18.	1980	Ch. OTCH Fern Hill Act One, TD	m	Handler
19.	1980	Ch. OTCH Liberte's Elixir O'Carousel, TD	m	Schaal
20.	1980	Ch. Chilure's Fiama De La Corps, UDT, BAR	f	Franklin
21.	1981	Ch. Theriots La Fee, UDT	f	Theriot
22.	1981	Ch. Outlaw De Chateau Blanc, UDT	m	Mahaffey, DVM
23.	1981	Ch. Sunshine's Antares O'Kajon, UDT	m	Whitesides
24.	1981	Ch. Commander's Agamemmon, UDT	m	Horstman and Jett
25.	1981	Ch. Fern Hill Knave De Sharvonne, UDT	m	Hittesdorf
26.	1983	Ch. Theriots The Riot, UDT	f	Theriot
27.	1983	Ch. StarBright Bacho Noir, UDTX	f	Foley
28.	1983	Ch. Hi Time T'Regan De Aurora Reve, UDT	f	Liggett
29.	1984	Ch. High Times All Ready Rima, UDT	f	Cole and Rothstein
30.	1984	Ch. Bonheurs Perin De Kalyn, UDT	m	Millner
31.	1984	Ch. Chantilly Esprit De Joie, UDT, BAR	f	Hittesdorf
32.	1985	Ch. Eclipse Esprit De Joie, UDT	m	Scott
33.	1985	Ch. Drifter Esprit De Joie, UDT	m	Eckelman
34.	1985	Ch. Locknor A RePeter, UDT	m	Treanor

	Year	Name of Dog	Sex	Owner(s)
35.	1985	Ch. Bilgay's Hi Times Nutmeg, UDT	f	Cooper
36.	1985	Ch. Hamadryade De Mont-Cenis, UDT	f	Manor Jr.
37.	1986	Ch. StarBright Cisco Kid, UDTX	m	Schultz
38.	1986	Ch. Sanroyals Yves Du Sabre, UDT	m	Wood, MD
39.	1987	Ch. HTCh. Theriots The Brat, UDT	f	Theriot
40.	1987	Ch. Jamaica Nemesis, UDTX	f	Hittesdorf
41.	1987	Ch. Snowflower Brady O'Liberte, UDTX	m	Schaal
42.	1987	Ch. UpTempo Haarve V Einem, UDT	m	MacManus
43.	1988	Ch. StarBright Champignon, UDTX	f	Foley and Blankley
44.	1989	Ch. HTCh. Ochiama's Luciana De La Corps, UDT	f	Franklin

OBEDIENCE TRIAL CHAMPIONS

Date Finished	Name of Dog	Sex	Owner
4-04-1979	Ch. Hi Times Tops With Theo, TD	m	Treanor
4-29-1979	Ch. Folie des Rogues Rouges	m	Brown
8-05-1979	Ch. Robiel Briget Fille de Ultra	f	Thompson
9-23-1979	Ch. Libertes Elixir O'Carousel	m	Schaal
10-17-1982	Brandiwynes Lady Mystique	f	McGrath
11-19-1982	Ch. Fern Hill Act One, TD	m	Handler
5-07-1983	Cin Lis A'Salem of Sandyhills	m	Hill
10-30-1983	Gabiama's Krista De La Corps, TD	f	Strong
11-13-1983	Brandiwynes Snooky Bear	m	McGrath
5-12-1984	Dusty of Sierra Shadows, TDX	f	Scott
9-23-1984	Hi Times Country Summer	f	Noble and Paull
3-01-1987	Ochiama's Legend De La Corps	m	Allen
7-26-1987	Cavalier's Tokay Kalee, TD	f	Harnedy
11-1988	Gabiama's Kaiser De La Corps	m	Janek

TDX TITLEHOLDERS

Year	Name of Dog	Sex	Owner
1981	Ch. Chimina's Etiene de la Corps, UDT	m	Franklin
1981	Ch. Winjammers One For The Road, CDX	m	Whitesides
1981	Ch. Starbright Bacho Noir, UDT	f	Foley
1982	Ch. Commander Foxfire of Glenoak, CDX	f	McHenry
1982	Ch. Starbright Champignon, UD	f	Foley and Blankley
1982	Ch. Ceejay's Adios Amigo, CDX	m	Rounsaville
1983	Ch. Maplewood Ezekiel O'Glenoak, CD	m	Rounsaville
1984	Ch. Starbright Cisco Kid, UDT	m	Schultz
1984	Ch. Corsair's Escapade	m	Whitesides and Behrens
1984	Ch. Yessit C'Est Tout	m	Deckert and Barlow
1984	Glenoak's Driftin' by Maplewood, CDX	m	Davis and McHenry
1984	Petit Chalet's Show'N'Go	m	Rounsaville and Wellman
1984	Snowflower Indian Paintbrush, UDT	f	Harris
1987	Crestar's Dione Til Dusk, CDX	f	Biggins and Steiner
1987	Liberte Fait De Purlaine, CDX	m	Koukkari
1987	Ch. Jamaica Nemesis, UDT	f	Hittesdorf
1988	Ch. Artful Dodger of Anduin	m	Simonsen
1988	Ch. A-Astra StarBright Folly, CD	f	Foley and Blankley
1988	OTCh Dusty of Sierra Shadows	f	Scott
1988	Ch. Cramoisi Chenil D'Chardonney, CD	m	Kirk and Beeler
1988	Ch. Snowflower Brady O'Liberte, UDT	m	Schaal
1988	HTCh. Winjammers Tuff Act Too, CD	m	VanEseltine
1988	Ch. Liberte's High Noon	m	Schaal

ABTC HERDING TRIAL CHAMPIONS

Date	Name of Dog	Sex	Owner
1-15-84	Am. Can. Ch. Hi Times Top of the Crop, Am. Can. UDT, BAR, OTDds, STDc	f	Morgan
5-29-84	Am. Can. Ch. Winjammers On The Rise, CDX, Can. CD, OTDds, STDc	m	Thal
8-10-84	Am. Can. Ch. Winjammers On The Move, CD, TD, STDdsc	f	Burgess and Morgan
8-10-84	Am. Can. Ch. Winjammers Tuff Act To Follow, Am. Can. CD, STDds	m	Morgan
8-16-84	Ch. Ochiama's Luciana de la Corps, CDX, AD, SchH. I, STDds	f	Franklin
10-13-84	Winjammers Spit In Yer Eye, OTDds, STDc	m	Morgan
10-15-84	Ch. Winjammers Top Of The Crop Jr., Am. Can. CD, STDds	f	Thal
11-07-84	Ch. Chilure's Fiama de la Corps, UDT, BAR, SchH. I, AD, STDds	f	Franklin
1-20-85	Yessit's Cadenza, UD	f	Sams
4-28-85	Ch. Winjammers Snake In The Grass, STDds	m	Thal
10-06-85	Ch. Desaray's Chapter Two, STDd	f	Morgan and Morgan
5-26-86	Sandyhill Zared de Loup Noir, STDds	m	Morgan
9-01-86	Ch. Winjammers Without A Doubt, Am. Can. CDX, OTDd	f	Morlan
11-02-86	Ch. Theriot's The Brat, UDT, AD, VB	f	Theriot
8-15-87	Ch. Sumar's Academy Award, CDX, STDd	m	Weiss and Bless
3-20-88	Winjammers Top This	f	Nofs and Morgan
6-4-88	Winjammers Webe Aimin Ta Pleaz	f	Dirks

Date	Name of Dog	Sex	Owner
6-12-88	Winjammers Apparition, Am. Can. CD	m	Pews
6-12-88	Winjammers For The Love Of Ewe	m	Morgan
7-2-88	Winjammers Tuff Act Too, CD, TDX, Can. CD, TD, STDds	m	VanEseltine
7-2-88	Winjammers Webe Never Cloudy	f	Dirks
9-4-88	Ch. Matiama's Machoman De La Corps, CD	m	Franklin
11-13-88	Ch. Winjammers Wisecrack, CD	m	Kingsley
2-18-89	Ch. Winjammers Tuff To Top, CD	f	LaFear
2-18-89	Ch. Winjammers To Top It Off, CD	m	LaFear
2-18-89	Am. Can. Ch. Winjammers Sequel, CD	m	Morlan

BAR AWARDS WINNERS (THROUGH 1988)

Gender	Name	Title	C-BAR	O-BAR
D	Achates Esprit de Joie	C-BAR	1985	
B	Aimee du Bon Chateau	BAR	1973	1976
B	Alsace de Mont-Cenis	C-BAR	1986	
D	Andre de Chateau Blanc	BAR	1979	1978
B	Apaula de Spice	C-BAR	1981	
B	Ardeche de Mont-Cenis	C-BAR	1986	
B	Belle de Chateau Blanc	BAR	1981	1979
B	Bichette Sur le Qui Vive Araby	BAR	1985	1981
B	Bluehavens Dena Vedette Noir	C-BAR	1987	
B	Bonheur du Val de Tonnerre	C-BAR	1978	
D	Bonheur Ruarri Mactire	BAR	1985	1985
B	Bonheurs Bobbins N'Pins	BAR	1974	1974
D	Bonheurs D'Artagnon	BAR	1976	1976
B	Bonheurs Nova du Sang Royal	C-BAR	1984	
D	Brigadier de la Brigade	C-BAR	1973	
B	Brillance de Mont-Cenis	BAR	1982	1981
B	Cavaliers High Sierra Mahogany	C-BAR	1987	
D	Chagall du Masque Noir	BAR	1983	1983
B	Chant de Braise Rouge	C-BAR	1975	
B	Chantilly Esprit de Joie	BAR	1989	1988
B	Charlyn du Chalet Belgique	C-BAR	1986	
D	Chateaubriand	BAR	1975	1977
B	Chilures Fiama De La Corps	BAR	1987	1983
D	Columbine Nikit	BAR	1976	1977
B	Commanders Dare O'Wanderlord	C-BAR	1987	
D	Commanders Fire Away	C-BAR	1985	
B	Commanders Win d'Braise Rouge	C-BAR	1983	
D	Corsairs Beaujangles	C-BAR	1988	

Gender	Name	Title	C-BAR	O-BAR
D	Corsairs Frostfire Cyclone	C-BAR	1987	
D	Crocs Blancs Diablo O'Hi Time	C-BAR	1980	
D	Cyrano de Chateau Blanc	BAR	1974	1976
D	D'Artagnone du Falaise	BAR	1971	1972
D	Daktary de Chateau Blanc	BAR	1977	1980
D	Dali de la Pouroffe	C-BAR	1986	
D	Dandy du Clos Saint Jacques	BAR	1969	1970
B	Danseuse D'Elegance	C-BAR	1988	
D	Darass de la Pouroffe	C-BAR	1988	
B	Debonaire Debra Vedette Noir	C-BAR	1987	
B	Dentelle du Val de Tonnerre	BAR	1973	1974
B	Douceur du Vent de Bayville	BAR	1983	1987
B	Duchesse de la Belle Edita	BAR	1986	1988
B	Eau-de-Vie du Val de Tonnerre	C-BAR	1978	
B	Eglantine de Chateau Blanc	C-BAR	1980	
D	Elysee de Mont-Cenis	BAR	1986	1985
B	Faola de Chateau Blanc	C-BAR	1981	
B	Fillette de Fauve Charbonne	O-BAR		1976
D	Flair de Fauve Charbonne	C-BAR	1975	
B	Frostfires Cher O'Vedette Noir	C-BAR	1986	
B	Frostfires Innovation	BAR	1982	1981
B	Frostfires Ipso Facto	C-BAR	1985	
B	Galaxy de Chateau Blanc	BAR	1977	1980
D	Geronimo de Chateau Blanc	C-BAR	1980	
D	Hi Times C-Sam O'Crocs Blancs	BAR	1984	1987
D	Hi Times Kanook of Crocs Blanc	BAR	1977	1981
D	Hi Times Let It Be De La Corps	O-BAR		1979
B	Hi Times O K So Show Me	C-BAR	1987	
B	Hi Times Sweet Polly Purebred	C-BAR	1981	

Gender	Name	Title	C-BAR	O-BAR
B	Hi Times Top Of The Crop	BAR	1984	1986
B	Hi-Line Querido	BAR	1976	1977
B	Hiltons Cookie Chip of Patana	C-BAR	1975	
B	Hiltons Joli Fleur de Lis	C-BAR	1985	
B	Hiltons Wicked Witch	C-BAR	1981	
B	Ingenue de Petite Chalet	BAR	1982	1981
B	Jasmine de Cledeville	BAR	1970	1970
B	Javondis Allure De La Corps	BAR	1988	1980
D	Joker of Georjune	BAR	1971	1973
B	Justa Flare of Georjune	BAR	1971	1972
B	Kajons Kashmier of Sanroyale	C-BAR	1983	
B	Kajons Sherry	C-BAR	1987	
D	Kajons Slaughter	C-BAR	1980	
B	Kalyns Zazarac de Bonheur	BAR	1984	1984
B	Kandice de Fauve Charbonne	BAR	1970	1973
B	Katie de Fauve Charbonne	BAR	1971	1971
D	Kenny de Cledeville	BAR	1971	1977
B	Kiki de Fauve Charbonne	C-BAR	1970	
D	Kis-Tams Candide Pataud	C-BAR	1974	
B	Kis-Tams Renee	C-BAR	1969	
B	Kriquette de Fauve Charbonne	BAR	1976	1976
B	La Mariee du Val de Tonnerre	C-BAR	1983	
B	La Verite de Chateau Blanc	C-BAR	1984	
D	Lancer de Chateau Blanc	BAR	1980	1983
B	Linda du Clos Saint Jacques	BAR	1972	1971
D	Mars de Fauve Charbonne	BAR	1971	1974
B	Martins Chris of Sunfire	BAR	1977	1977
B	Mystique de Fauve Charbonne	BAR	1974	1976
D	Nugget de Fauve Charbonne	C-BAR	1988	
B	Oondine of Georjune	BAR	1981	1975

Gender	Name	Title	C-BAR	O-BAR
B	Oradea de Braise Ardente	C-BAR	1975	
B	Orellana de Braise Ardente	BAR	1975	1979
B	Ouka du Val D'Orge	BAR	1973	1976
D	Our Valient du Garde Roux	C-BAR	1977	
D	Ovation de Chateau Blanc	C-BAR	1988	
B	Patanas Fame of Georjune	BAR	1979	1980
B	Paulmars Cosmic Agena	BAR	1979	1981
D	Rajah D'Antre du Louve	BAR	1982	1986
B	Reginas Echo de Bonheur	BAR	1977	1984
B	Rob-Lyn's Ange Acajou	BAR	1974	1977
B	Romance de Noir et Or	C-BAR	1974	
B	Rouyn de Braise Rouge	C-BAR	1978	
B	Sabrina de Flambeau Rouge	BAR	1976	1978
B	Sachet de Flambeau Rouge	C-BAR	1985	
D	Sandy Haze Prince of Hearts	BAR	1974	1976
B	Sanroyales Giselle	C-BAR	1984	
B	Sanroyales Humoresque	C-BAR	1986	
D	Sanroyales the Hustler	C-BAR	1986	
B	Satin de Fauve Charbonne	BAR	1976	1976
D	Scorpio de Fauve Charbonne	BAR	1978	1981
B	Snowflower Chavon	BAR	1987	1988
B	Solar Flash	C-BAR	1985	
B	StarBright Black Brocade	BAR	1987	1988
D	StarBright Bonne Chance	C-BAR	1988	
B	StarBright Bouquetiere	BAR	1985	1985
B	Tammi Candide	C-BAR	1970	
B	Tanzy de Landas	BAR	1975	1976
B	Tiejjos Sweet Tart	C-BAR	1987	
B	Umber de Sharvonne	BAR	1984	1986
B	Up Tempo Naima	BAR	1986	1986

Gender	Name	Title	C-BAR	O-BAR
B	Von Duncans Feux D'Artifice	C-BAR	1988	
B	Wallendales Tabatha	C-BAR	1979	
B	Wayfarers Nadia du Rochemont	C-BAR	1973	
D	Wayfarers Pacemaker	C-BAR	1978	
B	Wayfarers Prize Package	C-BAR	1974	
B	Whirlwinds Amber O'Frost Fire	BAR	1984	1986
B	Winjammers Hi Time Souvenir	BAR	1984	1985
B	Winjammers I'Ma Hi Timer	O-BAR		1986
B	Wyelands Ashawna	O-BAR		1987
D	Yamin van 'T Hof Melyn	BAR	1982	1982

Glossary

ABTC—American Belgian Tervuren Club. The national breed club.

ABTC Obedience System. A point scale system used by the ABTC to determine the top ten obedience Tervuren each year. The dog must be owner-handled and receives one point for a score of 195, up to fifteen points for a 200 score earned at an AKC trial. See also Delaney and Shuman systems.

AD (or ET)—Ausdauer. A Schutzhund title, a working test of endurance and obedience for dog and handler.

AKC—American Kennel Club. The national all-breed dog club in the United States that issues AKC registrations.

ASCA—Australian Shepherd Club of America. This club sanctions many herding events at which Tervuren compete.

ATD—Advanced Trial Dog (ASCA). A third level of difficulty herding title; see STD for details.

BAR—Breeder's Achievement Record (ABTC). A title awarded to outstanding producers in conformation (C-BAR) and obedience (O-BAR). A dog holding both C-BAR and O-BAR simply is designated BAR.

BIS—Best in Show (AKC). The highest win bestowed to a dog at an AKC all-breed conformation dog show.

Brevet. See Ring Sport.

CAC—Certificate of Aptitude for Championship. A conformation certificate toward championship status available at noninternational dog shows (in FCI countries).

CACIB—Certificate d'Aptitude au Championnat de Beauté. A conformation award available to a representative of each sex in each variety at designated international FCI dog shows. Four of these are among the requirements for the title of International Champion of Beauty and International Champion.

CACIT. Working certificate required for eligibility for the title of International Champion.

CC—Challenge Certificate. A certificate awarded in conformation competition for the best dog and the best bitch in a breed at British championship shows. To become a champion, three CCs must be won under three different judges.

CD—Companion Dog (AKC). The basic title earned at an AKC licensed obedience trial, demonstrating that a dog has passed all sections of the Novice obedience classes, three different times under three different judges. Requirements include heeling on and off leash, standing for examination by the judge, coming when called and group stay exercises.

CDX—Companion Dog Excellent (AKC). The second obedience title that can be earned, obtainable after a dog has earned its CD and passes all portions of the Open obedience classes at three different trials under three different judges. Requirements include heeling off leash, recall (come) exercise with a drop on command, retrieving a dumbbell "on the flat," as well as over a jump, jumping a broad jump and group stay exercises with the handlers out of sight of the dogs.

CFCBB—Club Français du Chien de Berger Belge. The French Belgian Sheepdog Club; a member of SCC.

Ch.—Champion (AKC). A title awarded to a dog that has obtained fifteen points at AKC dog shows, including at least two "majors" (three to five points) under two different judges. The number of points is determined by the numbers of dogs defeated by winning the Winners class or a higher award. Dogs are judged on their adherence to the breed standard.

Delaney Obedience System. A point scale system to determine the yearly top ten obedience dogs in each breed, group and all breeds. Based upon wins, points are accumulated for class placements and High in Trial wins, basically one point per dog defeated. See also ABTC and Shuman systems.

Dog World Award. An award offered by the publishers of *Dog World* magazine for dogs meeting certain obedience, show or breeding accomplishments. Most frequently referred to in this book for dogs earning an obedience title in no more than the three required trials, with a score of 195 or greater in each trial. Also referred to as a *Will Judy* award.

FCI—Fédération Cynologique Internationale. The international governing body for most kennel clubs other than those in the United States, Canada and Britain.

FH—Faehrtenhund. A German advanced tracking title.

Groups. The seven divisions of breeds established by the AKC, based on the dogs' original purpose. The Belgian Tervuren is in the Herding Group.

HIC—Herding Instinct Certificate (ABTC). Any purebred Belgian Tervuren, six months of age or older, with or without prior exposure to or training on livestock, can be entered in an ABTC sanctioned herding instinct test. These tests are sponsored by any of the herding breed clubs, individual herding trainers and kennel or training clubs throughout the country. Those persons running the test must apply to the Herding Committee of the ABTC for sanction before an HIC can be awarded to any passing Tervuren at that test. Passing qualifications require that a dog express sustained interest in herding livestock, can be trained and controlled, demonstrate appropriate style and is not a threat to the health or safety of the livestock.

HIT—High in Trial (AKC). Also referred to as HSDT, the highest win bestowed to a dog at an obedience trial, awarded to the dog receiving the highest score. Can also refer to High in Trial at a livestock herding trial.

HTCh.—Herding Trial Champion (ABTC). Any purebred Belgian Tervuren at least six months of age that has earned the required points by placing in stock classes at ABTC approved herding trials is awarded an HTCh. An HTCh. is completed when a dog earns fifteen points. Points earned are based on a scale approved by the ABTC, and based on the number of dogs defeated in competition. An HIC counts for one point toward the HTCh.

Int.—International. A Schutzhund-related title that can only be earned by dogs holding a SchH. III. The requirements are the same from one country to another and are very demanding, particularly the obedience segment. Very few SchH. III dogs go on to acquire this prestigious title, just as very few CD obedience dogs advance to UD status.

Int. Ch.—International Champion (FCI). A championship title awarded on the basis of both beauty and working ability. The requirements for this title are: (1) four CACIB wins under different judges, with one being from an FCI judge from a different continent; (2) a passing score on a temperament (protection) test in an FCI country; (3) one leg on a CD (or its equivalent) in an FCI country; and (4) a passing score in a tracking test in an FCI country.

Int. Ch. of Beauty—International Champion of Beauty. A term used to designate dogs having won four CACIBs (with one from a judge from another continent), but not the working qualifications necessary for the International Champion title.

LOB. Stud book of the Belgian Kennel Club (not recognized by the FCI or the AKC).

LOF. Stud book of the French SCC. LOF registration papers are required by the AKC for registration on a French import.

LOSH—Livre des Origines St. Hubert. Stud book of the SRSH in Belgium. LOSH registration papers are required by the AKC for registration on a Belgian import.

OFA—Orthopedic Foundation for Animals. This foundation provides professional evaluation of hip X-rays on dogs over two years of age and certifies the results. An OFA number is assigned to each dog whose hips are certified.

OTCH—Obedience Trial Champion (AKC). The highest title bestowed upon an obedience dog. It is earned by a Utility-titled dog who obtains the required one hundred points that are accumulated by winning first or second places in Open B or Utility classes. The number of points won at any show is determined by the number of dogs defeated in the class.

OTD—Open Trial Dog (ASCA). A second level of difficulty herding title; see STD for details.

Ring Sport. A fast-growing, highly structured and sophisticated competition sport requiring extreme control over the dog. Brought to the United States from France in the late 1980s, it combines obedience, agility and protection work. Its four levels of increasing difficulty include Brevet (basic), Ring I, Ring II and Ring III.

SCC—Société Centrale Canine. The French national all-breed dog club (equivalent to the AKC), which issues LOF registrations.

SchH. I, II and III—Schutzhund levels I, II and III. Developed nearly a century ago and meaning "protection dog" in German, Schutzhund's purpose is to demonstrate the ability of a dog to serve man as companion, protector and tracker. Each test includes phases of obedience, protection and tracking that become increasingly more difficult with the three levels. The dog must pass all three phases at one test to earn the SchH. title. In the protection segment the dog must not demonstrate shyness to gunshot and must protect his owner from a stranger by biting and sustaining attacks by the decoy with a stick and, importantly, must demonstrate good judgment and stop biting on command. The tracking portion becomes increasingly more difficult with the Schutzhund levels, beginning with a 400-foot track in SchH. I to a 1,200-foot track in SchH. III, each aged longer and with more turns and articles to find. Exact requirements for each SchH. level vary from country to country.

Select (ABTC). An award available only at ABTC National Specialty shows, it may be given by the judge to those dogs competing in the Best of Breed (Specials) class that the judge feels are of meritorious quality.

Shuman Obedience System. A point scale used to determine the yearly top ten of each breed, group and all breeds. Based upon scores earned by Open and Utility dogs only, a dog receives one point for each qualifying score, up to a possible eight points for a perfect 200 score. See also ABTC and Delaney systems.

SR—Subject Recommended. A dog judged of sufficient quality for breeding at the French Belgian Club's (CFCBB) annual Specialty show.

SRSH—Société Royale de Saint Hubert. Belgium's national all-breed dog club (equivalent to the AKC), which issues LOSH registrations.

STD—Started Trial Dog (ASCA). A first level of difficulty herding title earned by passing at two ASCA tests under two different judges. The type of stock used will be designated after the title: d = ducks, s = sheep, c = cattle. OTD and ATD are advanced levels of difficulty.

TD—Tracking Dog (AKC). Title earned by a dog passing an AKC licensed tracking test, at which it must demonstrate the ability to follow an unmarked track laid out by a stranger. The track must be at least one-half hour but no more than two hours old. It covers a distance of between 440 and 500 yards and contains at least two right-angle turns well out in the open. The dog must find the tracklayer's article at the end of the track.

TDI—Therapy Dogs International. A title obtained by many dogs that are used as therapy dogs in nursing homes and hospitals. To obtain the TDI title the dog must be obedience trained and reliable off leash on stay commands under distracting conditions and when exposed to wheelchairs, crutches and people with unusual motions. The owner must demonstrate responsibility, agree to keep his dog in good health and carry insurance coverage for liability.

TDX—Tracking Dog Excellent (AKC). An advanced title awarded to a TD dog passing a TDX course at an AKC licensed event. The track, which is laid by a stranger, must be three to five hours old. It covers a distance of 800 to 1,000 yards, contains at least three right angle turns and is crossed in two places by more recent tracks. The dog must find four articles left along the track by the tracklayer.

TNT—Tervuren News Tales. Official newsletter of the American Belgian Tervuren Club.

TT—Temperament Test (passed). Administered by the American Temperament Test Society (ATTS), the TT is awarded to a dog that demonstrates mental stability and reasonable courage when exposed to a set routine of normal and unusual people, sounds and footing.

UD—Utility Dog (AKC). The third level of AKC obedience titles, earned by a CDX dog that passes all portions of the Utility classes at three trials, under three different judges. Includes an exercise of signals only (no verbal commands), finding two of the handler's articles by scent from other like articles and retrieving them, taking direction to retrieve one of three gloves, a heeling stand with an examination by the judge and a directed jumping exercise that includes leaving the handler's side and going to a point opposite the handler across the ring.

VB—Traffic Secure Companion. A Schutzhund title in which the dog must perform obedience work under both normal conditions and heavy traffic with severe distraction.

WH—Wachhund. A Schutzhund title that roughly translates into Watch Dog title. The dog is tested in obedience and guarding of areas and articles.

Honor those of graying muzzle,
Those of unquestioning loyalty,
Devotedly giving their best,
Asking only for love in return.